P9-BBN-571

Everyman, I will go with thee,
and be thy guide

Henry James

THE OTHER HOUSE

Introduction by

TONY TANNER
University of Cambridge

Consultant Editor for this volume

CHRISTOPHER BIGSBY
University of East Anglia

EVERYMAN
J. M. DENT · LONDON
CHARLES E. TUTTLE
VERMONT

This edition first published by Everyman Paperbacks in 1966
Introduction and other critical apparatus © J. M. Dent 1996

J. M. Dent
Orion Publishing Group
Orion House
5 Upper St Martin's Lane
London WC2H 9EA
and
Charles E. Tuttle Co. Inc.
28 South Main Street
Rutland, Vermont 05701, USA

Typeset in Sabon by CentraCet Ltd, Cambridge
Printed in Great Britain by
The Guernsey Press Co. Ltd, Guernsey, C. I.

British Library Cataloguing-in-Publication Data
is available upon request.

ISBN 0 460 87806 9

CONTENTS

NOTE ON THE AUTHOR AND EDITOR

HENRY JAMES was born on 15 April 1843 in New York City. His wealthy father travelled extensively, and the James children spent their childhood divided between the US and Europe. James was educated on both continents, but returned to the United States in the early 1860s, where he began to write short stories and reviews for the *Atlantic Monthly, The Nation* and the *North American Review*. Attracted by the European cultural environment, James managed to secure a position as the *New York Tribune* correspondent in Paris, in 1875. He moved to England later that year, and decided to make it his permanent home. James resided in London until 1897, when he retired to Lamb House, in Rye. In 1914, upon the outbreak of World War I, the author became involved in the war effort, and devoted much time and energy to the support of the British troops. Disturbed by the United States government's reluctance to enter the war, James adopted British citizenship in 1915, and received an Order of Merit in 1916. Shortly thereafter, his health deteriorating, James died of a stroke in Lamb House on 28 February, 1916.

James's writing career was long and productive. He published nearly thirty novels and novellas, in addition to a myriad of short stories, travel sketches and critical essays. His best-known works include *Daisy Miller* (1878), *The Portrait of a Lady* (1881), *The Bostonians* (1886), *The Turn of the Screw* (1898), *The Wings of the Dove* (1902), *The Ambassadors* (1903) and *The Golden Bowl* (1904).

TONY TANNER is Professor of English and American Literature at Cambridge University, and a fellow of King's College, Cambridge. He is the author of numerous books, the most recent being *Venice Desired* (Blackwell, 1992) and *Henry James and the Art of Non-Fiction* (Georgia University Press, 1994).

CHRONOLOGY OF JAMES'S LIFE

Year	Age	Life
1843		Born on 15 April in New York City
1843-5	0-2	James family travels abroad
1845-7	2-4	Family returns to New York and moves to Albany
1847-55	4-12	Family moves to New York City
1855-8	12-15	Family travels abroad; James educated in Europe (Geneva, Paris, Boulogne)

CHRONOLOGY OF HIS TIMES

Year	Literary Context	Historical Events
1843	Dickens, *A Christmas Carol, Martin Chuzzlewit*	
1844–5	Browning, *Dramatic Romances and Lyrics*	
1846	Balzac, *La Cousine Bette*	
1847	Thackeray, *Vanity Fair* Charlotte Brontë, *Jane Eyre* Emily Brontë, *Wuthering Heights* Balzac, *Le Cousin Pons*	
1848	Dickens, *Dombey and Son*	European Revolutions California Gold Rush
1850	Dickens, *David Copperfield* Hawthorne, *The Scarlet Letter* Turgenev, *A Month in the Country* Death of Balzac	
1851	Melville, *Moby-Dick*	Great Exhibition
1852		Louis Napoleon proclaimed Emperor of France
1853	Dickens, *Bleak House*	
1854–6	Dickens, *Hard Times*	Crimean War
1855	Trollope, *The Warden*	
1856	Turgenev, *Rudin*	
1857	Dickens, *Little Dorrit* Elizabeth Barrett Browning, *Aurora Leigh* Trollope, *Barchester Towers* Flaubert, *Madame Bovary*	Indian Mutiny

Year	Age	Life
1858–9	15–16	Family returns to US and moves to Newport
1859–60	16–17	Family travels to Europe; James studies in Geneva and Bonn
1860–2	17–19	Family returns to Newport
1862–3	19–20	James enters Harvard Law School; withdraws from law school to commence writing
1864	21	'A Tragedy of Error' published (unsigned) in *Continental Monthly*. Begins writing reviews for *North American Review*
1865	22	Publishes first signed story, 'The Story of a Year' in *Atlantic Monthly*. Writes reviews for *The Nation*
1869–70	26–7	European tour
1870	27	Beloved cousin, Minny Temple, dies. Returns to Cambridge, Masachusetts
1871	28	Publishes first novel, *Watch and Ward*, in *Atlantic Monthly*

Year	Literary Context	Historical Events
1858	George Eliot, *Scenes of Clerical Life* Trollope, *Doctor Thorne* Dickens, *A Tale of Two Cities*	
1859	George Eliot, *Adam Bede* Trollope, *The Bertrams*	Darwin, *The Origin of Species*
1860	George Eliot, *The Mill on the Floss* Turgenev, *On the Eve* Hawthorne, *The Marble Faun*	
1861	Dickens, *Great Expectations* George Eliot, *Silas Marner* Turgenev, *Fathers and Sons*	American Civil War begins
1861–5		Presidency of Lincoln
1862	Flaubert, *Salammbô*	
1863	George Eliot, *Romola*	
1864	Trollope, *Can You Forgive Her?*	
1865	Dickens, *Our Mutual Friend*	End of American Civil War; assassination of Lincoln
1866	Dostoevsky, *Crime and Punishment* George Eliot, *Felix Holt*	
1867	Zola, *Thérèse Raquin* Trollope, *Phineas Finn*	Marx, *Das Kapital* I
1868	Dostoevsky, *The Idiot* Trollope, *He Knew He Was Right*	Gladstone Prime Minister
1869	Flaubert, *L'Education sentimentale* Tolstoy, *War and Peace*	Suez Canal opened
1870	Death of Dickens	Franco-Prussian War; fall of Napoleon III Education Act
1871	George Eliot, *Middlemarch*	Darwin, *The Descent of Man*

Year	Age	Life
1872–4	29–31	Visits Europe with sister Alice. Writes travel sketches for *The Nation*
1875	32	*Roderick Hudson* serialised in *Atlantic Monthly*. Publishes *A Passionate Pilgrim and Other Tales*. Tries living in New York, but decides to return to Europe; arranges to write Paris letters for *New York Tribune*
1875–6	32–3	Arrives in Paris and meets Turgenev, Flaubert, Zola, Daudet, Maupassant; moves to London in December
1877	34	Publishes *The American*. Meets Robert Browning and George du Maurier
1878	35	Publishes *Daisy Miller* to international acclaim; also publishes 'An International Episode', and *The Europeans*
1879	36	Publishes *Hawthorne*; *Confidence* serialised in *Scribner's*
1880	37	Meets Constance Fenimore Woolson. Publishes *Washington Square*; *The Portrait of a Lady* begins to appear in *Macmillan's Magazine* and *Atlantic Monthly*
1881	38	*The Portrait of a Lady* published in novel form
1882	39	Visits US; death of parents
1883	40	Death of brother Wilky
1886	43	Publishes *The Bostonians*, *The Princess Casamassima*
1888	45	Publishes *The Aspern Papers*, *The Reverberator*

Year	Literary Context	Historical Events
1873	Tolstoy, *Anna Karenina*	
1874	Hardy, *Far from the Madding Crowd*	Disraeli Prime Minister First Impressionist exhibition in Paris Factory Act
1875	George Eliot, *Daniel Deronda*	Invention of telephone
1876	Twain, *Tom Sawyer*	
1878	Hardy, *The Return of the Native*	
1880	Dostoevsky, *The Brothers Karamazov* Deaths of George Eliot and Flaubert	Gladstone Prime Minister
1881		Married Woman's Property Act; Irish Land Act
1883	Maupassant, *Une Vie*	Fabian Society founded Death of Marx
1884	Twain, *The Adventures of Huckleberry Finn*	
1885	Howells, *The Rise of Silas Lapham* Maupassant, *Bel Ami* Zola, *Germinal*	Salisbury Prime Minister
1886	Stevenson, *The Strange Case of Dr Jekyll and Mr Hyde*	Year of the 'Great Upheaval' (USA): 700,000 on strike; demand for eight-hour day
1887		Queen Victoria's Golden Jubilee
1889	Death of Browning	

Year	Age	Life
1890	47	Publishes *The Tragic Muse*; turns to play-writing
1892	49	Death of sister, Alice
1894	51	Constance Fenimore Woolson commits suicide in Italy
1895	52	Booed off stage on opening night of *Guy Domville*. Returns to fiction writing
1897	54	Publishes *The Spoils of Poynton, What Maisie Knew*. Settles at Lamb House, in Rye. Begins friendship with Joseph Conrad
1898	55	Publishes *The Turn of the Screw, In the Cage*
1899	56	Publishes *The Awkward Age*
1901	58	Publishes *The Sacred Fount*
1902	59	Publishes *The Wings of the Dove*
1903	60	Publishes *The Ambassadors*. Meets Edith Wharton
1904	61	Publishes *The Golden Bowl*
1905	62	Visits USA; delivers lectures

Year	Literary Context	Historical Events
1890	Wilde, *Picture of Dorian Gray*	William James, *Principles of Psychology*
1891	Hardy, *Tess of the d'Urbervilles* Gissing, *New Grub Street* Howells, *A Modern Instance*	
1892		Gladstone Prime Minister
1894		Death of Alexander III; accession of Nicholas II
1895	Hardy, *Jude the Obscure* Conrad, *Almayer's Folly* Wells, *The Time Machine* Wilde, *The Importance of Being Earnest*	Trial of Oscar Wilde Salisbury Prime Minister Marconi's 'wireless' telegraphy
1896	Chekhov, *The Seagull*	Klondike Gold Rush
1897	Conrad, *The Nigger of the 'Narcissus'*	Queen Victoria's Diamond Jubilee
1899	Chopin, *The Awakening* Norris, *McTeague*	
1899–1902		Boer War
1900	Dreiser, *Sister Carrie* Conrad, *Lord Jim* Wells, *Love and Mr Lewisham* Chekhov, *Uncle Vanya* Death of Wilde	Freud, *Interpretation of Dreams*
1901	Kipling, *Kim*	Death of Queen Victoria; accession of Edward VII
1901–9		Presidency of Theodore Roosevelt
1902	William James, *Varieties of Religious Experience* Conrad, *Heart of Darkness*	Balfour Prime Minister
1904	Conrad, *Nostromo*	Russo-Japanese War begins
1905	Wells, *Kipps* Edith Wharton, *The House of Mirth* Forster, *Where Angels Fear to Tread*	First Russian Revolution

Year	Age	Life
1907	64	Publishes *The American Scene*. Travels in France with Edith Wharton; visits Henrik Andersen in Italy
1907–9	64–6	Publishes the New York Edition of his fiction
1910	67	Death of brothers William and Robertson
1911	68	Receives honorary degree from Harvard
1912	69	Receives honorary degree from Oxford
1913	70	Publishes first autobiographical memoir, *A Small Boy and Others*
1914	71	Publishes second autobiographical memoir, *Notes of a Son and Brother*
1915	72	Becomes British subject
1916	73	Awarded Order of Merit; dies on 28 February

Year	Literary Context	Historical Events
1906	Sinclair, *The Jungle*	
1907	Adams, *The Education of Henry Adams* Conrad, *The Secret Agent* William James, *Pragmatism*	
1908	Forster, *A Room with a View*	Asquith Prime Minister
1909	Wells, *Ann Veronica* and *Tono-Bungay*	First Ford Model T car
1910	Wells, *Mr Polly* Forster, *Howards End* Death of Tolstoy	Death of Edward VII; accession of George V
1911	Conrad, *Under Western Eyes* Mann, *Death in Venice* Edith Wharton, *Ethan Frome*	
1912		The *Titanic* disaster
1913	Lawrence, *Sons and Lovers* Edith Wharton, *The Custom of the Country* Proust, *Swann's Way*	Panama Canal opened
1914	Joyce, *Dubliners*	Outbreak of World War I
1915	Lawrence, *The Rainbow* Ford Madox Ford, *The Good Soldier*	
1916	Joyce, *A Portrait of the Artist as a Young Man*	LLoyd George Prime Minister Russian Revolution

INTRODUCTION

In his memoir on Henry James, written shortly after his death, Ford Madox Ford says of James's art:

> He can convey an impression, an atmosphere of what you will with literally nothing. Embarrassment, chastened happiness – for his happiness is always tinged with regret – greed, horror, social vacuity – he can give you it all with a purely blank page. His characters will talk about rain, about the opera, about the moral aspects of the selling of Old Masters to the New Republic, and those conversations will convey to your mind that the quiet talkers are living in an atmosphere of horror, of bankruptcy, of passion hopeless as the Dies Irae! That is the supreme trick of art today, since that is how we really talk about the musical glasses whilst our lives crumble to pieces around us.

Ford's *The Good Soldier* is his most Jamesian novel – with its uncertainties and hesitations, its gaps and incompletions, its silences and sadnesses; the sense of accumulating horrors beneath the maintained civilities, the crumbling of lives under the cut-glass manners. It was originally entitled *The Saddest Story*, which the publishers rejected, presumably because they felt the times were already sad enough (it was published in 1915). Few people realise that this was, in fact, a quotation from James, a nod of acknowledgement, as it were, to the master. He retained it in the opening line. 'This is the saddest story I ever heard.' In *The Other House*, we read: 'Tony looked as if he were retracing the saddest story on earth.' Ford's novel, rightly, became an acknowledged modern classic. James's novel, unjustly, has suffered almost complete neglect.

An anonymous reviewer of the time recognised that the novel was something special.

> The appearance of a new book by Mr Henry James is always an event to the connoisseur of letters. It cannot be stated too explicitly

or published too widely that *The Other House* is an event of the first order. In a small way it is a revolution. Mr James has done something new. His name has been for long a synonym for cleverness and conscious skill, but on laying down this volume the reader is forced to confess that henceforward, if the writer so wills, it is also a synonym for power. The book has grip.

The reviewer is right; the novel is – still – 'gripping'. It has a power which is, at least, different in kind from that of James's previous work. We do not measure the power of a novel by the number of violently terminated lives it contains, but it is worth remarking that this is James's one and only murder novel.

In his Notebooks, James records the moments of the novel's incubation. It offers a marvellous insight into the way his mind worked – teasing and tracing out the latent possibilities of a subject.

26 December (34 De Vere Gardens)

I have been sitting here in the firelight – on this quiet afternoon of the empty London Christmastide, trying to catch hold of the tail of an idea, of a 'subject'. Vague, dim forms of imperfect conceptions seem to brush across one's face with a blur of suggestion, a flutter of impalpable wings ... Is there something for a tale, is there something for a play, in something that might be a little like the following. It is the *play* that I am looking for, but it is worth noting, all the same, for the *other* possibility.

Very briefly, I imagine a young man who has lost his wife and who has a little girl, the only issue of that prematurely frustrated union. He has very solemnly, and on his honour, promised his wife, on her deathbed, that, *du vivant* of their child, he will not marry again. He has given her this absolutely sacred assurance and she has died believing him. She has had a reason, a deep motive for her demand – the overwhelming dread of a stepmother. She has had one herself – a stepmother who rendered her miserable, darkened and blighted her youth. She wishes to preserve her own little girl from such a fate. For five years all goes well – the husband doesn't think of marrying again. He delights in the child, watches over her growth and looks forward to her future. Then, inevitably, fatally he meets a girl with whom he falls deeply in love – in love as he hadn't *begun* to be with his poor dead wife. She returns his affection, his passion; but he sees the phantom of his solemn vow, his sacred promise rise terribly before him. In the presence of it he falters, and while the girl stands obviously ready to surrender herself, he hangs back, he tries to resist the current that sweeps him along. *Or*, there is another figure intensely engaged in the action – and without whom it would present no drama. This is the figure of a young woman who loves him, who has loved him from the moment she has seen him, who has seen him, known him, *du vivant* of his wife. The circumstances of this personage are all questions to determine.

Initially, then, James was drawn to the narrative possibilities of the obstacles to passion thrown up by the vow, and the consequent anguished irresoluteness of the hero. Then he sees that it will only become drama if the situation is complicated by the passion of another woman, and he begins to shift his interest to what he calls his Bad Heroine. Note that he is thinking in terms of a play.

The curtain rises on Act II, 5 years later. My hero has never married, of course – no more has my Bad Heroine. She is fearfully in love with my Hero. He meanwhile has fallen in love with my Good Heroine, who ignorantly and innocently returns his passion. My Bad Heroine is frightfully afraid the two will marry ... Then my young lady takes a decision – she determines to poison the child – on the calculation that suspicion will fall on her rival. She does so – and on the theory of *motive* – suspicion *does* fall on the wretched girl. There are two persons to figure as the *public*, the judging, wondering, horrified world, the doctor and a convenient older woman who has been in the first act. Suspicion descends – it is *constatée* [certified] that the child is poisoned: the question is who has done it? ... The child recovers, demanding the Good Heroine, and the attempt of the Bad Heroine is condoned and covered up by the doctor – who has aspired to her hand! – and the man who first loved her. The Hero at the '*request*' of his little daughter determines on a union with the Good Heroine; and the other woman is got off by the doctor and the 2d *amoureux*. As I so barbarously and roughly jot the story down, I seem to feel in it the stuff of a play ...

This is greatly edited, but even from what I have quoted ideas can be seen growing as James writes himself into the imagined

situation. And they went on growing. The child is finally not
poisoned but drowned; and instead of recovering, it dies. But
the Bad Heroine, now a murderess, is still 'got off', and the
conventional retributions of the law are excluded. And, at this
stage, James still saw it all as making a play. Which takes us,
briefly, to the matter of James and the theatre.

Between the years of 1890 and 1895, James made a concerted
effort to write successfully for the theatre (for full details see the
volume in Leon Edel's magisterial biography of Henry James
entitled *The Treacherous Years*). He had already written six
plays at the time of the above Notebook entry (only one had
been produced), and he was even then working on his seventh
play, *Guy Domville*. This play had a catastrophic reception
when it was staged a year later. A shattered James returned to
the novel and *The Other House* is one of the first fruits of his
slightly traumatised post-theatre years (the others were *The
Spoils of Poynton* and *What Maisie Knew*, and all three novels
have features in common – they all concern struggles for
possession; of a man, of a houseful of beautiful things, of a child
respectively). But if James fled from the theatre, he took a lot of
theatrical experience with him; and, from the point of view of
this novel, the crucial experience was his exposure to Ibsen.

In 1891 he saw Elizabeth Robbins play the heroine in Ibsen's
Hedda Gabler, and this occasioned an important essay by James
on 'Henrik Ibsen'. In describing Hedda Gabler, as acted by
Elizabeth Robbins, James could be outlining the figure of Rose
Armiger (described as being like an actress) in his own future
novel.

> It is the portrait of a nature ... and of a state of nerves as well as
> of soul, a state of temper, of health, of chagrin, of despair ... We
> receive Hedda ripe for her catastrophe, and if we ask for anteced-
> ents and explanations we must simply find them in her character.
> Her motives are just her passions. What the four acts show us is
> these motives and that character – complicated, strange, irrecon-
> cilable, infernal – playing themselves out ... The 'use' of Hedda
> Gabler is that she acts on others and that even her most disagree-
> able qualities have the privilege, thoroughly undeserved doubtless,
> but equally irresistible, of becoming a part of the history of others.
> And then one isn't so sure she is wicked, and by no means sure

(especially when she is represented by an actress who makes the point ambiguous) that she is disagreeable. She is various and sinuous and graceful, complicated and natural; she suffers, she struggles, she is human, and by that fact exposed to a dozen interpretations, to the importunity of our suspense. Wrought with admirable closeness is the whole tissue of relations between the five people whom the author sets in motion and on whose behalf he asks of us so few concessions.

In James's novel it will be six main characters, plus two (Doctor Ramage and Mrs Beever) who serve as what James had described as 'the judging, wondering, horrified world'. And James does not just take his ambiguous 'bad' heroine from Ibsen. In its confined, claustrophobic, inward-looking atmosphere; in what James noted in Ibsen as 'the pervasive air of small interests and standards, the signs of limited local life' and the 'parochial or suburban stamp', this whole novel is close to the Ibsenite play James undoubtedly hoped it would become. And what James admired more generally in Ibsen matched his own deepest proclivity – 'his admirable talent for producing an intensity of interest by means incorruptibly quiet, by an almost demure preservation of the appearances of the usual in which we see him juggle with difficulty and danger and which constitutes, as it were, his only coquetry'. Though James does note three aspects of Ibsen's work which amount to a signal missingness – 'I mean of course the absence of humour, the absence of free imagination, and the absence of style'. In his novel, James remedies the deficiencies.

James did in fact do a scenario for a three-act play to be called *The Promise*, but it was never put on and the script has not survived. Fortunately, a friend suggested he turn it into a serial for the *Illustrated London News*, which was where the novel we have now first appeared. As a novel, *The Other House* still bears very visible marks of its theatrical incubation. It falls into three distinct parts (acts) with each part clearly organised as a series of scenes. The characters enter and leave as if on cue – as one comes in from the garden, another goes out into the hall – leading, for the most part, to a series of increasingly charged and dramatic conversations, or confrontations, between all the people involved – seemingly between every possible

combination of two you can get out of eight. The accessories
are minimal: the men smoke cigarettes at awkward moments
(Paul eats buns); there is much play with 'the paraphernalia of
tea'; there are dolls and a birthday cake for poor, doomed Effie;
various pieces of furniture are mentioned; there are hats and
parasols. It is invariably quiet – 'the great showy clock ticked
in the scented silence'. Characters may pace restlessly, stand
stupefied, sit down in confusion, rush in breathlessly (though
awkward movements are rare), or just stroll amiably around.
The most violent act (on stage, that is) occurs when Dennis
kicks the turned up corner of a rug in frustration. During the
second act, the shadows lengthen in the garden, while through-
out the last act a deepening dusk seeps into the house. Each
section ends at a point of drama – with the announcement that
Julia is dying; the discovery of the body of young Effie; and the
disappearance of Rose into the night. The tensions grow, and
shocks give way to horrors until it is a 'black, bloody nightmare'
not only for Dennis, but, varyingly, for everyone. But the
manners remain impeccable; the civilised surface holds. 'Tony,
agitated as she could see, but with complete command of his
manners ...' 'To look at him was to recognise the value of
appearances.' Characters, even in distress, invariably find 'the
right tone'. Everyone instinctively behaves so as to 'establish a
superficial harmony'. There is unashamed reference to 'the
necessary falsehood'. 'In this way the trick was successfully
played – they found their feet.' 'It would lead to exactly nothing
– that had been settled all round in advance. This was a happy,
lively provision that kept everything down, made sociability a
cool, public, out-of-door affair, without a secret or a mystery
...' Except, of course, there are secrets and there will be
mysteries. Even Rose is 'constitutionally averse to making
unmeasured displays', but when her passion can no longer be
'kept down' and breaks cover, the smooth skin of the sociable
surface is hideously gashed. Only briefly, however. The tear is
soon healed over, though leaving what aching inner wounds we
are left to surmise. These are the sort of people Ford Madox
Ford was describing.

For James, the advantages of the novel over the stage are
many and crucial (even if it took him some time, and a grievous
disappointment, to realise it). There is, for example, the not

inconsiderable matter of James's humour. Doctor Ramage (as important a figure as doctors are in Ibsen) 'had a face so candid and circular that it suggested a large white pill'. You might certainly find a pale man to play the Doctor – but you would lose that priceless pill. 'The butler retired like a conscientious Minister retiring from untenable office.' Try staging that – particularly nowadays when that is precisely what Ministers *don't* do! More generally though, what James could not put on stage was just his imagery, and so much of the important action – the humour, the imaginative play, the style – occurs precisely there. 'They faced each other over the deep waters of the accumulated and the undiscussed.' You could do the first four words on stage, but not the rest. Or again: 'They stood looking at each other like a pair who, walking on a frozen lake, suddenly have in their ears the great crack of ice.' Once more, the first six words on stage, but the vital ones which follow can only be thought. When things come to a climax and characters find themselves in 'the agony of the actual' and having to name awful facts, they speak 'with a drop, before the red real, of all vain terms'. Here, the 'real' is indeed real enough, and red enough – hopeless murderous passion, and a killed child. There are times when all the terms are vain. But, for the most part, James is lamenting 'our sad want of signs for shades and degrees', and it is his incomparably nuanced amplifying, supplementing narrative commentary which seeks to supply that want.

The amplification is everywhere. 'Mrs Beever was so "early Victorian" as to be almost prehistoric – was constructed to move amid massive mahogany and sit upon banks of Berlin-wool.' It is crucial in establishing character: Tony has 'a certain quality of passive excess which was the note of the whole man and which, for an attentive eye, began with his neckties and ended with his intonations'. 'His presence was, anywhere and at any time, as much as ever the clock at the moment it strikes.' It is a vivid image, but I do not know what an actor would do with it; any more than I can see how an actress would convey the following – 'Rose stood there opposite him with a fine, rich urgency.' It is James who adds a whole extra dimension to the actual goings-on. When Tony comes downstairs after his dying wife has exacted the fatal promise – which nobody yet knows – he says 'She's there – it's all right. But ah, my dear people – !'

There is a lot of James in that ' – !', the always greater drama of what James calls 'the dominant unspeakable'. But here James goes on – 'And he passed his hand, with the vivid gesture of brushing away an image, over a face of which the essential radiance was visible even through perturbation.' I suppose this could just about be a stage direction; but pity the poor actor trying to juggle radiance and perturbation. As with – 'his face was a combat of mystifications'. Even more with the following, after Tony realises that both Rose (whom he does not love) and Jean (whom he does) adore him: 'He was in bliss with a great chill and in despair with a great lift, and confused and assured and alarmed.' The fact is that there are inner states so contradictory and mixed and confused that only patient, or inspired, analysis can convey them. Shakespeare can do it on the stage but his drama is unique. James needs the space of the novel.

James loved old English houses. Thus, in his journal: 'It was the old houses that fetched me – Montacute, the admirable; Barrington, that superb Ford Abbey, and several smaller ones ... These delicious old houses, in the long August days, in the south of England air, on the soil over which so much has passed and out of which so much has come, rose before me like a series of visions.' There are many important great houses in his fiction – Gardencourt, Poynton, Fawns – and all the action of this novel takes place in two well-appointed houses – Eastmead (rather old-fashioned, as befits Mrs Beever) and Bounds (more modern – Tony Bream's taste). But they are not among James's great houses; they seem more suburban – stock-broker belt, we would now call them. This is appropriate enough since both families are in banking. They also provide that apparently secure, placid, comfortable, solidly respectable (to the point of primness) atmosphere in which Rose Armiger is to explode. For it is she, of course, who is the source of all the drama in this otherwise peaceable upper-middle class kingdom.

When Jean first sees Rose she thinks her 'awfully plain'. Then Rose smiles, and 'the ambiguity that Mrs Beever had spoken of lighted up – an ambiguity worth all the dull prettiness in the world'. And it is that ambiguity which makes her by far the most interesting character in the book. All the others are, one feels, in their own ways, rather uncomplicatedly decent – even the 'brilliant, joking gentleman' Tony Bream. It is Rose who introduces complexity into the suburban serenity. That she is in the grip of a distinctly non-suburban passion is signalled early on. 'If there had been anyone at that moment to see her face, such an observer would have found it strangely, tragically convulsed: she had the appearance of holding in with extraordinary force some passionate sob or cry, some smothered impulse of anguish.' Tony does not realise what is happening, the passion he has aroused – 'the unexpected had sprung up before him'. 'What he saw, without understanding it, was the final snap of her tremendous tension, the end of her wonderful false calm.' It is only later that he realises what is written in her face. 'What Tony Bream saw was a circumstance of which he had already had glimpses; but for some reason or other it was now written with a largeness that made it resemble a printed poster on a wall ... This message was simply Rose Armiger's whole face, exquisite and tragic in its appeal ... He could meet it only with a compassion as unreserved as itself.' Here is perhaps the central moment in the book (it occurs almost exactly halfway):

> Their eyes met, and he again felt himself in the presence of what, in them, shortly before, had been so deep, so exquisite. It represented something that no lapse could long quench – something that gave out the measureless white ray of a light steadily revolving. She could sometimes turn it away, but it was always somewhere; and now it covered him with a great cold lustre that made everything for the moment look hard and ugly – made him also feel the chill of a complication for which he had not allowed. (p. 101)

That chill settles on the book: it is at this point that things begin to darken.

Rose shows the darkest side of her ruthless passion in two subsequent confrontations. In the first, she has the audacity to suggest to Jean that she, Rose, is worried about what Jean might do to the child in order that she might marry Tony. 'Jean turned again upon her companion a face bewildered and alarmed: unguardedly stepping into water that she had believed shallow, she found herself caught up in a current of fast-moving depths – a cold, full tide that set straight out to sea. '"Where *am* I?" her scared silence seemed for the moment to ask.' Well out of her emotional depth, as James's sustained aqueous image makes clear.

Jean had got up before these remarks had gone far, but even though she fell back a few steps her dismay was a force that condemned her to take them in. 'God forbid I should understand you,' she panted; 'I only make out that you say and mean horrible things and that you're doing your best to seek a quarrel with me from which you shall derive some advantage that, I'm happy to feel, is beyond my conception.' Both the women were now pale as death, and Rose was brought to her feet by the pure passion of this retort. (p. 153)

These are two women fighting over the same man, and, as their passions flare up, the suburbs are, briefly, on fire. Jean is left 'sick with the aftertaste of her encounter'. With her breathtakingly brazen accusation, Rose has broken all the tacit rules of civilised interchange. Instead of the usual cordial conversational potions she has poured a poisoned draught.

Perhaps even more shocking is the scene in which, playing quite shamelessly on his sturdy decency and ingrained sense of honour, she effectively forces her much abused suitor, Dennis Vidal, to lie for her, covering up the murder he knows she has committed. ' "So you can't abandon me – you can't . . . You're mine!" ' She then takes hold of him in the most chilling embrace in the book.

He submitted, with no movement but to close his eyes before the new-born dread of her caress. Yet he took the caress when it came – the dire confession of her hard embrace, the long entreaty of her stony kiss. He might still have been a creature trapped in steel; after she had let him go he still stood at a loss how to turn. (p. 186)

After she has done the deed, we are told that 'Rose's mask was the mask of Medusa.' Dennis has indeed been petrified; standing by Rose and seeing her through requires that he also be a man of steel. He utters the necessary falsehood – 'He spoke with a clearness that proved the steel surface he had in a few minutes forged for his despair.' It is Dennis who, at the end, carries Rose away into the night and an imponderable future.

So why don't they hand her over to the police, since all eight of them (but no-one else) know that she drowned Effie – ' "She forced her in. She held her down. She left her." ' – and her attempts to implicate Jean are an almost immediate failure? It cannot simply be that they want to keep up the good name of the district – though I suppose that eminent banking families would particularly deprecate having a murder attached to their names. One hardly feels that the good Doctor Ramage would participate in a crude neighbourhood cover-up. It is more to do with the nature of the case, with the sad, horrible hopelessness of Rose's passion. '"Don't come near such a thing; don't touch it; don't know it!"' cries Tony to Dennis, telling him that he has unwittingly intruded '"on obscure, unhappy things, on suffering and danger and death"'. The knowledge cannot be eluded; though it may be, in time, frozen over, as it were. Life goes on, and, it is intimated, Tony and Jean will, some time in the post-ravage future, get married. But the 'thing', the 'unutterable horror' *is* 'obscure'. Perhaps a hopeless but insuperable passion always is: when Dennis cries out helplessly '"it's not I, it's not she, it's not you, it's not anyone"', he is speaking a kind of truth. I'm not suggesting a communal guilt – Rose's is the only hand in the water – but it takes more than one person to make a situation. And how much encouragement did Tony give Rose – who must have been a good deal more interesting, at least, than dear, sweet Jean? When Jean learns that it is his – and everyone's – intention to 'let her go' – she is incredulous – '"And yet you condone the atrocity – ?"' There follows a crucial exchange.

'I must tell you all,' he said once more. 'I knew it – I always knew it. And I made her come.'
'You were kind to her – as you're always kind.'
'No; I was more than that. And I should have been less.'
His face showed a rift in the blackness. 'I remember.'
She followed him in pain and at a distance. 'You mean you liked it?'
'I liked it – whilst I was safe. Then I grew afraid.'
'Afraid of what?'
'Afraid of everything. You don't know – but we're abysses. At least *I'm* one!' he groaned. He seemed to sound the depth. 'There are other things. They go back far.'
'Don't tell me all,' said Jean. (p. 204)

Just what the 'it' was that Tony liked, and how much more than 'kind' he was to Rose, we will never know, just as Jean will never ask. Sex is never mentioned in these high suburban households. The nearest anyone comes to it is when Dennis admits to Rose, reluctantly as one feels, ' "your effect on – what shall I call it? ... On God knows what baser, obscurer part of me!" ' Sexual desire is the 'obscure' thing, behind all the other things – above everything else it is *the* 'dominant unspeakable' in the Jamesian world. But, above or below everything else, it is the most powerful part of 'the red real'. Rose's 'passion' is only an extreme case; and who knows how much Tony struck the tinder and stoked the fire – wittingly or unwittingly is, after a while, beside the point. We are to feel that the unambiguous judgements of the law would be too crude to be applied to the ambiguity that is Rose, and her ambiguously engendered passion. ' "Her doom will be to live." '

I have touched only on what strike me as some of the more notable features of this beautifully crafted, highly civilised novel, written when James is just about at the height of his powers. There are many other pleasures in the book – not least the exchanges between the rather officious Mrs Beever and her stolid, expressionless, bun-eating son, Paul. In truth, the whole novel is a continuous pleasure to read, as fresh today as it was a hundred years ago, even if our morals and manners have changed. Like all great artists, James, under the tea cups and the cigarettes, is dealing with matters that are unsuburban and unchanging. Late on in his life when he was working on the outline of a novel which he never finished, called *The Ivory Tower*, James suddenly writes in his Notebook – 'Oh blest *Other House* which gives me thus at every step a precedent, a support, a divine little light to walk by ...' It is a light we would be foolish to deprive ourselves of.

TONY TANNER

NOTE ON THE TEXT

The text of this Everyman edition is taken from the William Heinemann first edition published in 1896. Punctuation has been silently modernised according to Everyman house style.

THE OTHER HOUSE

BOOK ONE

CHAPTER I

Mrs Beever of Eastmead, and of 'Beever and Bream', was a close, though not a cruel observer of what went on, as she always said, at the other house. A great deal more went on there, naturally, than in the great clean, square solitude in which she had practically lived since the death of Mr Beever, who had predeceased by three years his friend and partner, the late Paul Bream of Bounds, leaving to his only son, the little godson of that trusted associate, the substantial share of the business in which his wonderful widow – she knew and rejoiced that she was wonderful – now had a distinct voice. Paul Beever, in the bloom of eighteen, had just achieved a scramble from Winchester to Oxford: it was his mother's design that he should go into as many things as possible before coming into the Bank. The Bank, the pride of Wilverley, the high clear arch of which the two houses were the solid piers, was worth an expensive education. It was, in the talk of town and county, 'hundreds of years' old, and as incalculably 'good' as a subject of so much infallible arithmetic could very well be. That it enjoyed the services of Mrs Beever herself was at present enough for her and an ample contentment to Paul, who inclined so little to the sedentary that she foresaw she should some day be as anxious at putting him into figures as she had in his childhood been easy about putting him into breeches. Half the ground moreover was held by young Anthony Bream, the actual master of Bounds, the son and successor of her husband's colleague.

She was a woman indeed of many purposes; another of which was that on leaving Oxford the boy should travel and inform himself: she belonged to the age that regarded a foreign tour not as a hasty dip, but as a deliberate plunge. Still another had for its main feature that on his final return he should marry the nicest girl she knew: that too would be a deliberate plunge, a plunge that would besprinkle his mother. It would do with the question what it was Mrs Beever's inveterate household practice to do with all loose and unarranged objects – it would get it out of the way. There would have been difficulty in saying whether it was a feeling for peace or for war, but her constant habit was to lay the ground bare for complications that as yet at least had never taken place. Her life was like a room prepared for a dance: the furniture was all against the walls. About the young lady in question she was perfectly definite; the nicest girl she knew was Jean Martle, whom she had just sent for at Brighton to come and perform in that character. The performance was to be for the benefit of Paul, whose midsummer return was at hand and in whom the imagination of alternatives was to be discouraged from the first. It was on the whole a comfort to Mrs Beever that he had little imagination of anything.

Jean Martle, condemned to Brighton by a father who was Mrs Beever's second cousin and whom the doctors, the great men in London, kept there, as this lady opined, because he was too precious wholly to lose and too boring often to see – Jean Martle would probably some day have money and would possibly some day have sense: even as regards a favoured candidate this marked the extent of Mrs Beever's somewhat dry expectations. They were addressed in a subordinate degree to the girl's 'playing', which was depended on to become brilliant, and to her hair, which was viewed in the light of a hope that it would with the lapse of years grow darker. Wilverley, in truth, would never know if she played ill; but it had an old-fashioned prejudice against loud shades in the natural covering of the head. One of the things his cousin had been invited for was that Paul should get used to her eccentric colour – a colour of which, on a certain bright Sunday of July, Mrs Beever noted afresh, with some alarm, the exaggerated pitch. Her young friend had arrived two days before and now – during the elastic interval from church to luncheon – had been despatched to Bounds with a message and some preliminary warnings. Jean knew that she should find there a house in some confusion, a new-born little girl, the first, a young mother not yet 'up', and an odd visitor, somewhat older than herself, in the person of Miss Armiger, a schoolfriend of Mrs Bream, who had made her appearance a month before that of the child and had stayed on, as Mrs Beever with some emphasis put it, 'right through everything'.

This picture of the situation had filled, after the first hour or two, much of the time of the two ladies, but it had originally included for Jean no particular portrait of the head of the family – an omission in some degree repaired, however, by the chance of Mrs Beever's having on the Saturday morning taken her for a moment into the Bank. They had had errands in the town, and Mrs Beever had wished to speak to Mr Bream, a brilliant, joking gentleman, who, instantly succumbing to their invasion and turning out a confidential clerk, had received them in his beautiful private room. 'Shall I like him?' Jean, with the sense of a widening circle, had, before this, adventurously asked. 'Oh, yes, if you notice him!' Mrs Beever had replied in obedience to an odd private prompting to mark him as insignificant. Later on, at the Bank, the girl noticed him enough to feel rather afraid of him: that was always with her the foremost result of being noticed herself. If Mrs Beever passed him over, this was in part to be accounted for by all that at Eastmead was usually taken for granted. The queen-mother, as Anthony Bream kept up the jest of calling her, would not have found it easy to paint off-hand a picture of the allied sovereign whom she was apt to regard as a somewhat restless vassal. Though he was a dozen years older than the happy young prince on whose behalf she exercised her regency, she had known him from his boyhood, and his strong points and his weak were alike an old story to her.

His house was new – he had on his marriage, at a vast expense, made it quite violently so. His wife and his child were new; new also in a marked degree was the young woman who had lately taken up her abode with him and who had the air of intending to remain till she should lose that quality. But Tony himself – this had always been his name to her – was intensely familiar. Never doubting that he was a subject she had mastered, Mrs Beever had no impulse to clear up her view by distributing her impressions. These impressions were as neatly pigeon-holed as her correspondence and her accounts – neatly, at least, save in so far as they were besprinkled with the dust of time. One of them might have been freely rendered into a hint that her young partner was a possible source of danger to her own sex. Not to her personally, of course; for herself, somehow, Mrs Beever was not of her own sex. If she *had* been a woman – she never thought of herself so loosely – she would, in spite of her age, have doubtless been conscious of peril. She now recognised none in life except that of Paul's marrying wrong, against which she had taken early measures. It would have been a misfortune therefore to feel a flaw in a security otherwise so fine. Was not perhaps the fact that she had a vague sense of exposure for Jean Martle a further motive for her not expatiating to that young lady on Anthony Bream? If any such sense operated, I hasten to add, it operated without Jean's having mentioned that at the Bank he had struck her as formidable.

Let me not fail equally to declare that Mrs Beever's general suspicion of him, as our sad want of signs for shades and degrees condemns me to call it, rested on nothing in the nature of evidence. If she had ever really uttered it she might have been brought up rather short on the question of grounds. There were certainly, at any rate, no grounds in Tony's having, before church, sent a word over to her on the subject of their coming to luncheon. 'Dear Julia, this morning, is really grand,' he had written. 'We've just managed to move her to her downstairs room, where they've put up a lovely bed and where the sight of all her things cheers and amuses her, to say nothing of the wide immediate outlook at her garden and her own corner of the terrace. In short the waves are going down and we're beginning to have our meals "regular". Luncheon may be rather late, but do bring over your charming little friend. How she lighted up yesterday my musty den! There will be another little friend, by the way – not of mine, but of Rose Armiger's, the young man to whom, as I think you know, she's engaged to be married. He's just back from China and comes down till tomorrow. Our Sunday trains are such a bore that, having wired him to take the other line, I'm sending to meet him at Plumbury.' Mrs Beever had no need to reflect on these few lines to be comfortably conscious that they summarised the nature of her neighbour – down to the 'dashed sociability', as she had heard the poor fellow, in sharp reactions, himself call it, that had made him scribble them and that always made him talk too much for a man in what, more than he, she held to be a 'position'. He was there in his premature bustle over his wife's slow recovery; he was there in his boyish impatience to improvise a feast; he was there in the simplicity with which he exposed himself to the depredations, to the possible avalanche, of Miss Armiger's belongings. He was there moreover in his free-handed way of sending six miles for a young man from China, and he was most of all there in his allusion to the probable lateness of luncheon. Many things in these days were new at the other house, but nothing was so new as the hours of meals. Mrs Beever had of old repeatedly dined there on the stroke of six. It will be seen that, as I began with declaring, she kept her finger on the pulse of Bounds.

CHAPTER 2

When Jean Martle, arriving with her message, was ushered into
the hall, it struck her at first as empty, and during the moment
that she supposed herself in sole possession she perceived it to
be showy and indeed rather splendid. Bright, large and high,
richly decorated and freely used, full of 'corners' and communi-
cations, it evidently played equally the part of a place of reunion
and of a place of transit. It contained so many large pictures
that if they hadn't looked somehow so recent it might have
passed for a museum. The shaded summer was in it now, and
the odour of many flowers, as well as the tick from the chimney-
piece of a huge French clock which Jean recognised as modern.
The colour of the air, the frank floridity, amused and charmed
her. It was not till the servant had left her that she became aware
she was not alone – a discovery that soon gave her an embarrassed minute. At the other end of the place appeared a young
woman in a posture that, with interposing objects, had made
her escape notice, a young woman bent low over a table at
which she seemed to have been writing. Her chair was pushed
back, her face buried in her extended and supported arms, her
whole person relaxed and abandoned. She had heard neither the
swing of the muffled door nor any footfall on the deep carpet,
and her attitude denoted a state of mind that made the messenger from Eastmead hesitate between quickly retreating on tiptoe
or still more quickly letting her know that she was observed.
Before Jean could decide her companion looked up, then rapidly
and confusedly rose. She could only be Miss Armiger, and she
had been such a figure of woe that it was a surprise not to see
her in tears. She was by no means in tears; but she was for an
instant extremely blank, an instant during which Jean remembered, rather to wonder at it, Mrs Beever's having said of her
that one really didn't know whether she was awfully plain or
strikingly handsome. Jean felt that one quite did know: she was

awfully plain. It may immediately be mentioned that about the charm of the apparition offered meanwhile to her own eyes Rose Armiger had not a particle of doubt: a slim, fair girl who struck her as a light sketch for something larger, a cluster of happy hints with nothing yet quite 'put in' but the splendour of the hair and the grace of the clothes – clothes that were not as the clothes of Wilverley. The reflection of these things came back to Jean from a pair of eyes as to which she judged that the extreme lightness of their grey was what made them so strange as to be ugly – a reflection that spread into a sudden smile from a wide, full-lipped mouth, whose regular office, obviously, was to produce the second impression. In a flash of small square white teeth this second impression was produced and the ambiguity that Mrs Beever had spoken of lighted up – an ambiguity worth all the dull prettiness in the world. Yes, one quite did know: Miss Armiger was strikingly handsome. It thus took her but a few seconds to repudiate every connection with the sombre image Jean had just encountered.

'Excuse my jumping out at you,' she said. 'I heard a sound – I was expecting a friend.' Jean thought her attitude an odd one for the purpose, but hinted a fear of being in that case in the way; on which the young lady protested that she was delighted to see her, that she had already heard of her, that she guessed who she was. 'And I daresay you've already heard of *me*.'

Jean shyly confessed to this, and getting away from the subject as quickly as possible, produced on the spot her formal credentials.

'Mrs Beever sent me over to ask if it's really quite right we should come to luncheon. We came out of church before the sermon, because of some people who were to go home with us. They're with Mrs Beever now, but she told me to come straight across the garden – the short way.'

Miss Armiger continued to smile. 'No way ever seems short enough for Mrs Beever!'

There was an intention in this, as Jean faintly felt, that was lost upon her; but while she was wondering her companion went on:

'Did Mrs Beever direct you to inquire of *me*?'

Jean hesitated. 'Of anyone, I think, who would be here to tell me in case Mrs Bream shouldn't be quite so well.'

'She isn't quite so well.'

The younger girl's face showed the flicker of a fear of losing her entertainment; on perceiving which the elder pursued:

'But we shan't romp or racket – shall we? We shall be very quiet.'

'Very, very quiet,' Jean eagerly echoed.

Her new friend's smile became a laugh, which was followed by the abrupt question: 'Do you mean to be long with Mrs Beever?'

'Till her son comes home. You know he's at Oxford, and his term soon ends.'

'And yours ends with it – you depart as he arrives?'

'Mrs Beever tells me I positively shan't,' said Jean.

'Then you positively won't. Everything is done here exactly as Mrs Beever tells us. Don't you like her son?' Rose Armiger asked.

'I don't know yet; it's exactly what she wants me to find out.'

'Then you'll have to be very clear.'

'But if I find out I don't?' Jean risked.

'I shall be very sorry for you!'

'I think then it will be the only thing in this love of an old place that I shan't have liked.'

Rose Armiger for a moment rested her eyes on her visitor, who was more and more conscious that she was strange and yet not, as Jean had always supposed strange people to be, disagreeable. 'Do you like *me*?' she unexpectedly inquired.

'How can I tell – at the end of three minutes?'

'*I* can tell – at the end of one! You must try to like me – you must be very kind to me,' Miss Armiger declared. Then she added: 'Do you like Mr Bream?'

Jean considered; she felt that she must rise to the occasion. 'Oh, immensely!' At this her interlocutress laughed again, and it made her continue with more reserve: 'Of course I only saw him for five minutes – yesterday at the Bank.'

'Oh, we know how long you saw him!' Miss Armiger exclaimed. 'He has told us all about your visit.'

Jean was slightly awe-stricken: this picture seemed to include so many people. 'Whom has he told?'

Her companion had the air of being amused at everything she said; but for Jean it was an air, none the less, with a kind of foreign charm in it. 'Why, the very first person was of course his poor little wife.'

'But I'm not to see *her*, am I?' Jean rather eagerly asked, puzzled by the manner of the allusion and but half suspecting it to be a part of her informant's general ease.

'You're not to see her, but even if you were she wouldn't hurt you for it,' this young lady replied. 'She understands his friendly way and likes above all his beautiful frankness.'

Jean's bewilderment began to look as if she too now, as she remembered, understood and liked these things. It might have been in confirmation of what was in her mind that she presently said: 'He told me I might see the wonderful baby. He told me he would show it to me himself.'

'I'm sure he'll be delighted to do that. He's awfully proud of the wonderful baby.'

'I suppose it's very lovely,' Jean remarked with growing confidence.

'Lovely! Do you think babies are ever lovely?'

Taken aback by this challenge, Jean reflected a little; she found, however, nothing better to say than, rather timidly: 'I like dear little children, don't you?'

Miss Armiger in turn considered. 'Not a bit!' she then replied. 'It would be very sweet and attractive of me to say I adore them; but I never pretend to feelings I can't keep up, don't you know? If you'd like, all the same, to see Effie,' she obligingly added, 'I'll so far sacrifice myself as to get her for you.'

Jean smiled as if this pleasantry were contagious. 'You won't sacrifice *her*?'

Rose Armiger stared. 'I won't destroy her.'

'Then do get her.'

'Not yet, not yet!' cried another voice – that of Mrs Beever, who had just been introduced and who, having heard the last words of the two girls, came, accompanied by the servant, down the hall. 'The baby's of no importance. We've come over for the mother. Is it true that Julia has had a bad turn?' she asked of Rose Armiger.

Miss Armiger had a peculiar way of looking at a person before speaking, and she now, with this detachment, delayed so long to answer Mrs Beever that Jean also rested her eyes, as if for a reason, on the good lady from Eastmead. She greatly admired her, but in that instant, the first of seeing her at Bounds, she perceived once for all how the difference of the setting made another thing of the gem. Short and solid, with rounded corners and full supports, her hair very black and very flat, her eyes very small for the amount of expression they could show, Mrs Beever was so 'early Victorian' as to be almost prehistoric – was constructed to move amid massive mahogany and sit upon banks of Berlin-wool. She was like an odd volume, 'sensibly' bound, of some old magazine. Jean knew that the great social event of her younger years had been her going to a fancy-ball in the character of an Andalusian, an incident of which she still carried a memento in the shape of a hideous fan. Jean was so constituted that she also knew, more dimly but at the end of five minutes, that the elegance at Mr Bream's was slightly provincial. It made none the less a medium in which Mrs Beever looked superlatively local. That indeed in turn caused Jean to think the old place still more of a 'love'.

'I believe our poor friend feels rather down,' Miss Armiger finally brought out. 'But I don't imagine it's of the least consequence,' she immediately added.

The contrary of this was, however, in some degree foreshadowed in a speech directed to Jean by the footman who had admitted her. He reported Mr Bream as having been in his wife's room for nearly an hour, and Doctor Ramage as having arrived some time before and not yet come out. Mrs Beever decreed, upon this news, that they must drop their idea of lunching and that Jean must go straight back to the friends who had been left at the other house. It was these friends who, on the way from church, had mentioned their having got wind of the rumour – the quick circulation of which testified to the compactness of Wilverley – that there had been a sudden change in Mrs Bream since the hour at which her husband's note was written. Mrs Beever dismissed her companion to Eastmead with a message for her visitors. Jean was to entertain them there in her stead and to understand that she might return to luncheon only in case of being sent for. At the door the girl paused and exclaimed rather wistfully to Rose Armiger: 'Well, then, give her my love!'

'Your young friend,' Rose commented, 'is as affectionate as she's pretty: sending her love to people she has never seen!'

'She only meant the little girl. I think it's rather nice of her,' said Mrs Beever. 'My interest in these anxieties is always confined to the mamma. I thought we were going so straight.'

'I dare say we are,' Miss Armiger replied. 'But Nurse told me an hour ago that I'm not to see her at all this morning. It will be the first morning for several days.'

Mrs Beever was silent a little. 'You've enjoyed a privilege altogether denied to *me*.'

'Ah, you must remember,' said Rose, 'that I'm Julia's oldest friend. That's always the way she treats me.'

Mrs Beever assented. 'Familiarly, of course. Well, you're not mine; but that's the way I treat you too,' she went on. 'You must wait with me here for more news, and be as still as a mouse.'

'Dear Mrs Beever,' the girl protested, 'I never made a noise in all my life!'

'You will some day – you're so clever,' Mrs Beever said.

'I'm clever enough to be quiet.' Then Rose added, less gaily: 'I'm the one thing of her own that dear Julia has ever had.'

Mrs Beever raised her eyebrows. 'Don't you count her husband?'

'I count Tony immensely; but in another way.'

Again Mrs Beever considered: she might have been wondering in what way even so expert a young person as this could count Anthony Bream except as a treasure to his wife. But what she presently articulated was: 'Do you call him "Tony" to himself?'

Miss Armiger met her question this time promptly. 'He has asked me to – and to do it even to Julia. Don't be afraid!' she exclaimed; 'I know my place and I shan't go too far. Of course he's everything to her now,' she continued, 'and the child is already almost as much; but what I mean is that if he counts for a great deal more, I, at least, go back a good deal further. Though I'm three years older we were brought together as girls by one of the strongest of all ties – the tie of a common aversion.'

'Oh, I know your common aversion!' Mrs Beever spoke with her air of general competence.

'Perhaps then you know that her detestable stepmother was, very little to my credit, my aunt. If her father, that is, was Mrs Grantham's second husband, my uncle, my mother's brother, had been the first. Julia lost her mother; I lost both my mother and my father. Then Mrs Grantham took me: she had shortly before made her second marriage. She put me at the horrid school at Weymouth at which she had already put her step-daughter.'

'You ought to be obliged to her,' Mrs Beever suggested, 'for having made you acquainted.'

'We are – we've never ceased to be. It was as if she had made us sisters, with the delightful position for me of the elder, the protecting one. But it's the only good turn she has ever done us.'

Mrs Beever weighed this statement with her alternative, her business manner. 'Is she really then such a monster?'

Rose Armiger had a melancholy headshake. 'Don't ask me about her – I dislike her too much, perhaps, to be strictly fair. For me, however, I daresay, it didn't matter so much that she was narrow and hard: I wasn't an easy victim – I could take care of myself, I could fight. But Julia bowed her head and suffered. Never was a marriage more of a rescue.'

Mrs Beever took this in with unsuspended criticism. 'And yet Mrs Grantham travelled all the way down from town the other day simply to make her a visit of a couple of hours.'

'That wasn't a kindness,' the girl returned; 'it was an injury, and I believe – certainly Julia believes – that it was a calculated one. Mrs Grantham knew perfectly the effect she would have, and she triumphantly had it. She came, she said, at the particular crisis, to "make peace". Why couldn't she let the poor dear alone? She only stirred up the wretched past and reopened old wounds.'

For answer to this Mrs Beever remarked with some irrelevancy: 'She abused *you* a good deal, I think.'

Her companion smiled frankly. 'Shockingly, I believe, but

that's of no importance to me. She doesn't touch me or reach me now.'

'Your description of her,' said Mrs Beever, 'is a description of a monstrous bad woman. And yet she appears to have got two honourable men to give her the last proof of confidence.'

'My poor uncle utterly withdrew his confidence when he saw her as she was. She killed him – he died of his horror of her. As for Julia's father, he's honourable if you like, but he's a muff. He's afraid of his wife.'

'And her "taking" you, as you say, who were no real relation to her – her looking after you and putting you at school: wasn't that,' Mrs Beever propounded, 'a kindness?'

'She took me to torment me – or at least to make me feel her hand. She has an absolute necessity to do that – it was what brought her down here the other day.'

'You make out a wonderful case,' said Mrs Beever, 'and if ever I'm put on my trial for a crime – say for muddling the affairs of the Bank – I hope I shall be defended by some one with your gift and your manner. I don't wonder,' she blandly pursued, 'that your friends, even the blameless ones, like this dear pair, cling to you as they do.'

'If you mean you don't wonder I stay on here so long,' said Rose good-humouredly, 'I'm greatly obliged to you for your sympathy. Julia's the one thing I have of my own.'

'You make light of our husbands and lovers!' laughed Mrs Beever. 'Haven't I had the pleasure of hearing of a gentleman to whom you're soon to be married?'

Rose Armiger opened her eyes – there was perhaps a slight affectation in it. She looked, at any rate, as if she had to make a certain effort to meet the allusion. 'Dennis Vidal?' she then asked.

'Lord, are there more than one?' Mrs Beever cried; after which, as the girl, who had coloured a little, hesitated in a way that almost suggested alternatives, she added: 'Isn't it a definite engagement?'

Rose Armiger looked round at the clock. 'Mr Vidal will be here this morning. Ask him how he considers it.'

One of the doors of the hall at this moment opened, and Mrs Beever exclaimed with some eagerness: 'Here he is, perhaps!' Her eagerness was characteristic; it was part of a comprehensive

vision in which the pieces had already fallen into sharp adjust-
ment to each other. The young lady she had been talking with
had in these few minutes, for some reason, struck her more
forcibly than ever before as a possible object of interest to a
youth of a candour greater even than any it was incumbent on a
respectable mother to cultivate. Miss Armiger had just given her
a glimpse of the way she could handle honest gentlemen as
'muffs'. She was decidedly too unusual to be left out of account.
If there was the least danger of Paul's falling in love with her it
ought somehow to be arranged that her marriage should
encounter no difficulty.

The person now appearing, however, proved to be only
Doctor Ramage, who, having a substantial wife of his own, was
peculiarly unfitted to promise relief to Mrs Beever's anxiety. He
was a little man who moved, with a warning air, on tiptoe, as if
he were playing some drawing-room game of surprises, and who
had a face so candid and circular that it suggested a large white
pill. Mrs Beever had once said with regard to sending for him:
'It isn't to take his medicine, it's to take *him*. I take him twice a
week in a cup of tea.' It was his tone that did her good. He had
in his hand a sheet of note-paper, one side of which was covered
with writing and with which he immediately addressed himself
to Miss Armiger. It was a prescription to be made up, and he
begged her to see that it was carried on the spot to the chemist's,
mentioning that on leaving Mrs Bream's room he had gone
straight to the library to think it out. Rose, who appeared to
recognise at a glance its nature, replied that as she was fidgety
and wanted a walk she would perform the errand herself. Her
bonnet and jacket were there; she had put them on to go to
church, and then, on second thoughts, seeing Mr Bream give it
up, had taken them off.

'Excellent for you to go yourself,' said the Doctor. He had an
instruction to add, to which, lucid and prompt, already
equipped, she gave full attention. As she took the paper from
him he subjoined: 'You're a very nice, sharp, obliging person.'

'She knows what she's about!' said Mrs Beever with much
expression. 'But what in the world is Julia about?'

'I'll tell you when *I* know, my dear lady.'

'Is there really anything wrong?'

'I'm waiting to find out.'

Miss Armiger, before leaving them, was waiting too. She had been checked on the way to the door by Mrs Beever's question, and she stood there with her intensely clear eyes on Doctor Ramage's face.

Mrs Beever continued to study it as earnestly. 'Then you're not going yet?'

'By no means, though I've another pressing call. I must have that thing from you first,' he said to Rose.

She went to the door, but there again she paused. 'Is Mr Bream still with her?'

'Very much with her – that's why I'm here. She made a particular request to be left for five minutes alone with him.'

'So Nurse isn't there either?' Rose asked.

'Nurse has embraced the occasion to pop down for her lunch. Mrs Bream has taken it into her head that she has something very important to say.'

Mrs Beever firmly seated herself. 'And pray what may that be?'

'She turned me out of the room precisely so that I shouldn't learn.'

'I think *I* know what it is,' their companion, at the door, put in.

'Then what is it?' Mrs Beever demanded.

'Oh, I wouldn't tell you for the world!' And with this Rose Armiger departed.

CHAPTER 4

Left alone with the lady of Eastmead, Doctor Ramage studied his watch a little absently. 'Our young friend's exceedingly nervous.'

Mrs Beever glanced in the direction in which Rose had disappeared. 'Do you allude to that girl?'

'I allude to dear Mrs Tony.'

'It's equally true of Miss Armiger; she's as worried as a pea on a pan. Julia, as far as that goes,' Mrs Beever continued, 'can never have been a person to hold herself together.'

'Precisely – she requires to be held. Well, happily she has Tony to hold her.'

'Then he's not himself in one of his states?'

Doctor Ramage hesitated. 'I don't quite make him out. He seems to have fifty things at once in his head.'

Mrs Beever looked at the Doctor hard. 'When does he ever not have? But I had a note from him only this morning – in the highest spirits.'

Doctor Ramage's little eyes told nothing but what he wanted. 'Well, whatever happens to him, he'll always have *them*!'

Mrs Beever at this jumped up. 'Robert Ramage,' she earnestly demanded, 'what *is* to happen to that boy?'

Before he had time to reply there rang out a sudden sound which had, oddly, much of the effect of an answer and which caused them both to start. It was the near vibration, from Mrs Bream's room, of one of the smart, loud electric bells which were for Mrs Beever the very accent of the newness of Bounds. They waited an instant; then the Doctor said quietly: 'It's for Nurse!'

'It's not for you?' The bell sounded again as she spoke.

'It's for Nurse,' Doctor Ramage repeated, moving nevertheless to the door he had come in by. He paused again to listen, and the door, the next moment thrown open, gave passage to a tall, good-looking young man, dressed as if, with much freshness, for church, and wearing a large orchid in his buttonhole. 'You rang for Nurse?' the Doctor immediately said.

The young man stood looking from one of his friends to the other. 'She's there – it's all right. But ah, my dear people – !' And he passed his hand, with the vivid gesture of brushing away an image, over a face of which the essential radiance was visible even through perturbation.

'How's Julia now?' Mrs Beever asked.

'Much relieved, she tells me, at having spoken.'

'Spoken of what, Tony?'

'Of everything she can think of that's conceivable – that's damnable.'

'If I hadn't known that she wanted to do exactly that,' said the Doctor, 'I wouldn't have given her the opportunity.'

Mrs Beever's eyes sounded her colleague of the Bank. 'You're upset, my poor boy – you're in one of your greatest states. Something painful to you has taken place.'

Tony Bream paid no attention to this remark; all his attention was for his other visitor, who stood with one hand on the door of the hall and an open watch, on which he still placidly gazed, in the other. 'Ramage,' the young man suddenly broke out, 'are you keeping something back? *Isn't* she safe?'

The good Doctor's small, neat face seemed to grow more genially globular. 'The dear lady is convinced, you mean, that her very last hour is at hand?'

'So much so,' Tony replied, 'that if she got you and Nurse away, if she made me kneel down by her bed and take her two hands in mine, what do you suppose it was to say to me?'

Doctor Ramage beamed. 'Why, of course, that she's going to perish in her flower. I've been through it so often!' he said to Mrs Beever.

'Before, but not after,' that lady lucidly rejoined. 'She has had her chance of perishing, but now it's too late.'

'Doctor,' said Tony Bream, '*is* my wife going to die?'

His friend hesitated a moment. 'When a lady's only symptom of that tendency is the charming volubility with which she dilates upon it, that's very well as far as it goes. But it's not quite enough.'

'She says she *knows* it,' Tony returned. 'But you surely know more than she don't you?'

'I know everything that can be known. I know that when, in certain conditions, pretty young mothers have acquitted themselves of that inevitable declaration, they turn over and go comfortably to sleep.'

'That's exactly,' said Tony, 'what Nurse must make her do.'

'It's exactly what she's doing.' Doctor Ramage had no sooner spoken than Mrs Bream's bell sounded for the third time. 'Excuse me!' he imperturbably added. 'Nurse calls me.'

'And doesn't she call me?' cried Tony.

'Not in the least.' The Doctor raised his hand with instant authority. 'Stay where you are!' With this he went off to his patient.

If Mrs Beever often produced, with promptitude, her theory that the young banker was subject to 'states', this habit, of which he was admirably tolerant, was erected on the sense of something in him of which even a passing observer might have caught a glimpse. A woman of still more wit than Mrs Beever, whom he had met on the threshold of life, once explained some accident to him by the words: 'The reason is, you know, that you're so exaggerated.' This had not been a manner of saying that he was inclined to overshoot the truth; it had been an attempt to express a certain quality of passive excess which was the note of the whole man and which, for an attentive eye, began with his neckties and ended with his intonations. To look at him was immediately to see that he was a collection of gifts, which presented themselves as such precisely by having in each case slightly overflowed the measure. He could do things – this was all he knew about them; and he was ready-made, as it were – he had not had to put himself together. His dress was just too fine, his colour just too high, his moustache just too long, his voice just too loud, his smile just too gay. His movement, his manner, his tone were respectively just too free, too easy and too familiar; his being a very handsome, happy, clever, active, ambitiously local young man was in short just too obvious. But the result of it all was a presence that was in itself a close contact, the air of immediate, unconscious, unstinted life, and of his doing what he liked and liking to please. One of his 'states', for Mrs Beever, was the state of his being a boy again, and the sign of it was his talking nonsense. It was not an example of that tendency, but she noted almost as if it were that almost as soon as the Doctor had left them he asked if she had not brought over to him that awfully pretty girl.

'She has been here, but I sent her home again.' Then his visitor added: 'Does she strike you as awfully pretty?'

'As pretty as a pretty song! I took a tremendous notion to her.'

'She's only a child – for mercy's sake don't show your notion too much!' Mrs Beever ejaculated.

Tony Bream gave his bright stare; after which, with his still brighter alacrity, 'I see what you mean: of course I won't!' he declared. Then, as if candidly and conscientiously wondering: 'Is it showing it too much to hope she'll come back to luncheon?'

'Decidedly – if Julia's so down.'

'That's only too much for Julia – not for *her*,' Tony said with his flurried smile. 'But Julia knows about her, hopes she's coming and wants everything to be natural and pleasant.' He passed his hand over his eyes again, and as if at the same time recognising that his tone required explanation, 'It's just because Julia's so down, don't you see?' he subjoined. 'A fellow can't stand it.'

Mrs Beever spoke after a pause during which her companion roamed rather jerkily about. 'It's a mere accidental fluctuation. You may trust Ramage to know.'

'Yes, thank God, I may trust Ramage to know!' He had the accent of a man constitutionally accessible to suggestion, and could turn the next instant to a quarter more cheering. 'Do you happen to have an idea of what has become of Rose?'

Again Mrs Beever, making a fresh observation, waited a little before answering. 'Do you now call her "Rose"?'

'Dear, yes – talking with Julia. And with *her*,' he went on as if he couldn't quite remember – 'do I too? Yes,' he recollected, 'I think I must.'

'What one must one must,' said Mrs Beever dryly. '"Rose", then, has gone over to the chemist's for the Doctor.'

'How jolly of her!' Tony exclaimed. 'She's a tremendous comfort.'

Mrs Beever committed herself to no opinion on this point, but it was doubtless on account of the continuity of the question that she presently asked: 'Who's this person who's coming today to marry her?'

'A very good fellow, I believe – and "rising": a clerk in some Eastern house.'

'And why hasn't he come sooner?'

'Because he has been at Hong Kong, or some such place, trying hard to pick up an income. 'He's "poor but pushing", she says. They've no means but her own two hundred.'

'Two hundred a year? That's quite enough for them!' Mrs Beever opined.

'Then you had better tell him so!' laughed Tony.

'I hope you'll back me up!' she returned; after which, before he had time to speak, she broke out with irrelevance: 'How is it she knows what Julia wanted to say to you?'

Tony, surprised, looked vague. 'Just now? Does she know? – I haven't the least idea.' Rose appeared at this moment behind the glass doors of the vestibule, and he added: 'Here she is.'

'Then you can ask her.'

'Easily,' said Tony. But when the girl came in he greeted her only with a lively word of thanks for the service she had just rendered; so that the lady of Eastmead, after waiting a minute, took the line of assuming with a certain visible rigour that he might have a reason for making his inquiry without an auditor. Taking temporary leave of him, she mentioned the visitors at home whom she must not forget. 'Then you won't come back?' he asked.

'Yes, in an hour or two.'

'And bring Miss What's-her-name?'

As Mrs Beever failed to respond to this, Rose Armiger added her voice. 'Yes – do bring Miss What's-her-name.' Mrs Beever, without assenting, reached the door, which Tony had opened for her. Here she paused long enough to be overtaken by the rest of their companion's appeal. 'I delight so in her clothes.'

'I delight so in her hair!' Tony laughed.

Mrs Beever looked from one of them to the other.

'Don't you think you've delight enough with what your situation here already offers?' She departed with the private determination to return unaccompanied.

CHAPTER 5

Three minutes later Tony Bream put his question to his other visitor. 'Is it true that you know what Julia a while ago had the room cleared in order to say to me?'

Rose hesitated. 'Mrs Beever repeated to you that I told her so? – Yes, then; I probably do know.' She waited again a little. 'The poor darling announced to you her conviction that she's dying.' Then at the face with which he greeted her exactitude: 'I haven't needed to be a monster of cunning to guess!' she exclaimed.

He had perceptibly paled: it made a difference, a kind of importance for that absurdity that it was already in other ears. 'She has said the same to you?'

Rose gave a pitying smile. 'She has done me that honour.'

'Do you mean today?'

'Today – and once before.'

Tony looked simple in his wonder. 'Yesterday?'

Rose hesitated again. 'No; before your child was born. Soon after I came.'

'She had made up her mind then from the first?'

'Yes,' said Rose, with the serenity of superior sense; 'she had laid out for herself that pleasant little prospect. She called it a presentiment, a fixed idea.'

Tony took this in with a frown. 'And you never spoke of it?'

'To you? Why in the world should I – when she herself didn't? I took it perfectly for what it was – an inevitable but unimportant result of the nervous depression produced by her stepmother's visit.'

Tony had fidgeted away with his hands in the pockets of his trousers. 'Damn her stepmother's visit!'

'That's exactly what I did!' Rose laughed.

'Damn her stepmother too!' the young man angrily pursued.

'Hush!' said the girl soothingly: 'we mustn't curse our relations before the Doctor!' Doctor Ramage had come back from his patient, and she mentioned to him that the medicine for which she had gone out would immediately be delivered.

'Many thanks,' he replied: 'I'll pick it up myself. I *must* run out – to another case.' Then with a friendly hand to Tony and a nod at the room he had quitted: 'Things are quiet.'

Tony, gratefully grasping his hand, detained him by it. 'And what was that loud ring that called you?'

'A stupid flurry of Nurse. I was ashamed of her.'

'Then why did you stay so long?'

'To have it out with your wife. She wants you again.'

Tony eagerly dropped his hand. 'Then I go!'

The Doctor raised his liberated member. 'In a quarter of an hour – not before. I'm most reluctant, but I allow her five minutes.'

'It may make her easier afterwards,' Rose observed.

'That's precisely the ground of my giving in. Take care, you know; Nurse will time you,' the Doctor said to Tony.

'So many thanks. And you'll come back?'

'The moment I'm free.'

When he had gone Tony stood there sombre. 'She wants to say it again – that's what she wants.'

'Well,' Rose answered, 'the more she says it the less it's true. It's not she who decides it.'

'No,' Tony brooded; 'it's not she. But it's not you and I either,' he soon went on.

'It's not even the Doctor,' Rose remarked with her conscious irony.

Her companion rested his troubled eyes on her. 'And yet he's as worried as if it were.' She protested against this imputation with a word to which he paid no heed. 'If anything should happen' – and his eyes seemed to go as far as his thought – 'what on earth do you suppose would become of me?'

The girl looked down, very grave. 'Men have borne such things.'

'Very badly – the real ones.' He seemed to lose himself in the effort to embrace the worst, to think it out. 'What should I do? where should I turn?'

She was silent a little. 'You ask me too much!' she helplessly sighed.

'Don't say that,' replied Tony, 'at a moment when I know so little if I mayn't have to ask you still more!' This exclamation made her meet his eyes with a turn of her own that might have struck him had he not been following another train. 'To you I can say it, Rose – she's inexpressibly dear to me.'

She showed him a face intensely receptive. 'It's for your affection for her that I've really given you mine.' Then she shook her head – seemed to shake out, like the overflow of a cup, her generous gaiety. 'But be easy. We shan't have loved her so much only to lose her.'

'I'll be hanged if we shall!' Tony responded. 'And such talk's a vile false note in the midst of a joy like yours.'

'Like mine?' Rose exhibited some vagueness.

Her companion was already accessible to the amusement of it. 'I hope that's not the way you mean to look at Mr Vidal!'

'Ah, Mr Vidal!' she ambiguously murmured.

'Shan't you then be glad to see him?'

'Intensely glad. But how shall I say it?' She thought a moment and then went on as if she found the answer to her question in Tony's exceptional intelligence and their comfortable intimacy. 'There's gladness and gladness. It isn't love's young dream; it's rather an old and rather a sad story. We've worried and waited – we've been acquainted with grief. We've come together a weary way.'

'I know you've had a horrid grind. But isn't this the end of it?'

Rose hesitated. 'That's just what he's to settle.'

'Happily, I see! Just look at him.'

The glass doors, as Tony spoke, had been thrown open by the butler. The young man from China was there – a short, meagre young man, with a smooth face and a dark blue double-breasted jacket. 'Mr Vidal!' the butler announced, withdrawing again, while the visitor, whose entrance had been rapid, suddenly and shyly faltered at the sight of his host. His pause, however, lasted but just long enough to enable Rose to bridge it over with the frankest maidenly grace; and Tony's quick sense of being out of place at this reunion was not a bar to the impression of her charming, instant action, her soft 'Dennis, Dennis!' her light, fluttered arms, her tenderly bent head and the short, bright stillness of her clasp of her lover. Tony shone down at them

with the pleasure of having helped them, and the warmth of it
was in his immediate grasp of the traveller's hand. He cut short
his embarrassed thanks – he was too delighted; and leaving him
with the remark that he would presently come back to show
him his room, he went off again to poor Julia.

CHAPTER 6

Dennis Vidal, when the door had closed on his host, drew again to his breast the girl to whom he was plighted and pressed her there with silent joy. She softly submitted, then still more softly disengaged herself, though in his flushed firmness he but partly released her. The light of admiration was in his hard young face – a visible tribute to what she showed again his disaccustomed eyes. Holding her yet, he covered her with a smile that produced two strong but relenting lines on either side of his dry, thin lips. 'My own dearest,' he murmured, 'you're still more so than one remembered!'

She opened her clear eyes wider. 'Still more what?'

'Still more of a fright!' And he kissed her again.

'It's you that are wonderful, Dennis,' she said; 'you look so absurdly young.'

He felt with his lean, fine brown hand his spare, clean brown chin. 'If I looked as old as I feel, dear girl, they'd have my portrait in the illustrated papers.'

He had now drawn her down upon the nearest sofa, and while he sat sideways, grasping the wrist of which he remained in possession after she had liberated her fingers, she leaned back and took him in with a deep air of her own. 'And yet it's not that you're exactly childish – or so extraordinarily fresh,' she went on as if to puzzle out, for her satisfaction, her impression of him.

'"Fresh", my dear girl!' He gave a little happy jeer; then he raised her wrist to his mouth and held it there as long as she would let him, looking at her hard. '*That's* the freshest thing I've ever been conscious of!' he exclaimed as she drew away her hand and folded her arms.

'You're worn, but you're not wasted,' she brought out in her kind but considering way. 'You're awfully well, you know.'

'Yes, I'm awfully well, I know' – he spoke with just the

faintest ring of impatience. Then he added: 'Your voice, all the
while, has been in my ears. But there's something you put into
it that *they* – out there, stupid things! – couldn't. Don't "size me
up" so,' he continued smiling; 'you make me nervous about
what I may seem to come to!'

They had both shown shyness, but Rose's was already gone.
She kept her inclined position and her folded arms; supported
by the back of the sofa, her head preserved, toward the side on
which he sat, its charming contemplative turn. 'I'm only thinking,' she said, 'that you look young just as a steel instrument of
the best quality, no matter how much it's handled, often looks
new.'

'Ah, if you mean I'm kept bright by use—!' the young man
laughed.

'You're polished by life.'

' "Polished" is delightful of you!'

'I'm not sure you've come back handsomer than you went,'
said Rose, 'and I don't know if you've come back richer.'

'Then let me immediately tell you I have!' Dennis broke in.

She received the announcement, for a minute, in silence: a
good deal more passed between this pair than they uttered.
'What I was going to say,' she then quietly resumed, 'is that I'm
awfully pleased with myself when I see that at any rate you're –
what shall I call you? – a made man.'

Dennis frowned a little through his happiness. 'With "yourself"? Aren't you a little pleased with me?'

She hesitated. 'With myself first, because I was sure of you
first.'

'Do you mean before I was of you? – I'm somehow not sure
of you yet!' the young man declared.

Rose coloured slightly; but she gaily laughed. 'Then I'm ahead
of you in everything!'

Leaning toward her with all his intensified need of her and
holding by his extended arm the top of the sofa-back, he worried
with his other hand a piece of her dress, which he had begun to
finger for want of something more responsive. 'You're as far
beyond me still as all the distance I've come.' He had dropped
his eyes upon the crumple he made in her frock, and her
own during that moment, from her superior height, descended
upon him with a kind of unseen appeal. When he looked up

again it was gone. 'What do you mean by a "made" man?' he asked.

'Oh, not the usual thing, but the real thing. A man one needn't worry about.'

'Thank you! The man not worried about is the man who muffs it.'

'That's a horrid, selfish speech,' said Rose Armiger. 'You don't deserve I should tell you what a success I now feel that you'll be.'

'Well, darling,' Dennis answered, 'that matters the less as I know exactly the occasion on which I shall fully feel it for myself.'

Rose manifested no further sense of this occasion than to go straight on with her idea. She placed her arm with frank friendship on his shoulder. It drew him closer, and he recovered his grasp of her free hand. With his want of stature and presence, his upward look at her, his small, smooth head, his seasoned sallowness and simple eyes, he might at this instant have struck a spectator as a figure actually younger and slighter than the ample, accomplished girl whose gesture protected and even a little patronised him. But in her vision of him she none the less clearly found full warrant for saying, instead of something he expected, something she wished and had her reasons for wishing, even if they represented but the gain of a minute's time. 'You're not splendid, my dear old Dennis – you're not dazzling, nor dangerous, nor even exactly distinguished. But you've a quiet little something that the tiresome time has made perfect, and that – just here where you've come to me at last – makes me immensely proud of you!'

She had with this so far again surrendered herself that he could show her in the ways he preferred how such a declaration touched him. The place in which he had come to her at last was of a nature to cause him to look about at it, just as to begin to inquire was to learn from her that he had dropped upon a crisis. He had seen Mrs Bream, under Rose's wing, in her maiden days; but in his eagerness to jump at a meeting with the only woman really important to him he had perhaps intruded more than he supposed. Though he expressed again the liveliest sense of the kindness of these good people, he was unable to conceal his disappointment at finding their inmate agitated also by something quite distinct from the joy of his arrival. 'Do you really think the poor lady will spoil our fun?' he rather resentfully put it to her.

'It will depend on what our fun may demand of her,' said Rose. 'If you ask me if she's in danger, I think not quite that: in such a case I must certainly have put you off. I dare say today will show the contrary. But she's so much to me – you know how much – that I'm uneasy, quickly upset; and if I seem to you flustered and not myself and not *with* you, I beg you to attribute it simply to the situation in the house.'

About this situation they had each more to say, and about many matters besides, for they faced each other over the deep waters of the accumulated and the undiscussed. They could keep no order and for five minutes more they rather helplessly played with the flood. Dennis was rueful at first, for what he seemed to have lighted upon was but half his opportunity; then he had an inspiration which made him say to his companion that they should both, after all, be able to make terms with any awkwardness by simply meeting it with a consciousness that their happiness had already taken form.

'Our happiness?' Rose was all interest.

'Why, the end of our delays.'

She smiled with every allowance. 'Do you mean we're to go out and be married this minute?'

'Well – almost; as soon as I've read you a letter.' He produced, with the words, his pocketbook.

She watched him an instant turn over its contents. 'What letter?'

'The best one I ever got. What have I done with it?' On his feet before her, he continued his search.

'From your people?'

'From my people. It met me in town, and it makes everything possible.'

She waited while he fumbled in his pockets; with her hands clasped in her lap she sat looking up at him. 'Then it's certainly a thing for me to hear.'

'But what the dickens have I done with it?' Staring at her, embarrassed, he clapped his hands, on coat and waistcoat, to other receptacles; at the end of a moment of which he had become aware of the proximity of the noiseless butler, upright in the high detachment of the superior servant who has embraced the conception of unpacking.

'Might I ask you for your keys, sir?'

Dennis Vidal had a light – he smote his forehead. 'Stupid – it's in my portmanteau!'

'Then go and get it!' said Rose, who perceived as she spoke, by the door that faced her, that Tony Bream was rejoining them. She got up, and Tony, agitated, as she could see, but with complete command of his manners, immediately and sociably said to Dennis that he was ready to guide him upstairs. Rose, at this, interposed. 'Do let Walker take him – I want to speak to you.'

Tony smiled at the young man. 'Will you excuse me then?' Dennis protested against the trouble he was giving, and Walker led him away. Rose meanwhile waited not only till they were out of sight and of earshot, but till the return of Tony, who, his hand on Vidal's shoulder, had gone with them as far as the door.

'Has he brought you good news?' said the master of Bounds.

'Very good. He's very well; he's all right.'

Tony's flushed face gave to the laugh with which he greeted this almost the effect of that of a man who had been drinking. 'Do you mean he's quite faithful?'

Rose always met a bold joke. 'As faithful as I! But your news is the thing.'

'Mine?' He closed his eyes a moment, but stood there scratching his head as if to carry off with a touch of comedy his betrayal of emotion.

'Has Julia repeated her declaration?'

Tony looked at her in silence. 'She has done something more extraordinary than that,' he replied at last.

'What has she done?'

Tony glanced round him, then dropped into a chair. He covered his face with his hands. 'I must get over it a little before I tell you!'

She waited compassionately for his nervousness to pass, dropping again, during the pause, upon the sofa she had just occupied with her visitor. At last as, while she watched him, his silence continued, she put him a question. 'Does she at any rate still maintain that she shan't get well?'

Tony removed his hands from his face. 'With the utmost assurance – or rather with the utmost serenity. But she treats that now as a mere detail.'

Rose wondered. 'You mean she's really convinced that she's sinking?'

'So she says.'

'But *is* she, good heavens? Such a thing isn't a matter of opinion: it's a fact or it's not a fact.'

'It's not a fact,' said Tony Bream. 'How can it be when one has only to see that her strength hasn't failed? She of course says it has, but she has a remarkable deal of it to show. What's the vehemence with which she expresses herself but a sign of increasing life? It's excitement, of course – partly; but it's also striking energy.'

'Excitement?' Rose repeated. 'I thought you just said she was "serene".'

Tony hesitated, but he was perfectly clear. 'She's calm about what she calls leaving me, bless her heart; she seems to have accepted that prospect with the strangest resignation. What she's uneasy, what she's in fact still more strangely tormented and exalted about, is another matter.'

'I see – the thing you just mentioned.'

'She takes an interest,' Tony went on, 'she asks questions, she sends messages, she speaks out with all her voice. She's delighted to know that Mr Vidal has at last come to you, and she told me to tell you so from her, and to tell *him* so – to tell you both, in fact, how she rejoices that what you've so long waited for is now so close at hand.'

Rose took this in with lowered eyes. 'How dear of her!' she murmured.

'She asked me particularly about Mr Vidal,' Tony continued – 'how he looks, how he strikes me, how you met. She gave me indeed a private message for him.'

Rose faintly smiled. 'A private one?'

'Oh, only to spare your modesty: a word to the effect that she answers for you.'

'In what way?' Rose asked.

'Why, as the charmingest, cleverest, handsomest, in every way most wonderful wife that ever any man will have had.'

'She *is* wound up!' Rose laughed. Then she said: 'And all the while what does Nurse think? – I don't mean,' she added with the same slight irony, 'of whether I shall do for Dennis.'

'Of Julia's condition? She wants Ramage to come back.'

Rose thought a moment. 'She's rather a goose, I think – she loses her head.'

'So I've taken the liberty of telling her.' Tony sat forward, his eyes on the floor, his elbows on his knees and his hands nervously rubbing each other. Presently he rose with a jerk. 'What do you suppose she wants me to do?'

Rose tried to suppose. 'Nurse wants you—?'

'No – that ridiculous girl.' Nodding back at his wife's room, he came and stood before the sofa.

Half reclining again, Rose turned it over, raising her eyes to him. 'Do you really mean something ridiculous?'

'Under the circumstances – grotesque.'

'Well,' Rose suggested, smiling, 'she wants you to allow her to name her successor.'

'Just the contrary!' Tony seated himself where Dennis Vidal had sat. 'She wants me to promise her she shall *have* no successor.'

His companion looked at him hard; with her surprise at something in his tone she had just visibly coloured. 'I see.' She was at a momentary loss. 'Do you call that grotesque?'

Tony, for an instant, was evidently struck by her surprise; then seeing the reason of it and blushing too a little, 'Not the idea, my dear Rose – God forbid!' he exclaimed. 'What I'm speaking of is the mistake of giving that amount of colour to her insistence – meeting her as if one accepted the situation as she represents it and were really taking leave of her.'

Rose appeared to understand and even to be impressed. 'You think that will make her worse?'

'Why, arranging everything as if she's going to die!' Tony sprang up afresh; his trouble was obvious and he fell into the restless pacing that had been his resource all the morning.

His interlocutress watched his agitation. 'Mayn't it be that if you do just that she'll, on the contrary, immediately find herself better?'

Tony wandered, again scratching his head. 'From the spirit of contradiction? I'll do anything in life that will make her happy, or just simply make her quiet: I'll treat her demand as intensely reasonable even, if it isn't better to treat it as an ado about nothing. But it stuck in my crop to lend myself, that way, to a death-bed solemnity. Heaven deliver us!' Half irritated and half anxious, suffering from his tenderness a twofold effect, he dropped into another seat with his hands in his pockets and his long legs thrust out.

'Does she wish it very solemn?' Rose asked.

'She's in dead earnest, poor darling. She wants a promise on my sacred honour – a vow of the most portentous kind.'

Rose was silent a little. 'You didn't give it?'

'I turned it off – I refused to take any such discussion seriously. I said: "My own darling, how can I meet you on so hateful a basis? Wait till you *are* dying!"' He lost himself an instant; then he was again on his feet. 'How in the world can she dream I'm capable—?' He hadn't patience even to finish his phrase.

Rose, however, finished it. 'Of taking a second wife? Ah, that's another affair!' she sadly exclaimed. 'We've nothing to do with that,' she added. 'Of course you understand poor Julia's feeling.'

'Her feeling?' Tony once more stood in front of her.

'Why, what's at the bottom of her dread of your marrying again.'

'Assuredly I do! Mrs Grantham naturally – *she's* at the bottom. She has filled Julia with the vision of my perhaps giving our child a stepmother.'

'Precisely,' Rose said, 'and if you had known, as I knew it, Julia's girlhood, you would do justice to the force of that horror.

It possesses her whole being – she would prefer that the child should die.'

Tony Bream, musing, shook his head with dark decision. 'Well, I would prefer that they neither of them should!'

'The simplest thing, then, is to give her your word.'

'My "word" isn't enough,' Tony said: 'she wants mystic rites and spells! The simplest thing, moreover, was exactly what I desired to do. My objection to the performance she demands was that this was just what it seemed to me not to be.'

'Try it,' said Rose, smiling.

'To bring her round?'

'Before the Doctor returns. When he comes, you know, he won't let you go back to her.'

'Then I'll go now,' said Tony, already at the door.

Rose had risen from the sofa. 'Be very brief – but be very strong.'

'I'll swear by all the gods – that or any other nonsense.' Rose stood there opposite to him with a fine, rich urgency which operated as a detention. 'I see you're right,' he declared. 'You always are, and I'm always indebted to you.' Then as he opened the door: 'Is there anything else?'

'Anything else?'

'I mean that you advise.'

She thought a moment. 'Nothing but that – for you to seem to enter thoroughly into her idea, to show her you understand it as she understands it herself.'

Tony looked vague. 'As she does?'

'Why, for the lifetime of your daughter.' As he appeared still not fully to apprehend, she risked: 'If you should lose Effie the reason would fail.'

Tony, at this, jerked back his head with a flush. 'My dear Rose, you don't imagine that it's as a *needed* vow—'

'That you would give it?' she broke in. 'Certainly I don't, any more than I suppose the degree of your fidelity to be the ground on which we're talking. But the thing is to convince Julia, and I said that only because she'll be more convinced if you strike her as really looking at what you subscribe to.'

Tony gave his nervous laugh. 'Don't you know I always "put down my name" – especially to "appeals" – in the most reckless way?' Then abruptly, in a different tone, as if with a passionate need to make it plain, 'I shall never, never, never,' he protested, 'so much as look at another woman!'

The girl approved with an eager gesture. 'You've got it, my dear Tony. Say it to her *that* way!' But he had already gone, and, turning, she found herself face to face with her lover, who had come back as she spoke.

CHAPTER 8

With his letter in his hand Dennis Vidal stood and smiled at her. 'What in the world has your dear Tony "got", and what is he to say?'

'To say? Something to his wife, who appears to have lashed herself into an extraordinary state.'

The young man's face fell. 'What sort of a state?'

'A strange discouragement about herself. She's depressed and frightened – she thinks she's sinking.'

Dennis looked grave. 'Poor little lady – what a bore for *us*! I remember her perfectly.'

'She of course remembers you,' Rose said. 'She takes the friendliest interest in your being here.'

'That's most kind of her in her condition.'

'Oh, her condition,' Rose returned, 'isn't quite so bad as she thinks.'

'I see.' Dennis hesitated. 'And that's what Mr Bream's to tell her.'

'That's a part of it.' Rose glanced at the document he had brought to her; it was in its envelope, and he tapped it a little impatiently on his left finger-tips. What she said, however, had no reference to it. 'She's haunted with a morbid alarm – on the subject, of all things, of his marrying again.'

'If she should die? She wants him not to?' Dennis asked.

'She wants him not to.' Rose paused a moment. 'She wants to have been the only one.'

He reflected, slightly embarrassed with this peep into a situation that but remotely concerned him. 'Well, I suppose that's the way women often feel.'

'I daresay it is.' The girl's gravity gave the gleam of a smile. 'I daresay it's the way *I* should.'

Dennis Vidal, at this, simply seized her and kissed her. 'You needn't be afraid – you'll be the only one!'

His embrace had been the work of a few seconds, and she had made no movement to escape from it; but she looked at him as if to convey that the extreme high spirits it betrayed were perhaps just a trifle mistimed. 'That's what I recommended him,' she dropped, 'to say to Julia.'

'Why, I should hope so!' Presently, as if a little struck, Dennis continued: 'Doesn't he want to?'

'Absolutely. They're all in all to each other. But he's naturally much upset and bewildered.'

'And he came to you for advice?'

'Oh, he comes to me,' Rose said, 'as he might come to talk of her with the mother that, poor darling, it's her misfortune never to have known.'

The young man's vivacity again played up. 'He treats you, you mean, as his mother-in-law?'

'Very much. But I'm thoroughly nice to him. People can do anything to me who are nice to Julia.'

Dennis was silent a moment; he had slipped his letter out of its cover. 'Well, I hope they're grateful to you for such devotion.'

'Grateful to me, Dennis? They quite adore me.' Then as if to remind him of something it was important he should feel: 'Don't you see what it is for a poor girl to have such an anchorage as this – such honourable countenance, such a place to fall back upon?'

Thus challenged, her visitor, with a moment's thought, did frank justice to her question. 'I'm certainly glad you've such jolly friends – one sees they're charming people. It has been a great comfort to me lately to know you were with them.' He looked round him, conscientiously, at the bright and beautiful hall. 'It *is* a good berth, my dear, and it must be a pleasure to live with such fine things. They've given me a room up there that's full of them – an awfully nice room.' He glanced at a picture or two – he took in the scene. 'Do they roll in wealth?'

'They're like all bankers, I imagine,' said Rose. 'Don't bankers always roll?'

'Yes, they seem literally to wallow. What a pity *we* ain't bankers, eh?'

'Ah, with my friends here their money's the least part of them,' the girl answered. 'The great thing's their personal goodness.'

Dennis had stopped before a large photograph, a great picture in a massive frame, supported, on a table, by a small gilded easel. 'To say nothing of their personal beauty! He's tremendously good-looking.'

Rose glanced with an indulgent sigh at a representation of Tony Bream in all his splendour, in a fine white waistcoat and a high white hat, with a stick and gloves and a cigar, his orchid, his stature and his smile. 'Ah, poor Julia's taste!'

'Yes,' Dennis exclaimed, 'one can see how he must have fetched her!'

'I mean the style of the thing,' said Rose.

'It isn't good, eh? Well, *you* know.' Then turning away from the picture, the young man added: 'They'll be after that fellow!'

Rose faltered. 'The people she fears?'

'The women-folk, bless 'em – if he should lose her.'

'I daresay,' said Rose. 'But he'll be proof.'

'Has he told you so?' Dennis smiled.

She met his smile with a kind of conscious bravado in her own. 'In so many words. But he assures me he'll calm her down.'

Dennis was silent a little: he had now unfolded his letter and run his eyes over it. 'What a funny subject for him to be talking about!'

'With me, do you mean?'

'Yes, and with his wife.'

'My dear man,' Rose exclaimed, 'you can imagine he didn't begin it!'

'Did *you*?' her companion asked.

She hesitated again, and then, 'Yes – idiot!' she replied with a quiet humour that produced, on his part, another demonstration of tenderness. This attempt she arrested, raising her hand, as she appeared to have heard a sound, with a quick injunction to listen.

'What's the matter?'

She bent her ear. 'Wasn't there a cry from Julia's room?'

'I heard nothing.'

Rose was relieved. 'Then it's only my nervousness.'

Dennis Vidal held up his letter. 'Is your nervousness too great to prevent your giving a moment's attention to this?'

'Ah, your letter!' Rose's eyes rested on it as if she had become conscious of it for the first time.

'It very intimately concerns our future,' said her visitor. 'I went up for it so that you should do me the favour to read it.'

She held out her hand promptly and frankly. 'Then give it to me – let me keep it a little.'

'Certainly; but kindly remember that I've still to answer it – I mean referring to points. I've waited to see you because it's from the "governor" himself – practically saying what he'll do for me.'

Rose held the letter; her large light eyes widened with her wonder and her sympathy. 'Is it something very good?'

Dennis prescribed, with an emphatic but amused nod at the paper, a direction to her curiosity. 'Read and you'll see!'

She dropped her eyes, but after a moment, while her left hand patted her heart, she raised them with an odd, strained expression. 'I mean is it really good enough?'

'That's exactly what I want you to tell me!' Dennis laughed out. A certain surprise at her manner was in his face.

While she noted it she heard a sound again, a sound this time explained by the opening of the door of the vestibule. Doctor Ramage had come back; Rose put down her letter. 'I'll tell you as soon as I have spoken to the Doctor.'

CHAPTER 9

The Doctor, eagerly, spoke to her first. 'Our friend has not come back?'

'Mine has,' said Rose with grace. 'Let me introduce Mr Vidal.' Doctor Ramage beamed a greeting, and our young lady, with her discreet gaiety, went on to Dennis: 'He too thinks all the world of me.'

'Oh, she's a wonder – she knows what to do! But you'll see that for yourself,' said the Doctor.

'I'm afraid you won't approve of me,' Dennis replied with solicitude. 'You'll think me rather in your patient's way.'

Doctor Ramage laughed. 'No indeed – I'm sure Miss Armiger will keep you out of it.' Then looking at his watch, 'Bream's not with her still?' he inquired of Rose.

'He came away, but he returned to her.'

'He shouldn't have done that.'

'It was by my advice, and I'm sure you'll find it's all right,' Rose returned. 'But you'll send him back to us.'

'On the spot.' The Doctor picked his way out.

'He's not at all easy,' Dennis pronounced when he had gone.

Rose demurred. 'How do you know that?'

'By looking at him. I'm not such a fool,' her visitor added with some emphasis, 'as you strike me as wishing to make of me.'

Rose candidly stared. 'As I strike you as wishing—?' For a moment this young couple looked at each other hard, and they both changed colour. 'My dear Dennis, what do you mean?'

He evidently felt that he had been almost violently abrupt; but it would have been equally evident to a spectator that he was a man of cool courage. 'I mean, Rose, that I don't quite know what's the matter with you. It's as if, unexpectedly, on my eager arrival, I find something or other between us.'

She appeared immensely relieved. 'Why, my dear child, of

course you do! Poor Julia's between us – much between us.' She faltered again; then she broke out with emotion: 'I may as well confess it frankly – I'm miserably anxious. Good heavens,' she added with impatience, 'don't you see it for yourself?'

'I certainly see that you're agitated and absent – as you warned me so promptly you would be. But remember you've quite denied to me the gravity of Mrs Bream's condition.'

Rose's impatience overflowed into a gesture. 'I've been doing that to deceive my own self!'

'I understand,' said Dennis kindly. 'Still,' he went on, considering, 'it's either one thing or the other. The poor lady's either dying, you know, or she ain't!'

His friend looked at him with a reproach too fine to be uttered. 'My dear Dennis – you're rough!'

He showed a face as conscientious as it was blank. 'I'm crude – possibly coarse? Perhaps I *am* – without intention.'

'Think what these people are to me,' said Rose.

He was silent a little. 'Is it anything so very extraordinary? Oh, I know,' he went on, as if he feared she might again accuse him of a want of feeling; 'I appreciate them perfectly – I do them full justice. Enjoying their hospitality here, I'm conscious of all their merits.' The letter she had put down was still on the table, and he took it up and fingered it a moment. 'All I mean is that I don't want you quite to sink the fact that I'm something to you too.'

She met this appeal with instant indulgence. 'Be a little patient with me,' she gently said. Before he could make a rejoinder she pursued: 'You yourself are impressed with the Doctor's being anxious. I've been trying not to think so, but I daresay you're right. There I've another worry.'

'The greater your worry, then, the more pressing our business.' Dennis spoke with cordial decision, while Rose, moving away from him, reached the door by which the Doctor had gone out. She stood there as if listening, and he continued: 'It's *me*, you know, that you've now to "fall back" upon.'

She had already raised a hand with her clear 'Hush!' and she kept her eyes on her companion while she tried to catch a sound. 'The Doctor said he would send him out of the room. But he doesn't.'

'All the better – for your reading this.' Dennis held out the letter to her.

She quitted her place. 'If he's allowed to stay, there must be something wrong.'

'I'm very sorry for them; but don't you call that a statement?'

'Ah, your letter?' Her attention came back to it, and, taking it from him, she dropped again upon the sofa with it. '*Voyons, voyons* this great affair!' – she had the air of trying to talk herself into calmness.

Dennis stood a moment before her. 'It puts us on a footing that really seems to me sound.'

She had turned over the leaf to take the measure of the document; there were three, large, close, neat pages. 'He's a trifle long-winded, the "governor"!'

'The longer the better,' Dennis laughed, 'when it's all in *that* key! Read it, my dear, quietly and carefully; take it in – it's really simple enough.' He spoke soothingly and tenderly, turning off to give her time and not oppress her. He moved slowly about the hall, whistling very faintly and looking again at the pictures, and when he had left her she followed him a minute with her eyes. Then she transferred them to the door at which she had just listened; instead of reading she watched as if for a movement of it. If there had been any one at that moment to see her face, such an observer would have found it strangely, tragically convulsed: she had the appearance of holding in with extraordinary force some passionate sob or cry, some smothered impulse of anguish. This appearance vanished miraculously as Dennis turned at the end of the room, and what he saw, while the great showy clock ticked in the scented stillness, was only his friend's study of what he had put before her. She studied it long, she studied it in silence – a silence so unbroken by inquiry or comment that, though he clearly wished not to seem to hurry her, he drew nearer again at last and stood as if waiting for some sign.

'Don't you call that really meeting a fellow?'

'I must read it again,' Rose replied without looking up. She turned afresh to the beginning, and he strolled away once more. She went through to the end; after which she said with tranquillity, folding the letter: 'Yes; it shows what they think of you.' She put it down where she had put it before, getting up as he came back to her. 'It's good not only for what he says, but for the way he says it.'

'It's a jolly bit more than I expected.' Dennis picked the letter up and, restoring it to its envelope, slipped it almost lovingly into a breastpocket. 'It does show, I think, that they don't want to lose me.'

'They're not such fools!' Rose had in her turn moved off, but now she faced him, so intensely pale that he was visibly startled; all the more that it marked still more her white grimace. 'My dear boy, it's a splendid future.'

'I'm glad it strikes you so!' he laughed.

'It's a great joy – you're all right. As I said a while ago, you're a made man.'

'Then by the same token, of course, you're a made woman!'

'I'm very, very happy about you,' she brightly conceded. 'The great thing is that there's more to come.

'Rather – there's more to come!' said Dennis. He stood meeting her singular smile. 'I'm only waiting for it.'

'I mean there's a lot behind – a general attitude. Read between the lines!'

'Don't you suppose I *have*, miss? I didn't venture, myself, to say that to you.'

'Do I have so to be prompted and coached?' asked Rose. 'I don't believe you even see all I mean. There are hints and tacit promises – glimpses of what may happen if you'll give them time.'

'Oh, I'll give them time!' Dennis declared. 'But he's really awfully cautious. You're sharp to have made out so much.'

'Naturally – I'm sharp.' Then, after an instant, 'Let me have the letter again,' the girl said, holding out her hand. Dennis promptly drew it forth, and she took it and went over it in silence once more. He turned away as he had done before, to give her a chance; he hummed slowly, to himself, about the room, and once more, at the end of some minutes, it appeared to strike him that she prolonged her perusal. But when he approached her again she was ready with her clear contentment. She folded the letter and handed it back to him. 'Oh, you'll do!' she proclaimed.

'You're really quite satisfied?'

She hesitated a moment. 'For the present – perfectly.' Her eyes were on the precious document as he fingered it, and something in his way of doing so made her break into incongruous gaiety. He had opened it delicately and been caught again by a passage. 'You handle it as if it were a thousand-pound note!'

He looked up at her quickly. 'It's much more than that. Capitalise his figure.'

'"Capitalise" it?'

'Find the invested sum.'

Rose thought a moment. 'Oh, I'll do everything for you but cipher! But it's millions.' Then as he returned the letter to his pocket she added: 'You should have that thing mounted in double glass – with a little handle like a handscreen.'

'There's certainly nothing too good for the charter of our liberties – for that's what it really is,' Dennis said. 'But you *can* face the music?' he went on.

'The music?' – Rose was momentarily blank.

He looked at her hard again. 'You have, my dear, the most extraordinary vacancies. The figure we're talking of – the poor, dear little figure. The five-hundred-and-forty,' he a trifle sharply explained. 'That's about what it makes.'

'Why, it seems to me a lovely little figure,' said the girl. 'To the "likes" of me, how can that be anything but a duck of an income? Then,' she exclaimed, 'think also of what's to come!'

'Yes – but I'm not speaking of anything you may bring.'

Rose wavered, judicious, as if trying to be as attentive as he desired. 'I see – without that. But I wasn't speaking of that either,' she added.

'Oh, *you* may count it – I only mean I don't touch it. And the going out – you take that too?' Dennis asked.

Rose looked brave. 'Why it's only for two years.'

He flushed suddenly, as with a flood of reassurance, putting his arms round her as round the fulfilment of his dream. 'Ah, my own old girl!'

She let him clasp her again, but when she disengaged herself they were somehow nearer to the door that led away to Julia Bream. She stood there as she had stood before, while he still held one of her hands; then she brought forth something that betrayed an extraordinary disconnection from all that had just preceded. 'I can't make out why he doesn't send him back!'

Dennis Vidal dropped her hand; both his own went into his

pockets, and he gave a kick to the turned-up corner of a rug. 'Mr Bream – the Doctor? Oh, they know what they're about!'

'The Doctor doesn't at all want him to be there. Something has happened,' Rose declared as she left the door.

Her companion said nothing for a moment. 'Do you mean the poor lady's gone?' he at last demanded.

'Gone?' Rose echoed.

'Do you mean Mrs Bream is dead?'

His question rang out so that Rose threw herself back in horror. 'Dennis – God forbid!'

'God forbid too, I say. But one doesn't know what you mean – you're too difficult to follow. One thing, at any rate, you clearly have in your head – that we must take it as possibly on the cards. That's enough to make it remarkably to the point to remind you of the great change that would take place in your situation if she *should* die.'

'What else in the world but that change am I thinking of?' Rose asked.

'You're not thinking of it perhaps so much in the connection I refer to. If Mrs Bream goes, your "anchorage", you call it, goes.'

'I see what you mean.' She spoke with the softest assent; the tears had sprung into her eyes and she looked away to hide them.

'One may have the highest possible opinion of her husband and yet not quite see you staying on here in the same manner with *him*.'

Rose was silent, with a certain dignity. 'Not quite,' she presently said with the same gentleness.

'The way therefore to provide against everything is – as I remarked to you a while ago – to settle with me this minute the day, the nearest one possible, for our union to become a reality.'

She slowly brought back her troubled eyes. 'The day to marry you?'

'The day to marry me of course!' He gave a short, uneasy laugh. 'What else?'

She waited again, and there was a fear deep in her face. 'I must settle it this minute?'

Dennis stared. 'Why, my dear child, when in the world if not now?'

'You can't give me a little more time?' she asked.

'More time?' His gathered stupefaction broke out. 'More time – after giving you years?'

'Ah, but just at the last, here – this news, this rush is sudden.'

'Sudden!' Dennis repeated. 'Haven't you known I was coming and haven't you known for what?'

She looked at him now with an effort of resolution in which he could see her white face harden; as if by a play of some inner mechanism something dreadful had taken place in it. Then she said with a painful quaver that no attempt to be natural could keep down: 'Let me remind you Dennis, that your coming was not at my request. You've come – yes; but you've come because you would. You've come in spite of me.'

He gasped, and with the mere touch of her tone his own eyes filled. 'You haven't wanted me?'

'I'm delighted to see you.'

'Then in God's name what do you mean? Where *are* we, and what are you springing on me?'

'I'm only asking you again, as I've asked you already, to be patient with me – to let me, at such a critical hour, turn round. I'm only asking you to bear with me – I'm only asking you to wait.'

'To wait for what?' He snatched the words out of her mouth. 'It's because I *have* waited that I'm here. What I want of you is three simple words – that you can utter in three simple seconds.' He looked about him, in his helpless dismay, as if to call the absent to witness. 'And you look at me like a stone. You open up an abyss. You give me nothing, nothing.' He paused, as it were, for a contradiction, but she made none; she had lowered her eyes and, supported against a table, stood there rigid and passive. Dennis sank into a chair with his vain hands upon his knees. 'What do you mean by my coming in spite of you? You never asked me not to – you've treated me well till now. It was my idea – yes; but you perfectly accepted it.' He gave her time to assent to this or to deny it, but she took none, and he continued: 'Don't you understand the one feeling that has possessed me and sustained me? Don't you understand that I've thought of nothing else every hour of my way? I arrived here with a longing for you that words can't utter; and now I see – though I couldn't immediately be sure – that I found you from the first constrained and unnatural.'

Rose, as he went on, had raised her eyes again; they seemed to follow his words in sombre submission. 'Yes, you must have found me strange enough.'

'And don't again say it's your being anxious—!' Dennis sprang up warningly. 'It's your being anxious that just makes me right.'

His companion shook her head slowly and ambiguously. 'I *am* glad you've come.'

'To have the pleasure of not receiving me?'

'I have received you,' Rose replied. 'Every word I've spoken to you and every satisfaction I've expressed is true, is deep. I do admire you, I do respect you, I'm proud to have been your friend. Haven't I assured you of my pure joy in your promotion and your prospects?'

'What do you call assuring me? You utterly misled me for some strange moments; you mystified me; I think I may say you trifled with me. The only assurance I'm open to is that of your putting your hand in mine as my wife. In God's name,' the young man panted, 'what has happened to you and what has changed you?'

'I'll tell you tomorrow,' said Rose.

'Tell me what I insist on?'

She cast about her. 'Tell you things I can't now.'

He sounded her with visible despair. 'You're not sincere – you're not straight. You've nothing to tell me, and you're afraid. You're only gaining time, and you've only been doing so from the first. I don't know what it's for – you're beyond me; but if it's to back out I'll be hanged if I give you a moment.'

Her wan face, at this, showed a faint flush; it seemed to him five years older than when he came in. 'You take, with your cruel accusations, a strange way to keep me!' the girl exclaimed. 'But I won't talk to you in bitterness,' she pursued in a different tone. 'That will drop if we do allow it a day or two.' Then on a sharp motion of his impatience she added: 'Whether you allow it or not, you know, I must take the time I need.'

He was angry now, as if she were not only proved evasion, but almost proved insolence; and his anger deepened at her return to this appeal that offered him no meaning. 'No, no, you must choose,' he said with passion, 'and if you're really honest you will. I'm here for you with all my soul, but I'm here for you now or never.'

'Dennis!' she weakly murmured.

'You do back out?'

She put out her hand. 'Goodbye.'

He looked at her as over a flood; then he thrust his hand behind him and glanced about for his hat. He moved blindly, like a man picking himself up from a violent fall – flung indeed suddenly from a smooth, swift vehicle. 'Goodbye.'

He quickly remembered that he had not brought in his hat, and also, the next instant, that even to clap it on wouldn't under the circumstances qualify him for immediate departure from Bounds. Just as it came over him that the obligation he had incurred must keep him at least for the day, he found himself in the presence of his host, who, while his back was turned, had precipitately reappeared and whose vision of the place had resulted in an instant question.

'Mrs Beever has not come back? Julia wants her – Julia must see her!'

Dennis was separated by the width of the hall from the girl with whom he had just enjoyed such an opportunity of reunion, but there was for the moment no indication that Tony Bream, engrossed with a graver accident, found a betrayal in the space between them. He had, however, for Dennis the prompt effect of a reminder to take care: it was a consequence of the very nature of the man that to look at him was to recognise the value of appearances and that he couldn't have dropped upon any scene, however disordered, without, by the simple fact, re-establishing a superficial harmony. His new friend met him with a movement that might have been that of stepping in front of some object to hide it, while Rose, on her side, sounding out like a touched bell, was already alert with her response. 'Ah,' said Dennis, to himself, 'it's for *them* she cares!'

'She has not come back, but if there's a hurry—' Rose was all there.

'There *is* a hurry. Some one must go for her.'

Dennis had a point to make that he must make on the spot. He spoke before Rose's rejoinder. 'With your increasing anxieties, Mr Bream, I'm quite ashamed to be quartered on you. Hadn't I really better be at the inn?'

'At the inn – to go from here? My dear fellow, are you mad?'

Tony sociably scoffed; he wouldn't hear of it. 'Don't be afraid; we've plenty of use for you – if only to keep this young woman quiet.'

'He can be of use this instant.' Rose looked at her suitor as if there were not the shadow of a cloud between them. 'The servants are getting luncheon. Will *you* go over for Mrs Beever?'

'Ah,' Tony demurred, laughing, 'we mustn't make him fetch and carry!'

Dennis showed a momentary blankness and then, in his private discomposure, jumped at the idea of escaping from the house and into the air. 'Do employ me,' he pleaded. 'I want to stretch my legs – I'll do anything.'

'Since you're so kind, then, and it's so near,' Tony replied. 'Mrs Beever's our best friend, and always the friend of our friends, and she's only across the river.'

'Just six minutes,' said Rose, 'by the short way. Bring her back with you.'

'The short way,' Tony pressingly explained, 'is through my garden and out of it by the gate on the river.'

'At the river you turn to the right – the little foot-bridge is *her* bridge,' Rose went on.

'You pass the gatehouse – empty and closed – at the other side of it, and there you are,' said Tony.

'In her garden – it's lovely. Tell her it's for Mrs Bream and it's important,' Rose added.

'My wife's calling aloud for her!' Tony laid his hand, with his flushed laugh, on the young man's shoulder.

Dennis had listened earnestly, looking at his companions in turn. 'It doesn't matter if she doesn't know in the least who I am?'

'She knows perfectly – don't be shy!' Rose familiarly exclaimed.

Tony gave him a great pat on the back which sent him off. 'She has even something particular to say to you! She takes a great interest in his relations with you,' he continued to Rose as the door closed behind their visitor. Then meeting in her face a certain impatience of any supersession of the question of Julia's state, he added, to justify his allusion, a word accompanied by the same excited laugh that had already broken from him. 'Mrs Beever deprecates the idea of any further delay in your marriage and thinks you've got quite enough to "set up" on. She pronounces your means remarkably adequate.'

'What does she know about our means?' Rose coldly asked.

'No more, doubtless, than I! But that needn't prevent her. It's the wish that's father to the thought. That's the result of her general goodwill to you.'

'She has no goodwill of any sort to me. She doesn't like me.' Rose spoke with marked dryness, in which moreover a certain surprise at the direction of her friend's humour was visible. Tony was now completely out of his groove; they indeed both were, though Rose was for the moment more successful in concealing her emotion. Still vibrating with the immense effort of the morning and particularly of the last hour, she could yet hold herself hard and observe what was taking place in her companion. He had been through something that had made his nerves violently active, so that his measure of security, of reality almost, was merged in the mere sense of the unusual. It was precisely this evidence of what he had been through that helped the girl's curiosity to preserve a waiting attitude – the firm surface she had triumphantly presented to each of the persons whom, from an early hour, she had had to encounter. But Tony had now the air of not intending to reward her patience by a fresh communication; it was as if some new delicacy had operated and he had struck himself as too explicit. He had looked astonished at her judgement of the lady of Eastmead.

'My dear Rose,' he said, 'I think you're greatly mistaken. Mrs Beever much appreciates you.'

She was silent at first, showing him a face worn with the ingenuity of all that in her interview with Dennis Vidal she had had to keep out of it and put into it. 'My dear Tony,' she then blandly replied, 'I've never known any one like you for not having two grains of observation. I've known people with only a little; but a little's a poor affair. You've absolutely none at all, and that, for your character, is the right thing: it's magnificent and perfect.'

Tony greeted this with real hilarity. 'I like a good square one between the eyes!'

'You can't like it as much as I like you for being just as you are. Observation's a second-rate thing; it's only a precaution – the refuge of the small and the timid. It protects our own ridicules and props up our defences. You may have ridicules – I don't say so; but you've no suspicions and no fears and no doubts; you're natural and generous and easy—'

'And beautifully, exquisitely stupid!' Tony broke in. '"Natural" – thank you! Oh, the horrible people who are natural! What you mean – only you're too charming to say it – is that I'm so utterly taken up with my own interests and feelings that I pipe about them like a canary in a cage. Not to have the things you mention, and above all not to have imagination, is simply not to have tact, than which nothing is more unforgivable and more loathsome. What lovelier proof of my selfishness could I be face to face with than the fact – which I immediately afterwards blushed for – that, coming in to you here a while ago, in the midst of something so important to you, I hadn't the manners to ask you so much as a question about it?'

'Do you mean about Mr Vidal – after he had gone to his room? You did ask me a question,' Rose said; 'but you had a subject much more interesting to speak of.' She waited an instant before adding: 'You spoke of something I haven't ceased to think of.' This gave Tony a chance for reference to his discharge of the injunction she had then laid upon him; as a reminder of which Rose further observed: 'There's plenty of time for Mr Vidal.'

'I hope indeed he's going to stay. I like his looks immensely,' Tony responded. 'I like his type; it matches so with what you've told me of him. It's the real thing – I wish we had him here.' Rose, at this, gave a small, confused cry, and her host went on: 'Upon my honour I do – I know a man when I see him. He's just the sort of fellow I personally should have liked to be.'

'You mean *you're* not the real thing?' Rose asked.

It was a question of a kind that Tony's good-nature, shining out almost splendidly even through trouble, could always meet with princely extravagance. 'Not a bit! I'm bolstered up with all sorts of little appearances and accidents. Your friend there has his feet on the rock.' This picture of her friend's position moved Rose to another vague sound – the effect of which, in turn, was to make Tony look at her more sharply. But he appeared not to impute to her any doubt of his assertion, and after an instant he reverted, with a jump, to a matter that he evidently wished not to drop. 'You must really, you know, do justice to Mrs Beever.

When she dislikes one it's not a question of shades or degrees. She's not an underhand enemy – she very soon lets one know it.'

'You mean by something she says or does?'

Tony considered a moment. 'I mean she gives you her reasons – she's eminently direct. And I'm sure she has never lifted a finger against you.'

'Perhaps not. But she will,' said Rose. 'You yourself just gave me the proof.'

Tony wondered. 'What proof?'

'Why, in telling Dennis that she had told you she has something special to say to him.'

Tony recalled it – it had already passed out of his mind. 'What she has to say is only what I myself have already said for the rest of us – that she hopes with all her heart things are now smooth for his marriage.'

'Well, what could be more horrid than that?'

'More horrid?' Tony stared.

'What has she to do with his marriage? Her interference is in execrable taste.'

The girl's tone was startling, and her companion's surprise augmented, showing itself in his lighted eyes and deepened colour. 'My dear Rose, isn't that sort of thing, in a little circle like ours, a permitted joke – a friendly compliment? We're all so *with* you.'

She had turned away from him. She went on, as if she had not heard him, with a sudden tremor in her voice – the tremor of a deep upheaval: 'Why does she give opinions that nobody wants or asks her for? What does she know of our relations or of what difficulties and mysteries she touches? Why can't she leave us alone – at least for the first hour?'

Embarrassment was in Tony's gasp – the unexpected had sprung up before him. He could only stammer after her as she moved away: 'Bless my soul, my dear child – you don't mean to say there *are* difficulties? Of course it's no one's business – but one hoped you were in quiet waters.' Across her interval, as he spoke, she suddenly faced round, and his view of her, with this, made him smite his forehead in his penitent, expressive way. 'What a brute I am not to have seen you're not quite happy, and not to have noticed that *he*—!' Tony caught himself up; the face offered him was the convulsed face that had not been offered Dennis Vidal. Rose literally glared at him; she stood there with her two hands on her heaving breast and something in all her aspect that was like the first shock of a great accident. What he saw, without understanding it, was the final snap of her tremendous tension, the end of her wonderful false calm. He misunderstood it in fact, as he saw it give way before him: he sprang at the idea that the poor girl had received a blow – a blow which her self-control up to within a moment only presented as more touchingly borne. Vidal's absence was there as a part of it: the situation flashed into vividness. 'His eagerness to leave you surprised me,' he exclaimed, 'and yours to make him go!' Tony thought again, and before he spoke his thought her eyes seemed to glitter it back. 'He has not brought you bad news – he has not failed of what we hoped?' He went to her with compassion and tenderness: 'You don't mean to say, my poor girl, that he doesn't meet you as you supposed he would?' Rose dropped, as he came, into a chair; she had burst into passionate tears. She threw herself upon a small table, burying her head in her arms, while Tony, all wonder and pity, stood above her and felt helpless as she sobbed. She seemed to have sunk under her wrong and to quiver with her pain. Her host, with his own recurrent pang, could scarcely bear it: he felt a sharp need of making some one pay. 'You don't mean to say Mr Vidal doesn't keep faith?'

'Oh, God! oh, God! oh, God!' Rose Armiger wailed.

Tony turned away from her with a movement which was a confession of incompetence; a sense moreover of the awkwardness of being so close to a grief for which he had no direct remedy. He could only assure her, in his confusion, of his deep regret that she had had a distress. The extremity of her collapse, however, was brief, a gust of passion after which she instantly showed the effort to recover. 'Don't mind me,' she said through her tears; 'I shall pull myself together; I shall be all right in a moment.' He wondered whether he oughtn't to leave her; and yet to leave her was scarcely courteous. She was quickly erect again, with her characteristic thought for others flowing out through her pain. 'Only don't let Julia know – that's all I ask of you. One's little bothers are one's little bothers – they're all in the day's work. Just give me three minutes. and I shan't show a trace.' She straightened herself and even smiled, patting her eyes with her crumpled handkerchief, while Tony marvelled at her courage and good humour.

'Of one thing you must be sure, Rose,' he expressively answered, 'that whatever happens to you, now or at any time, you've friends here and a home here that are yours for weal and woe.'

'Ah, don't say that,' she cried; 'I can scarcely bear it! Disappointments one can meet; but how in the world is one adequately to meet generosity? Of one thing you, on your side, must be sure: that no trouble in life shall ever make me a bore. It was because I was so awfully afraid to be one that I've been keeping myself in – and that has led, in this ridiculous way, to my making a fool of myself at the last. I knew a hitch was coming – I knew at least something was; but I hoped it would come and go without *this*!' She had stopped before a mirror, still dealing, like an actress in the wing, with her appearance, her make-up. She dabbed at her cheeks and pressed her companion to leave her to herself. 'Don't pity me, don't mind me; and, above all, don't ask any questions.'

'Ah,' said Tony in friendly remonstrance, 'your bravery makes it too hard to help you!'

'Don't try to help me – don't even want to. And don't tell any tales. Hush!' she went on in a different tone. 'Here's Mrs Beever!'

The lady of Eastmead was preceded by the butler, who, having formally announced her, announced luncheon as invidiously as if it had only been waiting for her. The servants at each house had ways of reminding her they were not the servants at the other.

'Luncheon's all very well,' said Tony, 'but who in the world's to eat it? Before *you* do,' he continued, to Mrs Beever, 'there's something I must ask of you.'

'And something I must ask too,' Rose added, while the butler retired like a conscientious Minister retiring from untenable office. She addressed herself to their neighbour with a face void, to Tony's astonishment, of every vestige of disorder. 'Didn't Mr Vidal come back with you?'

Mrs Beever looked incorruptible. 'Indeed he did!' she sturdily replied. 'Mr Vidal is in the garden of this house.'

'Then I'll call him to luncheon.' And Rose floated away, leaving her companions confronted in a silence that ended – as Tony was lost in the wonder of her presence of mind – only when Mrs Beever had assured herself that she was out of earshot.

'She has broken it off!' this lady then responsibly proclaimed.

Her colleague demurred. 'She? How do you know?'

'I know because he has told me so.'

'Already – in these few minutes?'

Mrs Beever hung fire. 'Of course I asked him first. I met him at the bridge – I saw he had had a shock.'

'It's Rose who has had the shock!' Tony returned. 'It's he who has thrown her over.'

Mrs Beever stared. 'That's *her* story?'

Tony reflected. 'Practically – yes.'

Again his visitor hesitated, but only for an instant. 'Then one of them lies.'

Tony laughed out at her lucidity 'It isn't Rose Armiger!'

'It isn't Dennis Vidal, my dear; I believe in him,' said Mrs Beever.

Her companion's amusement grew. 'Your operations are rapid.'

'Remarkably. I've asked him to come to me.'

Tony raised his eyebrows. 'To come to you?'

'Till he can get a train – tomorrow. He can't stay on here.'

Tony looked at it. 'I see what you mean.'

'That's a blessing – you don't always! I like him – he's my sort. And something seems to tell me I'm his!'

'I won't gracefully insult you by saying you're every one's,' Tony observed. Then, after an instant, 'Is he very much cut up?' he inquired.

'He's utterly staggered. He doesn't understand.'

Tony thought again. 'No more do I. But you'll console him,' he added.

'I'll feed him first,' said his neighbour. 'I'll take him back with me to luncheon.'

'Isn't that scarcely civil?'

'Civil to you?' Mrs Beever interposed. 'That's exactly what he asked me. I told him I would arrange it with you.'

'And you're "arranging" it, I see. But how can you take him if Rose is bringing him in?'

Mrs Beever was silent a while. 'She isn't. She hasn't gone to him. That was for *me*.'

Tony looked at her in wonder. 'Your operations are rapid,' he repeated. 'But I found her under the unmistakable effect of a blow.'

'I found her exactly as usual.'

'Well, that also was for you,' said Tony. 'Her disappointment's a secret.'

'Then I'm much obliged to you for mentioning it.'

'I did so to defend her against your bad account of her. But the whole thing's obscure,' the young man added with sudden weariness. 'I give it up!'

'*I* don't – I shall straighten it out.' Mrs Beever spoke with high decision. 'But I must see your wife first.'

'Rather! – she's waiting all this while.' He had already opened the door.

As she reached it she stopped again. 'Shall I find the Doctor with her?'

'Yes, by her request.'

'Then how is she?'

'Maddening!' Tony exclaimed; after which, as his visitor echoed the word, he went on: 'I mean in her dreadful obsession, to which poor Ramage has had to give way and which is the direct reason of her calling you.'

Mrs Beever's little eyes seemed to see more than he told her, to have indeed the vision of something formidable. 'What dreadful obsession?'

'She'll tell you herself.' He turned away to leave her to go, and she disappeared; but the next moment he heard her again on the threshold.

'Only a word to say that that child may turn up.'

'What child?' He had already forgotten.

'Oh, if you don't remember—!' Mrs Beever, with feminine inconsequence, almost took it ill.

Tony recovered the agreeable image. 'Oh, your niece? Certainly – I remember her hair.'

'She's not my niece, and her hair's hideous. But if she does come, send her straight home!'

'Very good,' said Tony. This time his visitor vanished.

CHAPTER 12

He moved a minute about the hall; then he dropped upon a sofa with a sense of exhaustion and a sudden need of rest; he stretched himself, closing his eyes, glad to be alone, glad above all to make sure that he could lie still. He wished to show himself he was not nervous; he took up a position with the purpose not to budge till Mrs Beever should come back. His house was in an odd condition, with luncheon pompously served and no one able to go to it. Poor Julia was in a predicament, poor Rose in another, and poor Mr Vidal, fasting in the garden, in a greater one than either. Tony sighed as he thought of this dispersal, but he stiffened himself resolutely on his couch. He wouldn't go in alone, and he couldn't even enjoy Mrs Beever. It next occurred to him that he could still less enjoy her little friend, the child he had promised to turn away; on which he gave a sigh that represented partly privation and partly resignation – partly also a depressed perception of the fact that he had never in all his own healthy life been less eager for a meal. Meanwhile, however, the attempt to stop pacing the floor was a success: he felt as if in closing his eyes he destroyed the vision that had scared him. He was cooler, he was easier, and he liked the smell of flowers in the dusk. What was droll, when he gave himself up to it, was the sharp sense of lassitude; it had dropped on him out of the blue and it showed him how a sudden alarm – such as, after all, he had had – could drain a fellow in an hour of half his vitality. He wondered whether, if he might be undisturbed a little, the result of this surrender wouldn't be to make him delightfully lose consciousness.

He never knew afterwards whether it was in the midst of his hope or on the inner edge of a doze just achieved that he became aware of a footfall betraying an uncertain advance. He raised his lids to it and saw before him the pretty girl from the other house, whom, for a moment before he moved, he lay there looking at. He immediately recognised that what had roused him was the fact that, noiselessly and for a few seconds, her eyes had rested on his face. She uttered a blushing 'Oh!' which deplored this effect of her propinquity and which brought Tony straight to his feet. 'Ah, good morning! How d'ye do?' Everything came back to him but her name. 'Excuse my attitude – I didn't hear you come in.'

'When I saw you asleep I'm afraid I kept the footman from speaking.' Jean Martle was much embarrassed, but it contributed in the happiest way to her animation. 'I came in because he told me that Cousin Kate's here.'

'Oh yes, she's here – she thought you might arrive. Do sit down,' Tony added with his prompt instinct of what, in his own house, was due from a man of some confidence to a girl of none at all. It operated before he could check it, and Jean was as passive to it as if he had tossed her a command; but as soon as she was seated, to obey him, in a high-backed, wide-armed Venetian chair which made a gilded cage for her flutter, and he had again placed himself – not in the same position – on the sofa opposite, he recalled the request just preferred by Mrs Beever. He was to send her straight home; yes, it was to be invited instantly to retrace her steps that she sat there panting and pink.

Meanwhile she was very upright and very serious; she seemed very anxious to explain. 'I thought it better to come, since she wasn't there. I had gone off to walk home with the Marshes – I was gone rather long; and when I came back she had left the house – the servants told me she must be here.'

Tony could only meet with the note of hospitality so logical a plea. 'Oh, it's all right – Mrs Beever's with Mrs Bream.' It was apparently all wrong – he must tell her she couldn't stay; but there was a prior complication in his memory of having invited her to luncheon. 'I wrote to your cousin – I hoped you'd come. Unfortunately she's not staying herself.'

'Ah, then, *I* mustn't!' Jean spoke with lucidity, but without quitting her chair.

Tony hesitated. 'She'll be a little while yet – my wife has something to say to her.'

The girl had fixed her eyes on the floor; she might have been reading there the fact that for the first time in her life she was regularly calling on a gentleman. Since this was the singular case she must at least call properly. Her manner revealed an earnest effort to that end, an effort visible even in the fear of a liberty if she should refer too familiarly to Mrs Bream. She cast about her with intensity for something that would show sympathy without freedom, and, as a result, presently produced: 'I came an hour ago, and I saw Miss Armiger. She told me she would bring down the baby.'

'But she didn't?'

'No, Cousin Kate thought it wouldn't do.'

Tony was happily struck. 'It will do – it shall do. Should you like to see her?'

'I thought I should like it very much. It's very kind of you.'

Tony jumped up. 'I'll show her to you myself.' He went over to ring a bell; then, as he came back, he added: 'I delight in showing her. I think she's the wonder of the world.'

'That's what babies always seem to me,' said Jean. 'It's so absorbing to watch them.'

These remarks were exchanged with great gravity, with stiffish pauses, while Tony hung about till his ring should be answered.

'Absorbing?' he repeated. 'Isn't it, preposterously? Wait till you've watched Effie!'

His visitor preserved for a while a silence which might have indicated that, with this injunction, her waiting had begun; but at last she said with the same simplicity: 'I've a sort of original reason for my interest in her.'

'Do you mean the illness of her poor mother?' He saw that she meant nothing so patronising, though her countenance fell with the reminder of this misfortune: she heard with awe that the unconscious child was menaced. 'That's a very good reason,' he declared, to relieve her. 'But so much the better if you've got another too. I hope you'll never want for one to be kind to her.'

She looked more assured. 'I'm just the person always to be.'

'Just the person—?' Tony felt that he must draw her out. She was now arrested, however, by the arrival of the footman, to whom he immediately turned. 'Please ask Gorham to be as good as to bring down the child.'

'Perhaps Gorham will think it won't do,' Jean suggested as the servant went off.

'Oh, she's as proud of her as I am! But if she doesn't approve

I'll take you upstairs. That'll be because, as you say you're just the person. I haven't the least doubt of it – but you were going to tell me why.'

Jean treated it as if it were almost a secret. 'Because she was born on *my* day.'

'Your birthday?'

'My birthday – the twenty-fourth.'

'Oh, I see; that's charming – that's delightful!' The circumstance had not quite all the subtlety she had beguiled him into looking for, but her amusing belief in it, which halved the date like a succulent pear, mingled oddly, to make him quickly feel that it had enough, with his growing sense that Mrs Beever's judgement of her hair was a libel. 'It's a most extraordinary coincidence – it makes a most interesting tie. Do, therefore, I beg you, whenever you keep your anniversary, keep also a little hers.'

'That's just what I was thinking,' said Jean. Then she added, still shy, yet suddenly almost radiant: 'I shall always send her something!'

'She shall do the same to you!' This idea had a charm even for Tony, who determined on the spot, quite sincerely, that he would, for the first years at least, make it his own charge. 'You're her very first friend,' he smiled.

'Am I?' Jean thought it wonderful news. 'Before she has even seen me!'

'Oh, those *are* the first. You're "handed down",' said Tony, humouring her.

She evidently deprecated, however, any abatement of her rarity. 'Why, I haven't seen her mother, either.'

'No, you haven't seen her mother. But you shall. And you have seen her father.'

'Yes, I have seen her father.' Looking at him as if to make sure of it, Jean gave this assertion the assent of a gaze so unrestricted that, feeling herself after an instant caught, as it were, in it, she turned abruptly away.

It came back to Tony at the same moment with a sort of coarseness that he was to have sent her home; yet now, somehow, as if half through the familiarity it had taken but these minutes to establish, and half through a perception of her extreme juvenility, his reluctance to tell her so had dropped. 'Do

you know I'm under a sort of dreadful vow to Mrs Beever?'
Then as she faced him again, wondering: 'She told me that if
you should turn up I was to pack you off.'

Jean stared with a fresh alarm. 'Ah, I shouldn't have stayed!'

'You didn't know it, and I couldn't show you the door.'

'Then I must go now.'

'Not a bit. I wouldn't have mentioned it – to consent to that.
I mention it for just the other reason – to keep you here as long
as possible. I'll make it right with Cousin Kate,' Tony continued.
'I'm not afraid of her!' he laughed. 'You produce an effect on
me for which I'm particularly grateful.' She was acutely sensitive; for a few seconds she looked as if she thought he might be
amusing himself at her expense. 'I mean you soothe me – at a
moment when I really want it,' he said with a gentleness from
which it gave him pleasure to see in her face an immediate
impression. 'I'm worried, I'm depressed, I've been threshing
about in my anxiety. You keep me cool – you're just the right
thing.' He nodded at her in clear kindness. 'Stay with me – stay
with me!'

Jean had not taken the flight of expressing a concern for his
domestic situation, but in the pity that flooded her eyes at this
appeal there was an instant surrender to nature. It was the
sweetness of her youth that had calmed him, but in the response
his words had evoked she already, on the spot, looked older.
'Ah, if I *could* help you!' she timidly murmured.

'Sit down again; sit down!' He turned away. 'Here's the
wonder of the world!' he exclaimed the next instant, seeing
Gorham appear with her charge. His interest in the apparition
almost simultaneously dropped, for Mrs Beever was at the
opposite door. She had come back, and Ramage was with her:
they stopped short together, and he did the same on catching
the direction, as he supposed, of his sharp neighbour's eyes. She
had an air of singular intensity; it was peculiarly embodied in a
look which, as she drew herself up, she shot straight past him
and under the reprobation of which he glanced round to see
Jean Martle turn pale. What he saw, however, was not Jean
Martle at all, but that very different person Rose Armiger, who,
by an odd chance and with Dennis Vidal at her side, presented
herself at this very juncture at the door of the vestibule. It was
at Rose Mrs Beever stared – stared with a significance doubtless

produced by this young lady's falsification of her denial that Mr Vidal had been actively pursued. She took no notice of Jean, who, while the rest of them stood about, testified to her prompt compliance with any word of Tony's by being the only member of the company in a chair. The sight of Mrs Beever's face appeared to have deprived her of the force to rise. Tony observed these things in a flash, and also how far the gaze of the Gorgon was from petrifying Rose Armiger, who, with a bright recovery of zeal by which he himself was wonderstruck, launched without delay a conscientious reminder of luncheon. It was on the table – it was spoiling – it was spoilt! Tony felt that he must gallantly support her. 'Let us at last go in then,' he said to Mrs Beever. 'Let us go in then,' he repeated to Jean and to Dennis Vidal. 'Doctor, you'll come too?'

He broke Jean's spell at a touch; she was on her feet; but the Doctor raised, as if for general application, a deterrent, authoritative hand. 'If you please, Bream – no banquet.' He looked at Jean, at Rose, at Vidal, at Gorham. 'I take the house in hand. We immediately subside.'

Tony sprang to him. 'Julia's worse?'

'No – she's the same.'

'Then I may go to her?'

'Absolutely not.' Doctor Ramage grasped his arm, linked his own in it and held him. 'If you're not a good boy I lock you up in your room. We immediately subside,' he said again, addressing the others; 'we go our respective ways and we keep very still. The fact is I require a hushed house. But before the hush descends Mrs Beever has something to say to you.'

She was on the other side of Tony, who felt, between them there, like their prisoner. She looked at her little audience, which consisted of Jean and Rose, of Mr Vidal and the matronly Gorham. Gorham carried in her ample arms a large white sacrifice, a muslin-muffled offering which seemed to lead up to a ceremony. 'I have something to say to you because Doctor Ramage allows it, and because we are both under pledges to Mrs Bream. It's a very peculiar announcement for me to have on my hands, but I've just passed her my promise, in the very strictest manner, to make it, before leaving the house, to every one it may concern, and to repeat it in certain other quarters.' She paused again, and Tony, from his closeness to her, could feel the tremor of her solid presence. She disliked the awkward-ness and the coercion, and he was sorry for her, because by this time he well knew what was coming. He had guessed his wife's extraordinary precaution, which would have been almost gro-tesque if it hadn't been so infinitely touching. It seemed to him that he gave the measure of his indulgence for it in overlooking the wound to his delicacy conveyed in the publicity she imposed. He could condone this in a tender sigh, because it meant that in consequence of it she'd now pull round. 'She wishes it as generally known as possible,' Mrs Beever brought out, 'that Mr Bream, to gratify her at a crisis which I trust she exaggerates, has assured her on his sacred honour that in the event of her death he will not again marry.'

'In the lifetime of her daughter, that is,' Doctor Ramage hastened to add.

'In the lifetime of her daughter,' Mrs Beever as clearly echoed.

'In the lifetime of her daughter!' Tony himself took up with an extravagance intended to offer the relief of a humorous treatment, if need be, to the bewildered young people whose embarrassed stare was a prompt criticism of Julia's discretion. It might have been in the spirit of a protest still more vehement that, at this instant, a small shrill pipe rose from the animated parcel with which Gorham, participating in the general awk-wardness, had possibly taken a liberty. The comical little sound created a happy diversion; Tony sprang straight to the child. 'So it *is*, my own,' he cried, 'a scandal to be talking of "lifetimes"!' He caught her from the affrighted nurse – he put his face down to hers with passion. Her wail ceased and he held her close to him; for a minute, in silence, as if something deep went out from him, he laid his cheek to her little cheek, burying his head under her veil. When he gave her up again, turning round, the hall was empty of every one save the Doctor, who signalled peremptorily to Gorham to withdraw. Tony remained there meeting his eyes, in which, after an instant, the young man saw something that led him to exclaim: 'How dreadfully ill she must be, Ramage, to have conceived a stroke in such taste!'

His companion drew him down to the sofa, patting, soothing, supporting him. 'You must bear it my dear boy – you must bear everything.' Doctor Ramage faltered. 'Your wife's exceedingly ill.'

BOOK TWO

It continued to be for the lady of Eastmead, as the years went on, a sustaining reflection that if in the matter of upholstery she yielded somewhat stiffly to the other house, so the other house was put out of all countenance by the mere breath of her garden. Tony could beat her indoors at every point, but when she took her stand on her lawn she could defy not only Bounds but Wilverley. Her stand, and still more her seat, in the summer days, was frequent there, as we easily gather from the fortified position in which we next encounter her. From May to October she was out, as she said, at grass, drawing from it most of the time a comfortable sense that on such ground as this her young friend's love of newness broke down. He might make his dinner-service as new as he liked; she triumphed precisely in the fact that her trees and her shrubs were old. He could hang nothing on his walls like her creepers and clusters; there was no velvet in his carpets like the velvet of her turf. She had everything, or almost everything – she had space and time and the river. No one at Wilverley had the river as she had it; people might say of course there was little of it to have, but of whatever there was she was in intimate possession. It skirted her grounds and improved her property and amused her guests; she always held that her free access made up for being, as people said, on the wrong side of it. If she had not been on the wrong side she would not have had the little stone foot-bridge which was her special pride and the very making of her picture, and which she had heard compared – she had an off-hand way of bringing it in – to a similar feature, at Cambridge, of one of the celebrated 'backs'. The other side was the side of the other house, the side for the view – the view as to which she entertained the merely qualified respect excited in us, after the first creative flush, by mysteries of our own making. Mrs Beever herself formed the view and the other house was welcome to it, especially to those parts of it enjoyed through the rare gaps in an interposing leafy lane. Tony had a gate which he called his river-gate, but you didn't so much as suspect the stream till you got well out of it. He had on his further quarter a closer contact with the town; but this was just what on both quarters she had with the country. Her approach to the town was by the 'long way' and the big bridge, and by going on, as she liked to do, past the Doctor's square red house. She hated stopping there, hated it as much as she liked his stopping at Eastmead: in the former case she seemed to consult him and in the latter to advise, which was the exercise of her wisdom that she decidedly preferred. Such degrees and dimensions, I hasten to add, had to do altogether with short relations and small things; but it was just the good lady's reduced scale that held her little world together. So true is it that from strong compression the elements of drama spring and that there are conditions in which they seem to invite not so much the opera-glass as the microscope.

Never, perhaps, at any rate, had Mrs Beever been more conscious of her advantages, or at least more surrounded with her conveniences, than on a beautiful afternoon of June on which we are again concerned with her. These blessings were partly embodied in the paraphernalia of tea, which had cropped up, with promptness and profusion, in a sheltered corner of the lawn and in the midst of which, waiting for custom, she might have been in charge of a refreshment-stall at a fair. Everything at the other house struck her as later and later, and she only regretted that, as the protest of her own tradition, she couldn't move in the opposite direction without also moving from the hour. She waited for it now, at any rate, in the presence of a large red rug and a large white tablecloth, as well as of sundry basket-chairs and of a hammock that swayed in the soft west wind; and she had meanwhile been occupied with a collection of parcels and pasteboard boxes that were heaped together on a bench. Of one of these parcels, enveloped in several layers of tissue-paper, she had just possessed herself, and, seated near her tea-table, was on the point of uncovering it. She became aware, at this instant, of being approached from behind; on which, looking over her shoulder and seeing Doctor Ramage, she straightway stayed her hands. These friends, in a long acquaintance, had dropped by the way so many preliminaries that

absence, in their intercourse, was a mere parenthesis and conversation in general scarce began with a capital. But on this
occasion the Doctor was floated to a seat not, as usual, on the
bosom of the immediately previous.

'Guess whom I've just overtaken on your doorstep. The young
man you befriended four years ago – Mr Vidal, Miss Armiger's
flame!'

Mrs Beever fell back in her surprise; it was rare for Mrs
Beever to fall back. 'He has turned up again?' Her eyes had
already asked more than her friend could tell. 'For what in the
world—?'

'For the pleasure of seeing you. He has evidently retained a
very grateful sense of what you did for him.'

'I did nothing, my dear man – I had to let it alone.'

'Tony's condition – of course I remember – again required
you. But you gave him a shelter,' said the Doctor, 'that
wretched day and that night, and he felt (it was evidently
much to him) that, in his rupture with his young woman, you
had the right instinct of the matter and were somehow on his
side.'

'I put him up for a few hours – I saved him, in time, the
embarrassment of finding himself in a house of death. But he
took himself off the next morning early – bidding me goodbye
only in a quiet little note.'

'A quiet little note which I remember you afterwards showed
me and which was a model of discretion and good taste. It
seems to me,' the Doctor went on, 'that he doesn't violate those
virtues in considering that you've given him the right to
reappear.'

'At the very time, and the only time, in so long a period that
his young woman, as you call her, happens also to be again in
the field!'

'That's a coincidence,' the Doctor replied, 'far too singular
for Mr Vidal to have had any forecast of it.'

'You didn't then tell him?'

'I told him nothing save that you were probably just where I
find you, and that, as Manning is busy with her tea-things, I
would come straight out for him and announce that he's there.'

Mrs Beever's sense of complications evidently grew as she
thought. 'By "there" do you mean on the doorstep?'

'Far from it. In the safest place in the world – at least when you're not in it.'

'In my own room?' Mrs Beever asked.

'In that austere monument to Domestic Method which you're sometimes pleased to call your boudoir. I took upon myself to show him into it and to close the door on him there. I reflected that you'd perhaps like to see him before any one else.'

Mrs Beever looked at her visitor with appreciation. 'You dear, sharp thing!'

'Unless, indeed,' the Doctor added, 'they have, in so many years, already met.'

'She told me only yesterday they haven't.'

'I see. However, as I believe you consider that she never speaks the truth, that doesn't particularly count.'

'I hold, on the contrary, that a lie counts double,' Mrs Beever replied with decision.

Doctor Ramage laughed. 'Then why have you never in your life told one? I haven't even yet quite made out,' he pursued, 'why – especially with Miss Jean here – you asked Miss Armiger down.'

'I asked her for Tony.'

'Because he suggested it? Yes, I know that.'

'I mean it,' said Mrs Beever, 'in a sense I think you don't know.' She looked at him a moment; but either her profundity or his caution were too great, and he waited for her to commit herself further. That was a thing she could always do rapidly without doing it recklessly. 'I asked her exactly on account of Jean.'

The Doctor meditated, but this seemed to deepen her depth. 'I give it up. You've mostly struck me as so afraid of every other girl Paul looks at.'

Mrs Beever's face was grave. 'Yes, I've always been; but I'm not so afraid of them as of those at whom Tony looks.'

Her interlocutor started. 'He's looking at Jean?'

Mrs Beever was silent a little. 'Not for the first time!'

Her visitor also hesitated. 'And do you think, Miss Armiger —?'

Mrs Beever took him up. 'Miss Armiger's better for him – since he must have somebody!'

'You consider she'd marry him?'

'She's insanely in love with him.'

The Doctor tilted up his chin; he uttered an expressive 'Euh! – She is indeed, poor thing!' he said. 'Since you frankly mention it, I as frankly agree with you, that I've never seen anything like it. And there's monstrous little I've not seen. But if Tony isn't crazy too—?'

'It's a kind of craze that's catching. He must think of that sort of thing.'

'I don't know what you mean by "thinking"! Do you imply that the dear man, on what we know—?' The Doctor couldn't phrase it.

His friend had greater courage. 'Would break his vow and marry again?' She turned it over, but at last she brought out: 'Never in the world.'

'Then how does the chance of his thinking of Rose help her?'

'I don't say it helps her. I simply say it helps poor me.'

Doctor Ramage was still mystified. 'But if they can't marry—?'

'I don't care whether they marry or not!'

She faced him with the bravery of this, and he broke into a happy laugh. 'I don't know whether most to admire your imagination or your morality.'

'I protect *my* girl,' she serenely declared.

Doctor Ramage made his choice. 'Oh, your morality!'

'In doing so,' she went on, 'I also protect my boy. That's the highest morality I know. I'll see Mr Vidal out here,' she added.

'So as to get rid of him easier?'

'My getting rid of him will depend on what he wants. He must take, after all,' Mrs Beever continued, 'his chance of meeting any embarrassment. If he plumps in without feeling his way—'

'It's his own affair – I see,' the Doctor said. What he saw was that his friend's diplomacy had suffered a slight disturbance. Mr Vidal was a new element in her reckoning; for if, of old, she had liked and pitied him, he had since dropped out of her problem. Her companion, who timed his pleasures to the minute, indulged in one of his frequent glances at his watch. 'I'll put it then to the young man – more gracefully than you do – that you'll receive him in this place.'

'I shall be much obliged to you.'

'But before I go,' Doctor Ramage inquired, 'where are all our friends?'

'I haven't the least idea. The only ones I count on are Effie and Jean.'

The Doctor made a motion of remembrance. 'To be sure – it's their birthday: that fellow put it out of my head. The child's to come over to you to tea, and just what I stopped for—'

'Was to see if I had got your doll?' Mrs Beever interrupted him by holding up the muffled parcel in her lap. She pulled away the papers. 'Allow me to introduce the young lady.'

The young lady was sumptuous and ample; he took her in his hands with reverence. 'She's splendid – she's positively human! I feel like a Turkish pasha investing in a beautiful Circassian. I feel too,' the Doctor went on, 'how right I was to depend, in the absence of Mrs Ramage, on your infallible taste.' Then restoring the effigy: 'Kindly mention how much I owe you.'

'Pay at the shop,' said Mrs Beever. 'They "trusted" me.'

'With the same sense of security that I had!' The Doctor got up. 'Please then present the object and accompany it with my love and a kiss.'

'You can't come back to give them yourself?'

'What do I ever give "myself", dear lady, but medicine?'

'Very good,' said Mrs Beever; 'the presentation shall be formal. But I ought to warn you that your beautiful Circassian will have been no less than the fourth.' She glanced at the parcels on the bench. 'I mean the fourth doll the child's to receive today.'

The Doctor followed the direction of her eyes. 'It's a regular slave-market – a perfect harem!'

'We've each of us given her one. Each, that is, except Rose.'

'And what has Rose given her?'

'Nothing at all.'

The Doctor thought a moment. 'Doesn't she like her?'

'She seems to wish it to be marked that she has nothing to do with her.'

Again Doctor Ramage reflected. 'I see – that's very clever.'

Mrs Beever, from her chair, looked up at him. 'What do you mean by "clever"?'

'I'll tell you some other time.' He still stood before the bench. 'There are no gifts for poor Jean?'

'Oh, Jean has had most of hers.'

'But nothing from *me*.' The Doctor had but just thought of her; he turned sadly away. 'I'm quite ashamed!'

'You needn't be, said Mrs Beever. 'She has also had nothing from Tony.'

He seemed struck. 'Indeed? On Miss Armiger's system?' His friend remained silent, and he went on: 'That of wishing it to be marked that he has nothing to do with her?'

Mrs Beever, for a minute, continued not to reply; but at last she exclaimed: 'He doesn't calculate!'

'That's bad – for a banker!' Doctor Ramage laughed. 'What then has she had from Paul?'

'Nothing either – as yet. That's to come this evening.'

'And what's it to be?'

Mrs Beever hesitated. 'I haven't an idea.'

'Ah, you *can* fib!' joked her visitor, taking leave.

CHAPTER 14

He crossed on his way to the house a tall parlourmaid who had
just quitted it with a tray which a moment later she deposited on
the table near her mistress. Tony Bream was accustomed to say
that since Frederick the Great's grenadiers there had never been
anything like the queen-mother's parlourmaids, who indeed on
field-days might, in stature, uniform and precision of exercise,
have affronted comparison with that formidable phalanx. They
were at once more athletic and more reserved than Tony liked to
see their sex, and he was always sure that the extreme length of
their frocks was determined by that of their feet. The young
woman, at any rate, who now presented herself, a young woman
with a large nose and a straight back, stiff cap-streamers, stiffer
petticoats and stiffest manners, was plainly the corporal of her
squad. There was a murmur and a twitter all around her; but she
rustled about the tea-table to a tune that quenched the voice of
summer. It left undisturbed, however, for awhile, Mrs Beever's
meditations; that lady was thoughtfully occupied in wrapping up
Doctor Ramage's doll. 'Do you know, Manning, what has
become of Miss Armiger?' she at last inquired.

'She went, ma'am, near an hour ago, to the pastrycook's.'

'To the pastrycook's?'

'She had heard you wonder, ma'am, she told me, that the
young ladies' birthday-cake hadn't yet arrived.'

'And she thought she'd see about it? Uncommonly good of
her!' Mrs Beever exclaimed.

'Yes, ma'am, uncommonly good of her.'

'Has it arrived, then, now?'

'Not yet, ma'am.'

'And Miss Armiger hasn't returned?'

'I think not, ma'am.'

Mrs Beever considered again. 'Perhaps she's waiting to bring
it.'

Manning indulged in a proportionate pause. 'Perhaps, ma'am – in a fly. And when it comes, ma'am, shall I fetch it out?'

'In a fly too? I'm afraid,' said Mrs Beever, 'that with such an incubation it will really require one.' After a moment she added: 'I'll go in and look at it first.' And then, as her attendant was about to rustle away, she further detained her. 'Mr Bream hasn't been over?'

'Not yet, ma'am.'

Mrs Beever consulted her watch. 'Then he's still at the Bank.'

'He must be indeed, ma'am.'

Tony's colleague appeared for a little to ponder this prompt concurrence; after which she said: 'You haven't seen Miss Jean?'

Manning bethought herself. 'I believe, ma'am, Miss Jean is dressing.'

'Oh, in honour—' But Mrs Beever's idea dropped before she finished her sentence.

Manning ventured to take it up. 'In honour of her birthday, ma'am.'

'I see – of course. And do you happen to have heard if that's what also detains Miss Effie – that she's dressing in honour of hers?'

Manning hesitated. 'I heard, ma'am, this morning that Miss Effie had a slight cold.'

Her mistress looked surprised. 'But not such as to keep her at home?'

'They were taking extra care of her, ma'am – so that she might be all right for coming.'

Mrs Beever was not pleased. 'Extra care? Then why didn't they send for the Doctor?'

Again Manning hesitated. 'They sent for Miss Jean, ma'am.'

'To come and look after her?'

'They often do, ma'am, you know. This morning I took in the message.'

'And Miss Jean obeyed it?'

'She was there an hour, ma'am.'

Mrs Beever administered a more than approving pat to the final envelope of her doll. 'She said nothing about it.'

Again Manning concurred. 'Nothing, ma'am.' The word sounded six feet high, like the figure she presented. She waited a moment and then, as if to close with as sharp a snap the last open door to the desirable, 'Mr Paul, ma'am,' she observed, 'if you were wanting to know, is out in his boat on the river.'

Mrs Beever pitched her parcel back to the bench. 'Mr Paul is never anywhere else!'

'Never, ma'am,' said Manning inexorably. She turned the next instant to challenge the stranger who had come down from the house. 'A gentleman, ma'am,' she announced; and, retiring while Mrs Beever rose to meet the visitor, drew, with the noise of a lawn-mower, a starched tail along the grass.

Dennis Vidal, with his hat off, showed his hostess a head over which not a year seemed to have passed. He had still his young, sharp, meagre look, and it came to her that the other time as well he had been dressed in double-breasted blue of a cut that made him sailorly. It was only on a longer view that she saw his special signs to be each a trifle intensified. He was browner, leaner, harder, finer; he even struck her as more wanting in height. These facts, however, didn't prevent another fact from striking her still more: what was most distinct in his face was that he was really glad to take her by the hand. That had an instant effect on her: she could glow with pleasure, modest matron as she was, at such an intimation of her having, so many years before, in a few hours, made on a clever young man she liked an impression that could thus abide with him. In the quick light of it she liked him afresh; it was as if their friendship put down on the spot a firm foot that was the result of a single stride across the chasm of time. In this indeed, to her clear sense, there was even something more to pity him for: it was such a dreary little picture of his interval, such an implication of what it had lacked, that there had been so much room in it for an ugly old woman at Wilverley. She motioned him to sit down with her, but she immediately remarked that before she asked him a question she had an important fact to make known. She had delayed too long, while he waited there, to let him understand that Rose Armiger was at Eastmead. She instantly saw at this that he had come in complete ignorance. The range of alarm in his face was narrow, but he coloured, looking grave; and after a brief debate with himself he inquired as to Miss Armiger's actual whereabouts.

'She has gone out, but she may reappear at any moment,' said Mrs Beever.

'And if she does, will she come out here?'

'I've an impression she'll change her dress first. That may take her a little time.'

'Then I'm free to sit with you ten minutes?'

'As long as you like, dear Mr Vidal. It's for you to choose whether you'll avoid her.'

'I dislike dodging – I dislike hiding,' Dennis returned; 'but I daresay that if I had known where she was I wouldn't have come.'

'I feel hatefully rude – but you took a leap in the dark. The absurd part of it,' Mrs Beever went on, 'is that you've stumbled on her very first visit to me.'

The young man showed a surprise which gave her the measure of his need of illumination. 'For these four years?'

'For these four years. It's the only time she has been at Eastmead.'

Dennis hesitated. 'And how often has she been at the other house?'

Mrs Beever smiled. 'Not even once.' Then as her smile broadened to a small, dry laugh, 'I can quite say *that* for her!' she declared.

Dennis looked at her hard. 'To your certain knowledge?'

'To my certain and absolute knowledge.' This mutual candour continued, and presently she said: 'But you – where do you come from?'

'From far away – I've been out of England. After my visit here I went back to my post.'

'And now you've returned with your fortune?'

He gave her a smile from which the friendliness took something of the bitter quality. 'Call it my *mis*fortune!' There was nothing in this to deprive Mrs Beever of the pleasant play of a professional sense that he had probably gathered such an independence as would have made him welcome at the Bank. On the other hand she caught the note of a tired grimness in the way he added: 'I've come back with that. It sticks to me!'

For a minute she spared him. 'You want her as much as ever?'

His eyes confessed to a full and indeed to a sore acceptance of that expression of the degree. 'I want her as much as ever. It's my constitutional obstinacy!'

'Which her treatment of you has done nothing to break down?'

'To break down? It has done everything in life to build it up.'

'In spite of the particular circumstance—?' At this point even Mrs Beever's directness failed.

That of her visitor, however, was equal to the occasion. 'The particular circumstance of her chucking me because of the sudden glimpse given her, by Mrs Bream's danger, of the possibility of a far better match?' He gave a laugh drier than her own had just been, the ring of an irony from which long, hard thought had pressed all the savour. 'That "particular circumstance", dear madam, is every bit that's the matter with me!'

'You regard it with extraordinary coolness, but I presumed to allude to it—'

'Because,' Dennis broke in with lucidity, 'I myself made no bones of doing so on the only other occasion on which we've met?'

'The fact that we both equally *saw*, that we both equally judged,' said Mrs Beever, 'was on that occasion really the only thing that had time to pass between us. It's a tie, but it's a slender one, and I'm all the more flattered that it should have had any force to make you care to see me again.'

'It never ceased to be my purpose to see you, if you would permit it, on the first opportunity. My opportunity,' the young man continued, 'has been precipitated by an accident. I returned to England only last week, and was obliged two days ago to come on business to Southampton. There I found I should have to go, on the same matter, to Marrington. It then appeared that to get to Marrington I must change at Plumbury—'

'And Plumbury,' said Mrs Beever, 'reminded you that you changed there, that it was from there you drove, on that horrible Sunday.'

'It brought my opportunity home to me. Without wiring you or writing you, without sounding the ground or doing anything I ought to have done, I simply embraced it. I reached this place an hour ago and went to the inn.'

She looked at him woefully. 'Poor dear young man!'

He turned it off. 'I do very well. Remember the places I've come from.'

'I don't care in the least where you've come from! If Rose weren't here I could put you up so beautifully.'

'Well, now that I know it,' said Dennis after a moment, 'I think I'm glad she's here. It's a fact the more to reckon with.'

'You mean to see her then?'

He sat with his eyes fixed, weighing it well. 'You must tell me two or three things first. Then I'll choose – I'll decide.'

She waited for him to mention his requirements, turning to her teapot, which had been drawing, so that she could meanwhile hand him a cup. But for some minutes, taking it and stirring it, he only gazed and mused, as if his curiosities were so numerous that he scarcely knew which to pick out. Mrs Beever at last, with a woman's sense for this, met him exactly at the right point. 'I must tell you frankly that if four years ago she was a girl most people admired—'

He caught straight on. 'She's still more wonderful now?'

Mrs Beever distinguished. 'I don't know about "wonderful", but she wears really well. She carries the years almost as you do, and her head better than any young woman I've ever seen. Life is somehow becoming to her. Every one's immensely struck with her. She only needs to get what she wants. She has in short a charm that I recognise.'

Her visitor stared at her words as if they had been a framed picture; the reflected colour of it made a light in his face. 'And you speak as one who, I remember, doesn't like her.'

The lady of Eastmead faltered, but there was help in her characteristic courage. 'No – I don't like her.'

'I see,' Dennis considered. 'May I ask then why you invited her?'

'For the most definite reason in the world. Mr Bream asked me to.'

Dennis gave his hard smile. 'Do you do everything Mr Bream asks?'

'He asks so little!'

'Yes,' Dennis allowed – 'if that's a specimen! Does he like her still?' he inquired.

'Just as much as ever.'

The young man was silent a few seconds. 'Do you mean he's in love with her?'

'He never was – in any degree.'

Dennis looked doubtful. 'Are you very sure?'

'Well,' said his hostess, 'I'm sure of the present. That's quite enough. He's not in love with her now – I have the proof.'

'The proof?'

Mrs Beever waited a moment. 'His request in itself. If he were in love with her he never would have made it.'

There was a momentary appearance on her companion's part of thinking this rather too fine; but he presently said: 'You mean because he's completely held by his death-bed vow to his wife?'

'Completely held.'

'There's no likelihood of his breaking it?'

'Not the slightest.'

Dennis Vidal exhaled a low, long breath which evidently represented a certain sort of relief. 'You're very positive; but I've a great respect for your judgement.' He thought an instant, then he pursued abruptly: 'Why did he wish her invited?'

'For reasons that, as he expressed them to me, struck me as natural enough. For the sake of old acquaintance – for the sake of his wife's memory.'

'He doesn't consider, then, that Mrs Bream's obsession, as you term it, had been in any degree an apprehension of Rose?'

'Why should he?' Mrs Beever asked. 'Rose, for poor Julia, was on the point of becoming your wife.'

'Ah! for all that was to prevent!' Dennis ruefully exclaimed.

'It was to prevent little enough, but Julia never knew how little. Tony asked me a month ago if I thought he might without awkwardness propose to Miss Armiger a visit to the other house. I said "No, silly boy!" and he dropped the question; but a week later he came back to it. He confided to me that he was ashamed for so long to have done so little for her; and she had behaved in a difficult situation with such discretion and delicacy that to have "shunted" her, as he said, so completely was a kind of outrage to Julia's affection for her and a slur upon hers for his wife. I said to him that if it would help him a bit I would address her a suggestion that she should honour me with her company. He jumped at that, and I wrote. *She* jumped, and here she is.'

Poor Dennis, at this, gave a spring, as if the young lady had come into sight. Mrs Beever reassured him, but he was on his feet and he stood before her. 'This then is their first meeting?'

'Dear, no! they've met in London. He often goes up.'

'How often?'

'Oh, irregularly. Sometimes twice a month.'

'And he sees her every time?'

Mrs Beever considered. 'Every time? I should think – hardly.'

'Then every other?'

'I haven't the least idea.'

Dennis looked round the garden. 'You say you're convinced that, in the face of his promise, he has no particular interest in her. You mean, however, of course, but to the extent of marriage.'

'I mean,' said Mrs Beever, 'to the extent of anything at all.' She also rose; she brought out her whole story. 'He's in love with another person.'

'Ah,' Dennis murmured, 'that's none of my business!' He nevertheless closed his eyes an instant with the cool balm of it. 'But it makes a lot of difference.''

She laid a kind hand on his arm. 'Such a lot, I hope, then, that you'll join our little party?' He looked about him again, irresolute, and his eyes fell on the packages gathered hard by, of which the nature was betrayed by a glimpse of flaxen curls and waxen legs. She immediately enlightened him. 'Preparations for a birthday visit from the little girl at the other house. She's coming over to receive them.'

Again he dropped upon a seat; she stood there and he looked up at her. 'At last we've got to business! It's *she* I've come to ask about.'

'And what do you wish to ask?'

'How she goes on – I mean in health.'

'Not very well, I believe, just today!' Mrs Beever laughed.

'Just today?'

'She's reported to have a slight cold. But don't be alarmed. In general she's splendid.'

He hesitated. 'Then you call it a good little life?'

'I call it a beautiful one!'

'I mean she won't pop off?'

'I can't guarantee that,' said Mrs Beever. 'But till she does—'

'Till she does?' he asked, as she paused.

She paused a moment longer. 'Well, it's a comfort to see her. You'll do that for yourself.'

'I shall do that for myself,' Dennis repeated. After a moment he went on: 'To be utterly frank, it was to do it I came.'

'And not to see me? Thank you! But I quite understand,' said Mrs Beever; 'you looked to me to introduce you. Sit still where you are, and I will.'

'There's one thing more I must ask you. You see; you know; you can tell me.' He complied but a minute with her injunction; again, nervously, he was on his feet. 'Is Miss Armiger in love with Mr Bream?'

His hostess turned away. 'That's the one question I can't answer.' Then she faced him again. 'You must find out for yourself.'

He stood looking at her. 'How shall I find out?'

'By watching her.'

'Oh, I didn't come to do *that*!' Dennis, on his side, turned away; he was visibly dissatisfied. But he checked himself; before him rose a young man in boating flannels, who appeared to have come up from the river, who had advanced noiselessly across the lawn and whom Mrs Beever introduced without ceremony as her 'boy'. Her boy blinked at Dennis, to whose identity he received no clue; and her visitor decided on a course. 'May I think over what you've said to me and come back?'

'I shall be very happy to see you again. But, in this poor place, what will you do?'

Dennis glanced at the river; then he appealed to the young man. 'Will you lend me your boat?'

'It's mine,' said Mrs Beever, with decision. 'You're welcome to it.'

'I'll take a little turn.' Raising his hat, Dennis went rapidly down to the stream.

Paul Beever looked after him. 'Hadn't I better show him—?' he asked of his mother.

'You had better sit right down there.' She pointed with sharpness to the chair Dennis had quitted, and her son submissively took possession of it.

CHAPTER 15

Paul Beever was tall and fat, and his eyes, like his mother's, were very small; but more even than to his mother nature had offered him a compensation for this defect in the extension of the rest of the face. He had large, bare, beardless cheeks and a wide, clean, candid mouth, which the length of the smooth upper lip caused to look as exposed as a bald head. He had a deep fold of flesh round his uncovered young neck, and his white flannels showed his legs to be all the way down of the same thickness. He promised to become massive early in life and even to attain a remarkable girth. His great tastes were for cigarettes and silence; but he was, in spite of his proportions, neither gross nor lazy. If he was indifferent to his figure he was equally so to his food, and he played cricket with his young townsmen and danced hard with their wives and sisters. Wilverley liked him and Tony Bream thought well of him: it was only his mother who had not yet made up her mind. He had done a good deal at Oxford in not doing any harm, and he had subsequently rolled round the globe in the very groove with which she had belted it. But it was exactly in satisfying that he a little disappointed her: she had provided so against dangers that she found it a trifle dull to be so completely safe. It had become with her a question not of how clever he was, but of how stupid. Tony had expressed the view that he was distinctly deep, but that might only have been, in Tony's florid way, to show that he himself was so. She would not have found it convenient to have to give the boy an account of Mr Vidal; but now that, detached from her purposes and respectful of her privacies, he sat there without making an inquiry, she was disconcerted enough slightly to miss the opportunity to snub him. On this occasion, however, she could steady herself with the possibility that her hour would still come. He began to eat a bun – his row justified that; and meanwhile she helped him to his tea. As she handed him the cup she challenged him with some sharpness. 'Pray, when are you going to give it?'

He slowly masticated while he looked at her. 'When do you think I had better?'

'Before dinner – distinctly. One doesn't know what may happen.'

'Do you think anything at all will?' he placidly asked.

His mother waited before answering. 'Nothing, certainly, unless you take some trouble for it.' His perception of what she meant by this was clearly wanting, so that after a moment she continued: 'You don't seem to grasp that I've done for you all I can do, and that the rest now depends on yourself.'

'Oh yes, mother, I grasp it,' he said without irritation. He took another bite of his bun and then added: 'Miss Armiger has made me quite do that.'

'Miss Armiger?' Mrs Beever stared; she even felt that her opportunity was at hand. 'What in the world has she to do with the matter?'

'Why I've talked to her a lot about it.'

'You mean she has talked to *you* a lot, I suppose. It's immensely like her.'

'It's like my dear mamma – that's whom it's like,' said Paul. 'She takes just the same view as yourself. I mean the view that I've a great opening and that I must make a great effort.'

'And don't you see that for yourself? Do you require a pair of women to tell you?' Mrs Beever asked.

Paul, looking grave and impartial, turned her question over while he stirred the tea. 'No, not exactly. But Miss Armiger puts everything so well.'

'She puts some things doubtless beautifully. Still, I should like you to be conscious of some better reason for making yourself acceptable to Jean than that another young woman, however brilliant, recommends it.'

The young man continued to ruminate, and it occurred to his mother, as it had occurred before, that his imperturbability was perhaps a strength. 'I am,' he said at last. 'She seems to make clear to me what I feel.'

Mrs Beever wondered. 'You mean of course Jean does.'

'Dear no – Miss Armiger!'

The lady of Eastmead laughed out in her impatience. 'I'm

delighted to hear you feel anything. You haven't often seemed
to me to feel.'

'I feel that Jean's very charming.'

She laughed again at the way he made it sound. 'Is that the
tone in which you think of telling her so?'

'I think she'll take it from me in any tone,' Paul replied. 'She
has always been most kind to me; we're very good friends, and
she knows what I want.'

'It's more than *I* do, my dear! That's exactly what you said to
me six months ago – when she liked you so much that she asked
you to let her alone.'

'She asked me to give her six months for a definite answer,
and she likes me the more for having consented to do that,' said
Paul. 'The time I've waited has improved our relations.'

'Well, then, they now must have reached perfection. You'll
get her definite answer, therefore, this very afternoon.'

'When I present the ornament?'

'When you present the ornament. You've got it safe, I hope?'

Paul hesitated; he took another bun. 'I imagine it's all right.'

'Do you only "imagine" – with a thing of that value? What
have you done with it?'

Again the young man faltered. 'I've given it to Miss Armiger.
She was afraid I'd lose it.'

'And you were not afraid she would?' his mother cried.

'Not a bit. She's to give it back to me on this spot. She wants
me too much to succeed.'

Mrs Beever was silent a little. 'And how much do you want
her to?'

Paul looked blank. 'In what?'

'In making a fool of you.' Mrs Beever gathered herself. 'Are
you in love with Rose Armiger, Paul?'

He judiciously weighed the question. 'Not in the least. I talk
with her of nobody and nothing but Jean.'

'And do you talk with Jean of nobody and nothing but Rose?'

Paul appeared to make an effort to remember. 'I scarcely talk
with her at all. We're such old friends that there's almost
nothing to say.'

'There's this to say, my dear – that you take too much for
granted!'

'That's just what Miss Armiger tells me. Give me, please,

some more tea.' His mother took his cup, but she looked at him hard and searchingly. He bore it without meeting her eyes, only turning his own pensively to the different dainties on the table. 'If I do take a great deal for granted,' he went on, 'you must remember that you brought me up to it.'

Mrs Beever found only after an instant a reply; then, however, she uttered it with an air of triumph. 'I may have brought you up – but I didn't bring up Jean!'

'Well, it's not of her I'm speaking,' the young man good-humouredly rejoined; 'though I might remind you that she has been here again and again, and month after month, and has always been taught – so far as you could teach her – to regard me as her inevitable fate. Have *you* any real doubt,' he went on, 'of her recognising in a satisfactory way that the time has come?'

Mrs Beever transferred her scrutiny to the interior of her teapot. 'No!' she said after a moment.

'Then what's the matter?'

'The matter is that I'm nervous, and that your stolidity makes me so. I want you to behave to me as if you cared – and I want you still more to behave so to her.' Paul made, in his seat, a movement in which his companion caught, as she supposed, the betrayal of a sense of oppression; and at this her own worst fear broke out. 'Oh, don't tell me you *don't* care – for if you do I don't know what I shall do to you!' He looked at her with an air he sometimes had, which always aggravated her impatience, an air of amused surprise, quickened to curiosity, that there should be in the world organisms capable of generating heat. She had thanked God, through life, that she was cold-blooded, but now it seemed to face her as a Nemesis that she was a volcano compared with her son. This transferred to him the advantage she had so long monopolised, that of always seeing, in any relation or discussion, the other party become the spectacle, while, sitting back in her stall, she remained the spectator and even the critic. She hated to perform to Paul as she had made others perform to herself; but she determined on the instant that, since she was condemned to do so, she would do it to some purpose. She would have to leap through a hoop, but she would land on her charger's back. The next moment Paul was watching her while she shook her little flags at him. 'There's one thing, my dear, that I can give you my word of honour for – the fact that if the influence that congeals, that paralyses you, happens by any chance to be a dream of what may be open to you in any other quarter, the sooner you utterly dismiss that dream the better it will be not only for your happiness, but for your dignity. If you entertain – with no matter how bad a conscience – a vain fancy that you've the smallest real chance of making the smallest real impression on anybody *else*, all I can say is that you prepare for yourself very nearly as much discomfort as you prepare disgust for your mother.' She paused a moment; she felt, before her son's mild gape, like a trapezist in pink tights. 'How much susceptibility, I should like to know, has Miss Armiger at her command for your great charms?'

Paul showed her a certain respect; he didn't clap her – that is he didn't smile. He felt something, however, which was indicated, as it always was, by the way his eyes grew smaller: they contracted at times, in his big, fair face, to mere little conscious points. These points he now directed to the region of the house. 'Well, mother,' he quietly replied, 'if you would like to know it, hadn't you better ask her directly?' Rose Armiger had come into view; Mrs Beever, turning, saw her approach, bareheaded, in a fresh white dress, under a showy red parasol. Paul, as she drew near, left his seat and strolled to the hammock, into which he immediately dropped. Extended there, while the great net bulged and its attachments cracked with his weight, he spoke with the same plain patience. 'She has come to give me up the ornament.'

'The great cake has at last arrived, dear lady!' Rose gaily announced to Mrs Beever, who waited, before acknowledging the news, long enough to suggest to her son that she was perhaps about to act on his advice.

'I'm much obliged to you for having gone to see about it,' was, however, what, after a moment, Miss Armiger's hostess instructed herself to reply.

'It was an irresistible service. I shouldn't have got over on such a day as this,' said Rose, 'the least little disappointment to dear little Jean.'

'To say nothing, of course, of dear little Effie,' Mrs Beever promptly rejoined.

'It comes to the same thing – the occasion so mixes them up. They're interlaced on the cake – with their initials and their candles. There are plenty of candles for each,' Rose laughed, 'for their years have been added together. It makes a very pretty number!'

'It must also make a very big cake,' said Mrs Beever.

'Colossal.'

'Too big to be brought out?'

The girl considered. 'Not so big, you know,' she archly replied, 'as if the candles had to be yours and mine!' Then holding up the 'ornament' to Paul, she said: 'I surrender you my trust. Catch!' she added with decision, making a movement to toss him a small case in red morocco, which, the next moment, in its flight through the air, without altering his attitude, he intercepted with one hand.

Mrs Beever's excited mistrust dropped at the mere audacity of this: there was something perceptibly superior in the girl who could meet half way, so cleverly, a suspicion she was quite conscious of and much desired to dissipate. The lady of East-mead looked at her hard, reading her desire in the look she gave back. 'Trust me, trust me,' her eyes seemed to plead; 'don't at all events think me capable of any self-seeking that's stupid or poor. I may be dangerous to myself, but I'm not so to others; least of all am I so to you.' She had a presence that was, in its way, like Tony Bream's: it made, simply and directly, a difference in any personal question exposed to it. Under its action, at all events, Mrs Beever found herself suddenly feeling that she could after all trust Rose if she could only trust Paul. She glanced at that young man as he lay in the hammock, and saw that in spite of the familiarity of his posture – which indeed might have been assumed with a misleading purpose – his diminished pupils, fixed upon their visitor, still had the expression imparted to them by her own last address. She hesitated; but while she did so Rose came straight up to her and kissed her. It was the very first time, and Mrs Beever blushed as if one of her secrets had been surprised. Rose explained her impulse only with a smile; but the smile said vividly: 'I'll polish him off!'

This brought a response to his mother's lips. 'I'll go and inspect the cake!'

Mrs Beever took her way to the house, and as soon as her back was turned her son got out of the hammock. An observer of the scene would not have failed to divine that, with some profundity of calculation, he had taken refuge there as a mute protest against any frustration of his interview with Rose. This young lady herself laughed out as she saw him rise, and her laugh would have been, for the same observer, a tribute to the natural art that was mingled with his obvious simplicity. Paul himself recognised its bearing and, as he came and stood at the tea-table, acknowledged her criticism by saying quietly: 'I was afraid dear mamma would take me away.'

'On the contrary; she has formally surrendered you.'

'Then you must let me perform her office and help you to some tea.'

He spoke with a rigid courtesy that was not without its grace, and in the rich shade of her umbrella, which she twirled repeatedly on her shoulder, she looked down with detachment at the table. 'I'll do it for myself, thank you; and I should like you to return to your hammock.'

'I left it on purpose,' the young man said. 'Flat on my back, that way, I'm at a sort of disadvantage in talking with you.'

'That's precisely why I made the request. I wish you to be flat on your back and to have nothing whatever to reply.' Paul immediately retraced his steps, but before again extending himself he asked her, with the same grave consideration, where in this case she would be seated. 'I shan't be seated at all,' she answered; 'I'll walk about and stand over you and bully you.' He tumbled into his net, sitting up rather more than before; and, coming close to it, she put out her hand. 'Let me see that object again.' He had in his lap the little box he had received from her, and at this he passed it back. She opened it, pressing on the spring, and, inclining her head to one side, considered afresh the mounted jewel that nestled in the white velvet. Then, closing the case with a loud snap, she restored it to him. 'Yes, it's very good; it's a wonderful stone, and she knows. But that alone, my dear, won't do it.' She leaned, facing him, against the tense ropes of the hammock, and he looked up at her. 'You take too much for granted.'

For a moment Paul answered nothing, but at last he brought out: 'That's just what I said to my mother you had already said when she said just the same.'

Rose stared an instant; then she smiled again. 'It's complicated, but I follow you! She has been waking you up.'

'She knows,' said her companion, 'that you advise me in the same sense as herself.'

'She believes it at last – her leaving us together was a sign of that. I have at heart perfectly to justify her confidence, for hitherto she has been so blind to her own interest as to suppose that, in these three weeks, you had been so tiresome as to fall in love with me.'

'I particularly told her I haven't at all.'

Paul's tone had at moments of highest gravity the gift of moving almost any interlocutor to mirth. 'I hope you'll be more convincing than that if you ever particularly tell any one you *have* at all!' the girl exclaimed. She gave a slight push to the hammock, turning away, and he swung there gently a minute.

'You mustn't ask too much of me, you know,' he finally said, watching her as she went to the table and poured out a cup of tea.

She drank a little and then, putting down the cup, came back to him. 'I should be asking too much of you only if you were asking too much of *her*. You're so far from that, and your position's so perfect. It's too beautiful, you know, what you offer.'

'I know what I offer and I know what I don't,' Paul returned; 'and the person we speak of knows exactly as well. All the elements are before her, and if my position's so fine it's there for her to see it quite as well as for you. I agree that I'm a decent sort, and that, as things are going, my business, my prospects, my guarantees of one kind and another, are substantial. But just these things, for years, have been made familiar to her, and nothing, without a risk of greatly boring her, can very well be added to the account. You and my mother say I take too much for granted; but I take only that.' This was a long speech for our young man, and his want of accent, his passionless pauses, made it seem a trifle longer. It had a visible effect on Rose Armiger, whom he held there with widening eyes as he talked. There was an intensity in her face, a bright sweetness that, when he stopped, seemed to give itself out to him as if to encourage him to go on. But he went on only to the extent of adding; 'All I mean is that if I'm good enough for her she has only to take me.'

'You're good enough for the best girl in the world,' Rose said with the tremor of sincerity. 'You're honest and kind; you're generous and wise.' She looked at him with a sort of intelligent pleasure, that of a mind fine enough to be touched by an exhibition of beauty even the most occult. 'You're so sound – you're so safe that it makes any relation with you a real luxury and a thing to be grateful for.' She shed on him her sociable approval, treating him as a happy product, speaking of him as of another person. 'I shall always be glad and proud that you've been, if only for an hour, my friend!'

Paul's response to this demonstration consisted in getting slowly and heavily to his feet. 'Do you think I *like* what you do to me?' he abruptly demanded.

It was a sudden new note, but it found her quite ready. 'I don't care whether you like it or not! It's my duty, and it's yours – it's the right thing.'

He stood there in his tall awkwardness; he spoke as if he had not heard her. 'It's too strange to have to take it from you.'

'Everything's strange – and the truest things are the strangest.

Besides, it isn't so extraordinary as that comes to. It isn't as if you had an objection to her; it isn't as if she weren't beautiful and good – really cultivated and altogether charming. It isn't as if, since I first saw her here, she hadn't developed in the most admirable way, and also hadn't, by her father's death, come into three thousand a year and into an opportunity for looking, with the red gold of her hair, in the deepest, daintiest, freshest mourning, lovelier far, my dear boy, than, with all respect, any girl who can ever have strayed before, or ever will again, into any Wilverley bank. It isn't as if, granting you do care for me, there were the smallest chance, should you try to make too much of it, of my ever doing anything but listen to you with a pained "Oh, dear!" pat you affectionately on the back and push you promptly out of the room.' Paul Beever, when she thus encountered him, quitted his place, moving slowly outside the wide cluster of chairs, while Rose, within it, turned as he turned, pressing him with deeper earnestness. He stopped behind one of the chairs, holding its high back and now meeting her eyes. 'If you do care for me,' she went on with her warm voice, 'there's a magnificent way you can show it. You can show it by putting into your appeal to Miss Martle something that she can't resist.'

'And what may she not be able to resist?' Paul inquired, keeping his voice steady, but shaking his chair a little.

'Why, *you* – if you'll only be a bit personal, a bit passionate, have some appearance of really desiring her, some that your happiness really depends on her.' Paul looked as if he were taking a lesson, and she gave it with growing assurance. 'Show her some tenderness, some eloquence, try some touch of the sort that goes home. Speak to her, for God's sake, the words that women like. We all like them, and we all feel them, and you can do nothing good without them. Keep well in sight that what you must absolutely do is *please* her.'

Paul seemed to fix his little eyes on this remote aim. 'Please her and please you.'

'It sounds odd, yes, lumping us together. But that doesn't matter,' said Rose. 'The effect of your success will be that you'll unspeakably help and comfort me. It's difficult to talk about it – my grounds are so deep, deep down.' She hesitated, casting about her, asking herself how far she might go. Then she decided, growing a little pale with the effort. 'I've an idea that has become a passion with me. There's a right I must see done – there's a wrong I must make impossible. There's a loyalty I must cherish – there's a memory I must protect. That's all I can say.' She stood there in her vivid meaning like the priestess of a threatened altar. 'If that girl becomes your wife – why then I'm at last at rest!'

'You get, by my achievement, what you want – I see. And, please, what do I get?' Paul presently asked.

'You?' The blood rushed back to her face with the shock of this question. 'Why, you get Jean Martle!' He turned away without a word, and at the same moment, in the distance, she saw the person whose name she had just uttered descend the great square steps. She hereupon slipped through the circle of chairs and rapidly met her companion, who stopped short as she approached. Rose looked him straight in the eyes. 'If you give me the peace I pray for, I'll do anything for you in life!' She left him staring and passed down to the river, where, on the little bridge, Tony Bream was in sight, waving his hat to her as he came from the other house.

CHAPTER 17

Rose Armiger, in a few moments, was joined by Tony, and they came up the lawn together to where Jean Martle stood talking with Paul. Here, at the approach of the master of Bounds, this young lady anxiously inquired if Effie had not been well enough to accompany him. She had expected to find her there; then, failing that, had taken for granted he would bring her.

'I've left the question, my dear Jean, in her nurse's hands,' Tony said. 'She had been bedizened from top to toe, and then, on some slight appearance of being less well, had been despoiled, denuded and disappointed. She's a poor little lamb of sacrifice. They were at her again, when I came away, with the ribbons and garlands; but there was apparently much more to come, and I couldn't answer for it that a single sneeze wouldn't again lay everything low. It's in the bosom of the gods. I couldn't wait.'

'You were too impatient to be with dear, delightful *us*,' Rose suggested.

Tony, with a successful air of very light comedy, smiled and inclined himself. 'I was too impatient to be with you, Miss Armiger.' The lapse of four years still presented him in such familiar mourning as might consort with a country nook on a summer afternoon; but it also allowed undiminished relief to a manner of addressing women which was clearly instinctive and habitual and which, at the same time, by good fortune, had the grace of flattery without phrases and of irony without impertinence. He was a little older, but he was not heavier; he was a little worn, but he was not worn dull. His presence was, anywhere and at any time, as much as ever the clock at the moment it strikes. Paul Beever's little eyes, after he appeared, rested on Rose with an expression which might have been that of a man counting the waves produced on a sheet of water by the plunge of a large object. For any like ripple on the fine surface of the younger girl he appeared to have no attention.

'I'm glad that remark's not addressed to *me*,' Jean said gaily; 'for I'm afraid I must immediately withdraw from you the light of my society.'

'On whom then do you mean to bestow it?'

'On your daughter, this moment. I must go and judge for myself of her condition.'

Tony looked at her more seriously. 'If you're at all really troubled about her I'll go back with you. You're too beautifully kind; they told me of your having been with her this morning.'

'Ah, you were with her this morning?' Rose asked of Jean in a manner to which there was a clear effort to impart the intonation of the casual, but which had in it something that made the person addressed turn to her with a dim surprise. Jean stood there in her black dress and her fair beauty; but her wonder was not of a sort to cloud the extraordinary radiance of her youth. 'For ever so long. Don't you know I've made her my peculiar and exclusive charge?'

'Under the pretext,' Tony went on, to Rose, 'of saving her from perdition. I'm supposed to be in danger of spoiling her, but Jean treats her quite *as* spoiled; which is much the greater injury of the two.'

'Don't go back, at any rate, please,' Rose said to him with soft persuasion. 'I never see you, you know, and I want just now particularly to speak to you.' Tony instantly expressed submission, and Rose, checking Jean, who, at this, in silence, turned to take her way to the bridge, reminded Paul Beever that she had just heard from him of his having, on his side, some special purpose of an interview with Miss Martle.

At this Paul grew very red. 'Oh yes, I should rather like to speak to you, please,' he said to Jean.

She had paused half way down the little slope; she looked at him frankly and kindly. 'Do you mean immediately?'

'As soon as you've time.'

'I shall have time as soon as I've been to Effie,' Jean replied. 'I want to bring her over. There are four dolls waiting for her.'

'My dear child,' Rose familiarly exclaimed, 'at home there are about forty! Don't you give her one every day or two?' she went on to Tony.

Her question didn't reach him; he was too much interested in

Paul's arrangement with Jean, on whom his eyes were fixed. 'Go, then – to be the sooner restored to us. And do bring the kid!' He spoke with jollity.

'I'm going in to change – perhaps I shall presently find you here,' Paul put in.

'You'll certainly find me, dear Paul. I shall be quick!' the girl called back. And she lightly went her way while Paul walked off to the house and the two others, standing together, watched her a minute. In spite of her black dress, of which the thin, voluminous tissue fluttered in the summer breeze, she seemed to shine in the afternoon light. They saw her reach the bridge, where, in the middle, she turned and tossed back at them a wave of her handkerchief; after which she dipped to the other side and disappeared.

'Mayn't I give you some tea?' Rose said to her companion. She nodded at the bright display of Mrs Beever's hospitality; Tony gratefully accepted her offer and they strolled on side by side. 'Why have you ceased to call me "Rose"?' she then suddenly demanded.

Tony started so that he practically stopped; on which she promptly halted. '*Have* I, my dear woman? I didn't know—' He looked at her and, looking at her, after a moment flagrantly coloured: he had the air of a man who sees something that operates as a warning. What Tony Bream saw was a circumstance of which he had already had glimpses; but for some reason or other it was now written with a largeness that made it resemble a printed poster on a wall. It might have been, from the way he took it in, a big yellow advertisement to the publicity of whose message no artifice of type was wanting. This message was simply Rose Armiger's whole face, exquisite and tragic in its appeal, stamped with a sensibility that was almost abject, a tenderness that was more than eager. The appeal was there for an instant with rare intensity, and what Tony felt in response to it he felt without fatuity or vanity. He could meet it only with a compassion as unreserved as itself. He looked confused, but he looked kind, and his companion's eyes lighted as with the sense of something that at last even in pure pity had come out to her. It was as if she let him know that since she had been at Eastmead nothing whatever had come out.

'When I was at Bounds four years ago,' she said, 'you called me "Rose" and you called our friend there' – she made a movement in the direction Jean had taken – 'nothing at all. Now you call her by name and you call me nothing at all.'

Tony obligingly turned it over. 'Don't I call you "Miss Armiger"?'

'Is that anything at all?' Rose effectively asked. 'You're conscious of some great difference.'

Tony hesitated; he walked on. 'Between you and Jean?'

'Oh, the difference between me and Jean goes without saying. What I mean is the difference between my having been at Wilverley then and my being here now.'

They reached the tea-table, and Tony, dropping into a chair, removed his hat. 'What have I called you when we've met in London?'

She stood before him closing her parasol. 'Don't you even know? You've called me nothing.' She proceeded to pour out tea for him, busying herself delicately with Mrs Beever's wonderful arrangements for keeping things hot. 'Have you by any chance been conscious of what I've called *you*?' she said.

Tony let himself, in his place, be served. 'Doesn't every one in the wide world call me the inevitable "Tony"? The name's dreadful – for a banker; it should have been a bar for me to that career. It's fatal to dignity. But then of course I haven't any dignity.'

'I think you haven't much,' Rose replied. 'But I've never seen any one get on so well without it; and, after all, you've just enough to make Miss Martle recognise it.'

Tony wondered. 'By calling me "Mr Bream"? Oh, for her I'm a greybeard – and I address her as I addressed her as a child. Of course I admit,' he added with an intention vaguely pacific, 'that she has entirely ceased to be that.'

'She's wonderful,' said Rose, handing him something buttered and perversely cold.

He assented even to the point of submissively helping himself. 'She's a charming creature.'

'I mean she's wonderful about your little girl.'

'Devoted, isn't she? That dates from long ago. She has a special sentiment about her.'

Rose was silent a moment. 'It's a little life to preserve and protect,' she then said. 'Of course!'

'Why, to that degree that she seems scarcely to think the child safe even with its infatuated daddy!'

Still on her feet beyond the table near which he sat, she had put up her parasol again, and she looked across at him from under it. Their eyes met, and he again felt himself in the presence of what, in them, shortly before, had been so deep, so exquisite. It represented something that no lapse could long quench – something that gave out the measureless white ray of a light steadily revolving. She could sometimes turn it away, but it was always somewhere; and now it covered him with a great cold lustre that made everything for the moment look hard and ugly – made him also feel the chill of a complication for which he had not allowed. He had had plenty of complications in life, but he had likewise had ways of dealing with them that were in general clever, easy, masterly – indeed often really pleasant. He got up nervously: there would be nothing pleasant in any way of dealing with this one.

CHAPTER 18

Conscious of the importance of not letting his nervousness show, he had no sooner pointlessly risen than he took possession of another chair. He dropped the question of Effie's security, remembering there was a prior one as to which he had still to justify himself. He brought it back with an air of indulgence which scarcely disguised, however, its present air of irrelevance. 'I'll gladly call you, my dear Rose, anything you like, but you mustn't think I've been capricious or disloyal. I addressed you of old – at the last – in the way in which it seemed most natural to address so close a friend of my wife's. But I somehow think of you here now rather as a friend of my own.'

'And that makes me so much more distant?' Rose asked, twirling her parasol.

Tony, whose plea had been quite extemporised, felt a slight confusion, which his laugh but inadequately covered. 'I seem to have uttered a *bêtise* – but I haven't. I only mean that a different title belongs, somehow, to a different character.'

'I don't admit my character to be different,' Rose said; 'save perhaps in the sense of its having become a little intensified. If I was here before as Julia's friend, I'm here still more as Julia's friend now.'

Tony meditated, with all his candour; then he gave a highly cordial, even if a slightly illogical assent. 'Of course you are – from your own point of view.' He evidently only wanted to meet her as far on the way to a quiet life as he could manage. 'Dear little Julia!' he exclaimed in a manner which, as soon as he had spoken, he felt to be such a fresh piece of pointlessness that, to carry it off, he got up again.

'Dear little Julia!' Rose echoed, speaking out loud and clear, but with an expression which, unlike Tony's, would have left on the mind of an ignorant auditor no doubt of its conveying a reference to the unforgotten dead.

Tony strolled towards the hammock. 'May I smoke a cigarette?' She approved with a gesture that was almost impatient, and while he lighted he pursued with genial gaiety: 'I'm not going to allow you to pretend that you doubt of my having dreamed for years of the pleasure of seeing you here again, or of the diabolical ingenuity that I exercised to enable your visit to take place in the way most convenient to both of us. You used to say the queen-mother disliked you. You see today how much!'

'She has ended by finding me useful,' said Rose. 'That brings me exactly to what I told you just now I wanted to say to you.'

Tony had gathered the loose net of the hammock into a single strand, and, while he smoked, had lowered himself upon it, sideways, in a posture which made him sit as in a swing. He looked surprised and even slightly disconcerted, like a man asked to pay twice. 'Oh, it isn't then what you did say —?'

'About your use of my name? No, it isn't that – it's something quite different.' Rose waited; she stood before him as she had stood before her previous interlocutor. 'It's to let you know the interest I take in Paul Beever. I take the very greatest.'

'You do?' said Tony approvingly. 'Well, you might go in for something worse!'

He spoke with a cheerfulness that covered all the ground; but she repeated the words as if challenging their sense. 'I might "go in" —?'

Her accent struck a light from them, put in an idea that had not been Tony's own. Thus presented, the idea seemed happy, and, in his incontrollable restlessness, his face more vividly brightening, he rose to it with a zeal that brought him for a third time to his feet. He smiled ever so kindly and, before he could measure his words or his manner, broke out: 'If you only really would, you know, my dear Rose!'

In a quicker flash he became aware that, as if he had dealt her a blow in the face, her eyes had filled with tears. It made the taste of his joke too bad. 'Are you gracefully suggesting that I shall carry Mr Beever off?' she demanded.

'Not from *me*, my dear – never!' Tony blushed and felt how much there was to rectify in some of his impulses. 'I think a lot of him and I want to keep my hand on him. But I speak of him frankly, always, as a prize, and I want something awfully good to happen to him. If you like him,' he hastened laughingly to add, 'of course it does happen – I see!'

He attenuated his meaning, but he had already exposed it, and he could perceive that Rose, with a kind of tragic perversity, was determined to get the full benefit, whatever it might be, of her impression or her grievance. She quickly did her best to look collected. 'You think he's safe then, and solid, and not so stupid as he strikes one at first?'

'Stupid? – not a bit. He's a statue in the block – he's a sort of slumbering giant. The right sort of tact will call him to life, the right sort of hand will work him out of the stone.'

'And it escaped you just now, in a moment of unusual expansion, that the right sort are mine?'

Tony puffed away at his cigarette, smiling at her resolutely through its light smoke. 'You do injustice to my attitude about you. There isn't an hour of the day that I don't indulge in some tribute or other to your great ability.'

Again there came into the girl's face her strange alternative look – the look of being made by her passion so acquainted with pain that even in the midst of it she could flower into charity. Sadly and gently she shook her head. 'Poor Tony!' Then she added in quite a different tone: 'What do you think of the difference of our ages?'

'Yours and Paul's? It isn't worth speaking of!'

'That's sweet of you – considering that he's only twenty-two. However, I'm not yet thirty,' she went on; 'and, of course, to gain time, one might press the thing hard.' She hesitated again; after which she continued: 'It's awfully vulgar, this way, to put the dots on the i's, but as it was you, and not I, who began it, I may ask if you really believe that if one should make a bit of an effort—?' And she invitingly paused, to leave him to complete a question as to which it was natural she should feel a delicacy.

Tony's face, for an initiated observer, would have shown that he was by this time watching for a trap; but it would also have shown that, after a moment's further reflection, he didn't particularly care if the trap should catch him. 'If you take such an interest in Paul,' he replied with no visible abatement of his preference for the stand-point of pleasantry, 'you can calculate better than I the natural results of drawing him out. But what I can assure you is that nothing would give me greater pleasure than to see you so happily "established", as they say – so honourably married, so affectionately surrounded and so thoroughly protected.'

'And all alongside of you here?' cried Rose.

Tony faltered, but he went on. 'It's precisely your being "alongside" of one that would enable one to see you.'

'It would enable one to see *you* – it would have that particular merit,' said Rose. 'But my interest in Mr Beever hasn't at all been of a kind to prompt me to turn the possibility over for myself. You can readily imagine how far I should have been in that case from speaking of it to you. The defect of your charming picture,' she presently added, 'is that an important figure is absent from it.'

'An important figure?'

'Jean Martle.'

Tony looked at the tip of his cigarette. 'You mean because there was at one time so much planning and plotting over the idea that she should make a match with Paul?'

'At one time, my dear Tony?' Rose exclaimed. 'There's exactly as much as ever, and I'm already – in these mere three weeks – in the very thick of it! Did you think the question had been quite dropped?' she inquired.

Tony faced her serenely enough – in part because he felt the extreme importance of so doing. 'I simply haven't heard much about it. Mrs Beever used to talk about it. But she hasn't talked of late.'

'She talked, my good man, no more than half an hour ago!' Rose replied.

Tony winced; but he stood bravely up; his cigarettes were an extreme resource. 'Really? And what did she say to you?'

'She said nothing to *me* – but she said everything to her son. She said to him, I mean, that she'll never forgive him if she doesn't hear from him an hour or two hence that he has at last successfully availed himself, with Miss Martle, of this auspicious day, as well as of the fact that he's giving her, in honour of it, something remarkably beautiful.'

Tony listened with marked attention, but without meeting his companion's eyes. He had again seated himself in the hammock, with his feet on the ground and his head thrown back; and he smoked freely, holding it with either hand. 'What is he giving her?' he asked after a moment.

Rose turned away; she mechanically did something at the table. 'Shouldn't you think she'd show it to you?' she threw over her shoulder.

While this shoulder, sensibly cold for the instant, was presented, he watched her. 'I daresay – if she accepts it.'

The girl faced him again. 'And won't she accept it?'

'Only – I should say – if she accepts *him*.'

'And won't she do that?'

Tony made a 'ring' with his cigarette. 'The thing will be for him to get her to.'

'That's exactly,' said Rose, 'what I want you to do.'

'Me?' He now stared at her. 'How can I?'

'I won't undertake to tell you how – I'll leave that to your ingenuity. Wouldn't it be a matter – just an easy extension – of existing relations? You saw just now that he appealed to her for his chance and that she consented to give it to him. What I wanted you to hear from me is that I feel how much interested you'll be in learning that this chance is of the highest importance for him and that I know with how good a conscience you'll throw your weight into the scale of his success.'

'My weight with the young lady? Don't you rather exaggerate my weight?' Tony asked.

'That question can only be answered by your trying it. It's a situation in which not to take an interest is – well, not your duty, you know,' said Rose.

Tony gave a smile which he felt to be a little pale; but there was still good-humour in the tone in which he protestingly and portentously murmured: 'Oh, my "duty"—!'

'Surely; if you see no objection to poor Mrs Beever's at last gathering the fruit of the tree she long ago so fondly and so carefully planted. Of course if you should frankly tell me you see one that I don't know—!' She looked ingenuous and hard. '*Do* you, by chance, see one?'

'None at all. I've never known a tree of Mrs Beever's of which the fruit hasn't been sweet.'

'Well, in the present case – sweet or bitter! – it's ready to fall. This is the hour the years have pointed to. You think highly of Paul—'

Tony Bream took her up. 'And I think highly of Jean, and therefore I must see them through? I catch your meaning. But have you – in a matter composed, after all, of ticklish elements – thought of the danger of one's meddling?'

'A great deal.' A troubled vision of this danger dawned even now in Rose's face. 'But I've thought still more of one's possible prudence – one's occasional tact.' Tony, for a moment, made no reply; he quitted the hammock and began to stroll about. Her anxious eyes followed him, and presently she brought out: 'Have you really been supposing that they've given it up?'

Tony remained silent; but at last he stopped short, and there was an effect of returning from an absence in the way he abruptly demanded: 'That who have given up what?'

'That Mrs Beever and Paul have given up what we're talking about – the idea of his union with Jean.'

Tony hesitated. 'I haven't been supposing anything at all!' Rose recognised the words for the first he had ever uttered to her that expressed even a shade of irritation, and she was unable to conceal that she felt, on the spot, how memorable this fact was to make them. Tony's immediate glance at her showed equally that he had instantly become aware of their so affecting her. He did, however, nothing to modify the impression: he only stood a moment looking across the river; after which he observed quietly: 'Here she is – on the bridge.'

He had walked nearer to the stream, and Rose had moved back to the tea-table, from which the view of the bridge was obstructed. 'Has she brought the child?' she asked.

'I don't make out – she may have her by the hand.' He approached again, and as he came he said: 'Your idea is really that I should speak to her now?'

'Before she sees Paul?' Rose met his eyes; there was a quick anguish of uncertainty in all her person. 'I leave that to you – since you cast a doubt on the safety of your doing so. I leave it,' said Rose, 'to your judgement – I leave it to your honour.'

'To my honour?' Tony wondered with a showy jerk of his head what the deuce his honour had to do with it.

She went on without heeding him. 'My idea is only that, whether you speak to her or not, she shall accept him. Gracious heavens, she *must*!' Rose broke out with passion.

'You take an immense interest in it!' Tony laughed.

'Take the same, then, yourself, and the thing will come off.' They stood a minute looking at each other, and more passed between them than had ever passed before. The result of it was that Rose had a drop from her strenuous height to sudden and beautiful gentleness. 'Tony Bream, I trust you.'

She had uttered the word in a way that had the power to make him flush. He answered peaceably, however, laughing again: 'I hope so, my dear Rose!' Then in a moment he added: 'I *will* speak.' He glanced again at the circuitous path from the bridge, but Jean had not yet emerged from the shrubbery by which it was screened. 'If she brings Effie will you take her?'

With her ominous face the girl considered. 'I'm afraid I can't do that.'

Tony gave a gesture of impatience. 'Good God, how you stand off from the poor little thing!'

Jean at this moment came into sight without the child. 'I shall never take her from *her*!' And Rose Armiger turned away.

CHAPTER 19

Tony went toward his messenger, who, as she saw Rose apparently leaving the garden, pressingly called out: 'Would *you*, Miss Armiger, very kindly go over for Effie? She wasn't even yet ready,' she explained as she came back up the slope with her friend, 'and I was afraid to wait after promising Paul to meet him.'

'He's not here, you see,' said Tony; 'it's he who, most ungallantly, makes you wait. Never mind; you'll wait with me.' He looked at Rose as they overtook her. 'Will you go and bring the child, as our friend here asks, or is such an act as that also, and still more, inconsistent with your mysterious principles?'

'You must kindly excuse me,' Rose said directly to Jean. 'I've a letter to write in the house. Now or never – I must catch the post.'

'Don't let us keep you, then,' Tony returned, 'I'll go over myself – as soon as Paul comes back.'

'I'll send him straight out.' And Rose Armiger retired in good order.

Tony followed her with his eyes; then he exclaimed: 'It's, upon my soul, as if she couldn't trust herself—!' His remark, which he checked, dropped into a snap of his fingers while Jean Martle wondered.

'To do what?' she asked.

Tony hesitated. 'To do nothing! The child's all right?'

'Perfectly right. It's only that the great Gorham has decreed that she's to have her usual little supper before she comes, and that, with her ribbons and frills all covered with an enormous bib, Effie had just settled down to that extremely solemn function.'

Tony in his turn wondered. 'Why shouldn't she have her supper here?'

'Ah, you must ask the great Gorham!'

'And didn't *you* ask her?'

'I did better – I divined her,' said Jean. 'She doesn't trust our kitchen.'

Tony laughed. 'Does she apprehend poison?'

'She apprehends what she calls "sugar and spice".'

'"And all that's nice"? Well, there's too much that's nice here, certainly! Leave the poor child then, like the little princess you all make of her, to her cook and her "taster," to the full rigour of her royalty, and stroll with me here till Paul comes out to you.' He looked at his watch and about at the broad garden where the shadows of the trees were still and the long afternoon had grown rich. 'This is remarkably peaceful, and there's plenty of time.' Jean concurred with a murmur as soft as the stir of the breeze, a 'Plenty, plenty', as serene as if, to oblige Tony Bream, so charming a day would be sure to pause in its passage. They went a few steps, but he stopped again with a question. 'Do you know what Paul wants of you?'

Jean looked a moment at the grass by her feet. 'I think I do.' Then raising her eyes without shyness, but with unqualified gravity, 'Do *you* know, Mr Bream?' she asked.

'Yes – I've just now heard.'

'From Miss Armiger?'

'From Miss Armiger. She appears to have had it from Paul himself.'

The girl gave out her mild surprise. 'Why has he told her?'

Tony hesitated. 'Because she's such a good person to tell things to.'

'Is it her immediately telling them again that makes her so?' Jean inquired with a faint smile.

Faint as this smile was, Tony met it as if he had been struck by it, and as if indeed, in the midst of an acquaintance which four years had now consecrated, he had not quite got used to being struck. That acquaintance had practically begun, on an unforgettable day, with his opening his eyes to it from an effort which had been already then the effort to forget – his suddenly taking her in as he lay on the sofa in his hall. From the way he sometimes looked at her it might have been judged that he had even now not taken her in completely – that the act of slow, charmed apprehension had yet to melt into accepted knowledge. It had in truth been made continuous by the continuous expansion of its object. If the sense of lying there on the sofa still sometimes came back to Tony, it was because he was interested in not interrupting by a rash motion the process taking place in the figure before him, the capricious rotation by which the woman peeped out of the child and the child peeped out of the woman. There was no point at which it had begun and none at which it would end, and it was a thing to gaze at with an attention refreshingly baffled. The frightened child had become a tall, slim nymph on a cloud, and yet there had been no moment of anything so gross as catching her in the act of change. If there had been he would have met it with some punctual change of his own; whereas it was his luxurious idea – unobscured till now – that in the midst of the difference so delightfully ambiguous he was free just *not* to change, free to remain as he was and go on liking her on trivial grounds. It had seemed to him that there was no one he had ever liked whom he could like quite so comfortably: a man of his age had had what he rather loosely called the 'usual' flashes of fondness. There had been no worrying question of the light this particular flash might kindle; he had never had to ask himself what his appreciation of Jean Martle might lead to. It would lead to exactly nothing – that had been settled all round in advance. This was a happy, lively provision that kept everything down, made sociability a cool, public, out-of-door affair, without a secret or a mystery – confined it, as one might say, to the breezy, sunny forecourt of the temple of friendship, forbidding it any dream of access to the obscure and comparatively stuffy interior. Tony had acutely remarked to himself that a thing could be led to only when there was a practicable road. As present to him today as on that other day was the little hour of violence – so strange and sad and sweet – which in his life had effectually suppressed any thoroughfare, making this expanse so pathless that, had he not been looking for a philosophic rather than a satiric term, he might almost have compared it to a desert. He answered his companion's inquiry about Rose's responsibility as an informant after he had satisfied himself that if she smiled exactly as she did it was only another illustration of a perfect instinct. That instinct, which at any time turned all talk with her away from flatness, told her that the right attitude for her now was the middle course between anxiety and resignation. 'If Miss Armiger hadn't spoken,' he said, 'I shouldn't have known. And of course I'm interested in knowing.'

'But why is she interested in your doing so?' Jean asked.

Tony walked on again. 'She has several reasons. One of them is that she greatly likes Paul and that, greatly liking him, she wishes the highest happiness conceivable for him. It occurred to her that as I greatly like a certain young lady I might not unnaturally desire for that young lady a corresponding chance, and that with a hint,' laughed Tony, 'that she really is about to have it, I might perhaps see my way to putting in a word for the dear boy in advance.'

The girl strolled beside him, looking quietly before her. 'How does she know,' she demanded, 'whom you "greatly like"?'

The question pulled him up a little, but he resisted the impulse, constantly strong in him, to stop again and stand face to face with her. He continued to laugh and after an instant he replied: 'Why, I suppose I must have told her.'

'And how many persons will she have told?'

'I don't care how many,' Tony said, 'and I don't think you need care either. Every one but she – from lots of observation – knows we're good friends, and it's because that's such a pleasant old story with us all that I feel as if I might frankly say to you what I have on my mind.'

'About what Paul may have to say?'

'The first moment you let him.'

Tony was going on when she broke in: 'How long have you had it on your mind?'

He found himself, at her challenge, just a trifle embarrassed. 'How long?'

'As it's only since Miss Armiger has told you that you've known there's anything in the air.'

This inquiry gave Tony such pause that he met it first with a laugh and then with a counter-appeal. 'You make me feel dreadfully dense! Do you mind my asking how long you yourself have known that what may be in the air is on the point of alighting?'

'Why, since Paul spoke to me.'

'Just now – before you went to Bounds?' Tony wondered. 'You were immediately sure that that's what he wants?'

'What else can he want? He doesn't want so much,' Jean added, 'that there would have been many alternatives.'

'I don't know what you call "much"!' Again Tony wondered. 'And it produces no more effect upon you—'

'Than I'm showing to you now?' the girl asked. 'Do you think me dreadfully stolid?'

'No, because I know that, in general, what you show isn't at all the full measure of what you feel. You're a great little mystery. Still,' Tony blandly continued, 'you strike me as calm – as quite sublime – for a young lady whose fate's about to be sealed. Unless, of course, you've regarded it,' he added, 'as sealed from far away back.'

They had strolled, in the direction they had followed, as far as they could go, and they necessarily stopped for a turn. Without taking up his last words Jean stood there and looked obscurely happy, as it seemed to him, at his recognition of her having appeared as quiet as she wished. 'You haven't answered my question,' she simply said. 'You haven't told me how long you've had it on your mind that you must say to me whatever it is you wish to say.'

'Why is it important I should answer it?'

'Only because you seemed positively to imply that the time of your carrying your idea about had been of the shortest. In the case of advice, if to advise is what you wish—'

'It *is* what I wish,' Tony interrupted; 'strangely as it may strike you that, in regard to such a matter as we refer to, one should be eager for such a responsibility. The question of time doesn't signify – what signifies is one's sincerity. I had an impression, I confess, that the prospect I a good while ago supposed you to have accepted had – what shall I call it? – rather faded away. But at the same time I hoped' – and Tony invited his companion to resume their walk – 'that it would charmingly come up again.'

Jean moved beside him and spoke with a colourless kindness which suggested no desire to challenge or cross-question, but a thoughtful interest in anything, in the connection in which they were talking, that he would be so good as to tell her and an earnest desire to be clear about it. Perhaps there was also in her manner just the visible tinge of a confidence that he would tell her the absolute truth. 'I see. You hoped it would charmingly come up again.'

'So that on learning that it *is* charmingly coming up, don't you see?' Tony laughed, 'I'm so agreeably agitated that I spill over on the spot. I want, without delay, to be definite to you about the really immense opinion I have of dear Paul. It can't do any harm, and it may do a little good, to mention that it has always seemed to me that we've only got to give him time. I mean, of course, don't you know,' he added, 'for him quite to distinguish himself.'

Jean was silent a little, as if she were thoroughly taking this home. 'Distinguish himself in what way?' she asked with all her tranquillity.

'Well – in every way,' Tony handsomely replied. 'He's full of stuff – there's a great deal of him: too much to come out all at once. Of course you know him – you've known him half your life; but I see him in a strong and special light, a light in which he has scarcely been shown to you and which puts him to a real test. He has ability; he has ideas; he has absolute honesty; and he has moreover a good stiff back of his own. He's a fellow of head; he's a fellow of heart. In short he's a man of gold.'

'He's a man of gold,' Jean repeated with punctual acceptance, yet as if it mattered much more that Tony should think so than that she should. 'It would be odd,' she went on, 'to be talking with you on a subject so personal to myself if it were not that I've felt Paul's attitude for so long past to be rather publicly taken for granted. He has felt it so, too, I think, poor boy, and for good or for ill there has been in our situation very little mystery and perhaps not much modesty.'

'Why *should* there be, of the false kind, when even the true has nothing to do with the matter? You and Paul are great people: he's the heir-apparent and you're the most eligible princess in the Almanach de Gotha. You can't be there and be hiding behind the window-curtain: you must step out on the balcony to be seen of the populace. Your most private affairs are affairs of state. At the smallest hint like the one I just mentioned even an old dunderhead like me catches on – he sees the strong reasons for Paul's attitude. However, it's not of that so much that I wanted to say a word. I thought perhaps you'd just let me touch on your own.' Tony hesitated; he felt vaguely disconcerted by the special quality of stillness that, though she moved beside him, her attention, her expectation put forth. It came over him that for the purpose of his plea she was almost too prepared, and this made him speculate. He stopped short again and, uneasily, 'May I light one more cigarette?' he asked. She assented with a flicker in her dim smile, and while he lighted he was increasingly conscious that she waited. He met the deep gentleness of her eyes and reflected afresh that if she was always beautiful she was beautiful at different times from different sources. What was the source of the impression she made on him at this moment if not a kind of refinement of patience, in which she seemed actually to hold her breath? 'In fact,' he said as he threw away his match, 'I *have* touched on it – I mean on the great hope we all have that you do see your way to meeting your friend as he deserves.'

'You "all" have it?' Jean softly asked.

Tony hesitated again. 'I'm sure I'm quite right in speaking for Wilverley at large. It takes the greatest interest in Paul, and I needn't at this time of day remind you of the interest it takes in yourself. But, I repeat, what I meant more particularly to utter was my own special confidence in your decision. Now that I'm fully enlightened it comes home to me that, as regards such a possibility as your taking your place here as a near neighbour and a permanent friend' – and Tony fixedly smiled – 'why, I can only feel the liveliest suspense. I want to make thoroughly sure of you!'

Jean took this in as she had taken the rest; after which she simply said: 'Then I think I ought to tell you that I shall not meet Paul in the way that what you're so good as to say seems to point to.'

Tony had made many speeches, both in public and in private, and he had naturally been exposed to replies of the incisive no less than of the massive order. But no check of the current had ever made him throw back his head quite so far as this brief and placid announcement. 'You'll not meet him—?'

'I shall never marry him.'

He undisguisedly gasped. 'In spite of all the reasons—?'

'Of course I've thought the reasons over – often and often. But there are reasons on the other side too. I shall never marry him,' she repeated.

CHAPTER 20

It was singular that though half an hour before he had not felt the want of the assurance he had just asked of her, yet now that he saw it definitely withheld it took an importance as instantly as a mirror takes a reflection. This importance was so great that he found himself suddenly scared by what he heard. He thought an instant with intensity. 'In spite of knowing that you'll disappoint' – he paused a little – 'the universal hope?'

'I know whom I shall disappoint; but I must bear that. I shall disappoint Cousin Kate.'

'Horribly,' said Tony.

'Horribly.'

'And poor Paul – to within an inch of his life.'

'No, not poor Paul, Mr Bream; not poor Paul in the least,' Jean said. She spoke without a hint of defiance or the faintest ring of bravado, as if for mere veracity and lucidity, since an opportunity quite unsought had been forced upon her. 'I know about poor Paul. It's all right about poor Paul,' she declared, smiling.

She spoke and she looked at him with a sincerity so distilled, as he felt, from something deep within her that to pretend to gainsay her would be in the worst taste. He turned about, not very brilliantly, as he was aware, to some other resource. 'You'll immensely disappoint your own people.'

'Yes, my mother and my grandmother – they both would like it. But they've never had any promise from me.'

Tony was silent awhile. 'And Mrs Beever – hasn't she had?'

'A promise? Never. I've known how much she has wanted it. But that's all.'

'Ah, that's a great deal,' said Tony. 'If, knowing how much she has wanted it, you've come back again and again, hasn't that been tantamount to giving it?'

Jean considered. 'I shall never come back again.'

'Ah, my dear child, what a way to treat us!' her friend broke out.

She took no notice of this; she only went on: 'Months ago – the last time I was here – an assurance, of a kind, was asked of me. But even then I held off.'

'And you've gone on with that intention?'

He had grown so serious now that he cross-questioned her, but she met him with a promptitude that was touching in its indulgence. 'I've gone on without an intention. I've only waited to see, to feel, to judge. The great thing seemed to me to be sure I wasn't unfair to Paul. I haven't been – I'm not unfair. He'll never say I've been – I'm sure he won't. I should have liked to be able to become his wife. But I can't.'

'You've nevertheless excited hopes,' said Tony. 'Don't you think you ought to consider that a little more?' His uneasiness, his sense of the unexpected, as sharp as a physical pang, increased so that he began to lose sight of the importance of concealing it; and he went on even while something came into her eyes that showed he had not concealed it. 'If you haven't meant not to do it, you've, so far as that goes, meant the opposite. Therefore something has made you change.'

Jean hesitated. 'Everything has made me change.'

'Well,' said Tony, with a smile so strained that he felt it almost pitiful, 'we've spoken of the disappointment to others, but I suppose there's no use in my attempting to say anything of the disappointment to me. That's not the thing that, in such a case, can have much effect on you.'

Again Jean hesitated: he saw how pale she had grown. 'Do I understand you tell me that you really *desire* my marriage?'

If the revelation of how he desired it had not already come to him the deep mystery of her beauty at this crisis might have brought it on the spot – a spectacle in which he so lost himself for the minute that he found no words to answer till she spoke again. 'Do I understand that you literally ask me for it?'

'I ask you for it – I ask you for it,' said Tony Bream.

They stood looking at each other like a pair who, walking on a frozen lake, suddenly have in their ears the great crack of the ice. 'And what are your reasons?'

'I'll tell you my reasons when you tell me yours for having changed.'

'I've not changed,' said Jean.

It was as if their eyes were indissolubly engaged. That was the way he had been looking a while before into another woman's, but he could think at this moment of the exquisite difference of Jean's. He shook his head with all the sadness and all the tenderness he felt he might permit himself to show just this once and never again. 'You've changed – you've changed.'

Then she gave up. 'Wouldn't you much rather I should never come back?'

'Far rather. But you *will* come back,' said Tony.

She looked away from him at last – turned her eyes over the place in which she had known none but emotions permitted and avowed, and again seemed to yield to the formidable truth. 'So you think I had better come back – so different?'

His tenderness broke out into a smile. 'As different as possible. As different as that will be just all the difference,' he added.

She appeared, with her averted face, to consider intently how much 'all' might in such a case practically amount to. But 'Here he comes' was what she presently replied.

Paul Beever was in sight, so freshly dressed that even at a distance his estimate of the requirements of the occasion was visible from his necktie to his boots. Adorned as it unmistakably had never been, his great featureless person moved solemnly over the lawn.

'Take him then – *take* him!' said Tony Bream.

Jean, intensely serious but with agitation held at bay, gave him one more look, a look so infinitely pacific that as, at Paul's nearer approach, he turned away from her, he had the sense of going off with a sign of her acceptance of his solution. The light in her face was the light of the compassion that had come out to him, and what was that compassion but the gage of a relief, of a promise? It made him walk down to the river with a step quickened to exhilaration; all the more that as the girl's eyes followed him he couldn't see in them the tragic intelligence he had kindled, her perception – from the very rhythm of the easy gait she had watched so often – that he really thought such a virtual confession to her would be none too lavishly repaid by the effort for which he had appealed.

Paul Beever had in his hand his little morocco case, but his glance also rested, till it disappeared, on Tony's straight and swinging back. 'I've driven him away,' he said.

'It was time,' Jean replied. 'Effie, who wasn't ready for me, must really come at last.' Then without the least pretence of unconsciousness she looked straight at the small object Paul carried.

Observing her attention to it he also dropped his eyes on it, while his hands turned it round and round in apparent uncertainty as to whether he had better present it to her open or shut. 'I hope you won't be as indifferent as Effie seems to be to the pretty trifle with which I've thought I should like to commemorate your birthday.' He decided to open the case and with its lifted lid he held it out to her. 'It will give me great pleasure if you'll kindly accept this little ornament.'

Jean took it from him – she seemed to study it a moment. 'Oh Paul, oh Paul!' – her protest was as sparing as a caress with the back of the hand.

'I thought you might care for the stone,' he said.

'It's a rare and perfect one – it's magnificent.'

'Well, Miss Armiger told me you would know.' There was a hint of relaxed suspense in Paul's tone.

Still holding the case open his companion looked at him a moment. 'Did *she* kindly select it?'

He stammered, colouring a little. 'No; mother and I did. We went up to London for it; we had the mounting designed and worked out. They took two months. But I showed it to Miss Armiger and she said you'd spot any defect.'

'Do you mean,' the girl asked, smiling, 'that if you had not had her word for that you would have tried me with something inferior?'

Paul continued very grave. 'You know well enough what I mean.'

Without again noticing the contents of the case she softly closed it and kept it in her hand. 'Yes, Paul, I know well enough what you mean.' She looked round her; then, as if her old familiarity with him were refreshed and sweetened: 'Come and sit down with me.' She led the way to a garden bench that stood at a distance from Mrs Beever's tea-table, an old green wooden bench that was a perennial feature of the spot. 'If Miss Armiger knows that I'm a judge,' she pursued as they went, 'it's, I think, because she knows everything – except one, which I know better than she.' She seated herself, glancing up and putting out her free hand to him with an air of comradeship and trust. Paul let it take his own, which he held there a minute. 'I know *you*.' She drew him down, and he dropped her hand; whereupon it returned to his little box, which, with the aid of the other, it tightly and nervously clasped. 'I can't take your present. It's impossible,' she said.

He sat leaning forward with his big red fists on his knees. 'Not for your birthday?'

'It's too splendid for that – it's too precious. And how can I take it for that when it isn't for that you offer it? How can I take so much, Paul, when I give you so little? It represents so much more than itself – a thousand more things than I've any right to let you think I can accept. I can't pretend not to know – I must meet you half way. I want to do that so much – to keep our relations happy, happy always, without a break or a cloud. They will be – they'll be beautiful. We've only to be frank. They *are* now: I feel it in the kind way you listen to me. If you hadn't asked to speak to me I should have asked it myself. Six months ago I promised I would tell you, and I've known the time was come.'

'The time is come, but don't tell me till you've given me a chance,' said Paul. He had listened without looking at her, his little eyes pricking with their intensity the remotest object they could reach. 'I want so to please you – to make you take a favourable view. There isn't a condition you may make, you know, of any sort whatever, that I won't grant you in advance. And if there's any inducement you can name that I've the least capacity to offer, please regard it as offered with all my heart. You know everything – you understand; but just let me repeat that all I am, all I have, all I can ever be or do –'

She laid her hand on his arm as if to help, not to stop him. 'Paul, Paul – you're beautiful!' She brushed him with the feather of her tact, but he reddened and continued to avert his big face, as if he were aware that the moment of such an assertion was scarcely the moment to venture to show it. 'You're such a gentleman!' Jean went on – this time with a tremor in her voice that made him turn.

'That's the sort of fine thing I wanted to say to *you*,' he said. And he was so accustomed, in any talk, to see his interlocutor suddenly laugh that his look of benevolence covered even her air of being amused by these words.

She smiled at him; she patted his arm. 'You've said to me far more than that comes to. I want you – oh, I want you so to be successful and happy!' And her laugh, with an ambiguous sob, suddenly changed into a burst of tears.

She recovered herself, but she had brought tears into his own eyes. 'Oh, that's of no consequence! I'm to understand that you'll never, never—?'

'Never, never.'

Paul drew a long, low breath. 'Do you know that every one has thought you probably would?'

'Certainly, I've known it, and that's why I'm glad of our talk. It ought to have come sooner. *You* thought I probably would, I think—'

'Oh, yes!' Paul artlessly broke in.

Jean laughed again while she wiped her eyes. 'That's why I call you beautiful. You had my possible expectation to meet.'

'Oh, yes!' he said again.

'And you were to meet it like a gentleman. I might have – but no matter. You risked your life – you've been magnificent.' Jean got up. 'And now, to make it perfect, you must take this back.'

She put the morocco case into his submissive hand, and he sat staring at it and mechanically turning it round. Unconsciously, musingly he threw it a little way into the air and caught it again. Then he also got up. 'They'll be tremendously down on us.'

'On "us"? On me, of course – but why on you?'

'For not having moved you.'

'You've moved me immensely. Before *me* – let no one say a word about you!'

'It's of no consequence,' Paul repeated.

'Nothing is, if we go on as we are. We're better friends than ever. And we're happy!' Jean announced in her triumph.

He looked at her with deep wistfulness, with patient envy. '*You* are!' Then his eyes took the direction to which her attention at that moment passed: they showed him Tony Bream coming up the slope with his little girl in his hand. Jean went down instantly to welcome the child, and Paul turned away with a grave face, giving at the same time another impulsive toss to the case containing the token she had declined.

CHAPTER 21

He directed his face to the house, however, only to find himself in the presence of his mother, who had come back to her tea-table and whom he saw veritably glare at the small object in his hands. From this object her scrutiny jumped to his own countenance, which, to his great discomfort, was not conscious of very successfully baffling it. He knew therefore a momentary relief when her observation attached itself to Jean Martle, whom Tony, planted on the lawn, was also undisguisedly watching and who was already introducing Effie to the treasure laid up in the shade of the tea-table. The girl had caught up the child on her strong young arm, where she sat robust and radiant, befrilled and besashed, hugging the biggest of the dolls; and in this position – erect, active, laughing, her rosy burden, almost on her shoulder, mingling its brightness with that of her crown of hair, and her other hand grasping, for Effie's further delight, in the form of another puppet from the pile, a still rosier imitation of it – anticipated quickly the challenge, which, as Paul saw, Mrs Beever was on the point of addressing her.

'Our wonderful cake's not coming out?'

'It's too big to transport,' said Mrs Beever: 'it's blazing away in the dining-room.'

Jean Martle turned to Tony. 'I may carry her in to see it?'

Tony assented. 'Only please remember she's not to partake.'

Jean smiled at him. 'I'll eat her share!' And she passed swiftly over the lawn while the three pair of eyes followed her.

'She looks,' said Tony, 'like the goddess Diana playing with a baby-nymph.'

Mrs Beever's attention came back to her son. 'That's the sort of remark one would expect to hear from *you*! You're not going with her?'

Paul showed vacant and vast. 'I'm going in.'

'To the dining-room?'

He wavered. 'To speak to Miss Armiger.'

His mother's gaze, sharpened and scared, had reverted to his morocco case. 'To ask her to keep that again?'

At this Paul met her with spirit. 'She may keep it for ever!' Giving another toss to his missile, while his companions stared at each other, he took the same direction as Jean.

Mrs Beever, disconcerted and flushed, broke out on the spot to Tony. 'Heaven help us all – she has refused him!'

Tony's face reflected her alarm. 'Pray, how do you know?'

'By his having his present to her left on his hands – a jewel a girl would jump at! I came back to hear it was settled—'

'And you haven't heard it's not!'

'What I haven't heard I've seen. That it's "not" sticks out of them! If she won't accept the gift,' Mrs Beever cried, 'how can she accept the giver?'

Tony's appearance, for some seconds, was an echo of her question. 'Why, she just promised me she would!'

This only deepened his neighbour's surprise 'Promised *you*—?'

Tony hesitated. 'I mean she left me to infer that I had determined her. She was so good as to listen most appreciatively to what I had to say.'

'And, pray, what had you to say?' Mrs Beever asked with austerity.

In the presence of a rigour so immediate he found himself so embarrassed that he considered. 'Well – everything. I took the liberty of urging Paul's claim.'

Mrs Beever stared. 'Very good of you! What did you think you had to do with it?'

'Why, whatever my great desire that she should accept him gave me.'

'Your great desire that she should accept him? This is the first I've heard of it.'

Once more Tony pondered. 'Did I never speak of it to you?'

'Never that I can remember. From when does it date?' Mrs Beever demanded.

'From the moment I really understood how much Paul had to hope.'

'How "much"?' the lady of Eastmead derisively repeated. 'It

wasn't so much that you need have been at such pains to make it less!'

Tony's comprehension of his friend's discomfiture was written in the smile of determined good humour with which he met the asperity of her successive inquiries; but his own uneasiness, which was not the best thing in the world for his temper, showed through this superficial glitter. He looked suddenly as blank as a man can look who looks annoyed. 'How in the world could I have supposed I was making it less?'

Mrs Beever faltered in her turn. 'To answer that question I should need to have been present at your appeal.'

Tony's eyes put forth a fire. 'It seems to me that your answer, as it is, will do very well for a charge of disloyalty. Do you imply that I didn't act in good faith?'

'Not even in my sore disappointment. But I imply that you made a gross mistake.'

Tony lifted his shoulders; with his hands in his pockets he had begun to fidget about the lawn – bringing back to her as he did so the worried figure that, in the same attitude, the day of poor Julia's death, she had seen pace the hall at the other house. 'But what the deuce then was I to do?'

'You were to let her alone.'

'Ah, but I should have had to begin that earlier!' he exclaimed with ingenuous promptitude.

Mrs Beever gave a laugh of despair. 'Years and years earlier!'

'I mean,' returned Tony with a blush, 'that from the first of her being here I made a point of giving her the impression of all the good I thought of Paul.'

His hostess continued sarcastic. 'If it was a question of making points and giving impressions, perhaps then you should have begun later still!' She gathered herself a moment; then she brought out: 'You should have let her alone, Tony Bream, because you're madly in love with her!'

Tony dropped into the nearest chair; he sat there looking up at the queen-mother. 'Your proof of that's my plea for your son?'

She took full in the face his air of pity for her lapse. 'Your plea was not for my son – your plea was for your own danger.'

'My own "danger"?' Tony leaped to his feet again in illustration of his security. 'Need I inform you at this time of day that I've such a thing as a conscience?'

'Far from it, my dear man. Exactly what I complain of is that you've quite too much of one.' And she gave him, before turning away, what might have been her last look and her last word. 'Your conscience is as big as your passion, and if both had been smaller you might perhaps have held your tongue!'

She moved off in a manner that added emphasis to her words, and Tony watched her with his hands still in his pockets and his long legs a little apart. He could turn it over that she accused him, after all, only of having been a particularly injurious fool. 'I was under the same impression as you,' he said ' – the impression that Paul was safe.'

This arrested and brought her sharply round. 'And were you under the impression that Jean was?'

'On my honour – as far as I'm concerned!'

'It's of course of you we're talking,' Mrs Beever replied. 'If you weren't her motive are you able to suggest who was?'

'Her motive for refusing Paul?' Tony looked at the sky for an inspiration. 'I'm afraid I'm too surprised and distressed to have a theory.'

'Have you one by chance as to why, if you thought them both so safe, you interfered?'

'"Interfered" is a hard word,' said Tony. 'I felt a wish to testify to my great sympathy with Paul from the moment I heard – what I didn't at all know – that this was the occasion on which he was, in more senses than one, to present his case.'

'May I go so far as to ask,' said Mrs Beever, 'if your sudden revelation proceeded from Paul himself?'

'No – not from Paul himself.'

'And scarcely from Jean, I suppose?'

'Not in the remotest degree from Jean.'

'Thank you,' she replied; 'you've told me.' She had taken her place in a chair and fixed her eyes on the ground. 'I've something to tell you myself, though it may not interest you so much.' Then raising her eyes: 'Dennis Vidal is here.'

Tony almost jumped. 'In the house?'

'On the river – paddling about.' After which, as his blankness grew, 'He turned up an hour ago,' she explained.

'And no one has seen him?'

'The Doctor and Paul. But Paul didn't know—'

'And didn't ask?' Tony panted.

'What does Paul ever ask? He's too stupid! Besides, with all my affairs, he sees my people come and go. Mr Vidal vanished when he heard that Miss Armiger's here.'

Tony went from surprise to mystification. 'Not to come back?'

'On the contrary, I hope, as he took my boat.'

'But he wishes not to see her?'

'He's thinking it over.'

Tony wondered. 'What, then, did he come for?'

Mrs Beever hung fire. 'He came to see Effie.'

'Effie?'

'To judge if you're likely to lose her.'

Tony threw back his head. 'How the devil does that concern him?'

Again Mrs Beever faltered; then, as she rose, 'Hadn't I better leave you to think it out?' she demanded.

Tony, in spite of his bewildered face, thought it out with such effect that in a moment he exclaimed: 'Then he still wants that girl?'

'Very much indeed. 'That's why he's afraid—'

Tony took her up. 'That Effie may die?'

'It's a hideous thing to be talking about,' said Mrs Beever. 'But you've perhaps not forgotten who were present—!'

'I've not forgotten who were present! I'm greatly honoured by Mr Vidal's solicitude,' Tony continued; 'but I beg you to tell him from me that I think I can take care of my child.'

'You must take more care than ever,' Mrs Beever pointedly observed. 'But don't mention him to *her*!' she as sharply added. Rose Armiger's white dress and red parasol had reappeared on the steps of the house.

CHAPTER 22

At the sight of the two persons in the garden Rose came straight down to them, and Mrs Beever, sombre and sharp, still seeking relief in the opportunity for satire, remarked to her companion in a manner at once ominous and indifferent that her guest was evidently in eager pursuit of him. Tony replied with gaiety that he awaited her with fortitude, and Rose, reaching them, let him know that as she had something more to say to him she was glad he had not, as she feared, quitted the garden. Mrs Beever hereupon signified her own intention of taking this course: she would leave their visitor, as she said, to Rose to deal with.

Rose smiled with her best grace. 'That's as I leave Paul to you. I've just been with him.'

Mrs Beever testified not only to interest, but to approval. 'In the library?'

'In the drawing-room.' Rose the next moment conscientiously showed by a further remark her appreciation of the attitude that, on the part of her hostess, she had succeeded in producing. 'Miss Martle's in the library.'

'And Effie?' Mrs Beever asked.

'Effie, of course, is where Miss Martle is.'

Tony, during this brief colloquy, had lounged away as restlessly as if, instead of beaming on the lady of Eastmead, Rose were watching the master of the other house. He promptly turned round. 'I say, dear lady, you know – be kind to her!'

'To Effie?' Mrs Beever demanded.

'To poor Jean.'

Mrs Beever, after an instant's reflection, took a humorous view of his request. 'I don't know why you call her "poor"! She has declined an excellent settlement, but she's not in misery yet.' Then she said to Rose: 'I'll take Paul first.'

Rose had put down her parasol, pricking the point of it, as if with a certain shyness, into the close, firm lawn. 'If you like, when you take Miss Martle—' She paused in deep contemplation of Tony.

'When I take Miss Martle?' There was a new encouragement in Mrs Beever's voice.

The apparent effect of this benignity was to make Miss Armiger's eyes widen strangely at their companion. 'Why, I'll come back and take the child.'

Mrs Beever met this offer with an alertness not hitherto markedly characteristic of her intercourse with Rose. 'I'll send her out to you.' Then by way of an obeisance to Tony, directing the words well at him: 'It won't indeed be a scene for that poor lamb!' She marched off with her duty emblazoned on her square satin back.

Tony, struck by the massive characters in which it was written there, broke into an indulgent laugh, yet even in his mirth he traced the satisfaction she took in letting him see that she measured with some complacency the embarrassment Rose might cause him. 'Does she propose to tear Miss Martle limb from limb?' he playfully inquired.

'Do you ask that,' said Rose, 'partly because you're apprehensive that it's what I propose to do to you?'

'By no means, my dear Rose, after your just giving me so marked a sign of the pacific as your coming round—'

'On the question,' Rose broke in, 'of one's relation to that little image and echo of her adored mother? That isn't peace, my dear Tony. You give me just the occasion to let you formally know that it's war.'

Tony gave another laugh. 'War?'

'Not on you – I pity you too much.'

'Then on whom?'

Rose hesitated. 'On any one, on every one, who may be likely to find that small child – small as she is! – inconvenient. Oh, I know,' she went on, 'you'll say I come late in the day for this and you'll remind me of how very short a time ago it was that I declined a request of yours to occupy myself with her at all. Only half an hour has elapsed, but what has happened in it has made all the difference.'

She spoke without discernible excitement, and Tony had already become aware that the face she actually showed him

was not a thing to make him estimate directly the effect
wrought in her by the incongruous result of the influence he had
put forth under pressure of her ardour. He needed no great
imagination to conceive that this consequence might, on the
poor girl's part, well be mainly lodged in such depths of her
nature as not to find an easy or an immediate way to the
surface. That he had her to reckon with he was reminded
as soon as he caught across the lawn the sheen of her white
dress; but what he most felt was a lively, unreasoning hope
that for the hour at least, and until he should have time to
turn round and see what his own situation exactly contained
for him, her mere incontestable cleverness would achieve a
revolution during which he might take breath. This was not a
hope that in any way met his difficulties – it was a hope that
only avoided them; but he had lately had a vision of something in which it was still obscure to him whether the bitter
or the sweet prevailed, and he was ready to make almost any
terms to be allowed to surrender himself to these first quick
throbs of response to what was at any rate an impression of
perfect beauty. He was in bliss with a great chill and in despair
with a great lift, and confused and assured and alarmed –
divided between the joy and the pain of knowing that what
Jean Martle had done she had done for Tony Bream, and done
full in the face of all he couldn't do to repay her. That Tony
Bream might never marry was a simple enough affair, but that
this rare creature mightn't suddenly figured to him as formidable and exquisite. Therefore he found his nerves rather indebted
to Rose for her being – if that was the explanation – too proud
to be vulgarly vindictive. She knew his secret, as even after
seeing it so freely handled by Mrs Beever he still rather artlessly
called the motive of his vain appeal; knew it better than before,
since she could now read it in the intenser light of the knowledge of it betrayed by another. If on this advantage he had no
reason to look to her for generosity, it was at least a comfort
that he might look to her for good manners. Poor Tony had
the full consciousness of needing to think out a line, but it
weighed somewhat against that oppression to feel that Rose
also would have it. He was only a little troubled by the idea
that, ardent and subtle, she would probably think faster than
he. He turned over a moment the revelation of these qualities

conveyed in her announcement of a change, as he might call it, of policy.

'What you say is charming,' he good-naturedly replied, 'so far as it represents an accession to the ranks of my daughter's friends. You will never without touching me remind me how nearly a sister you were to her mother; and I would rather express the pleasure I take in that than the bewilderment I feel at your allusion to any class of persons whose interest in her may not be sincere. The more friends she has, the better – I welcome you all. The only thing I ask of you,' he went on, smiling, 'is not to quarrel about her among yourselves.'

Rose, as she listened, looked almost religiously calm, but as she answered there was a profane quaver in her voice that told him with what an effort she achieved that sacrifice to form for which he was so pusillanimously grateful. 'It's very good of you to make the best of me; and it's also very clever of you, let me add, my dear Tony – and add with all deference to your goodness – to succeed in implying that any other course is open to you. You may welcome me as a friend of the child or not. I'm present for her, at any rate, and present as I've never been before.'

Tony's gratitude, suddenly contracting, left a little edge for irritation. 'You're present, assuredly, my dear Rose, and your presence is to us all an advantage of which, happily, we never become unconscious for an hour. But do I understand that the firm position among us that you allude to is one to which you see your way to attaching any possibility of permanence?'

She waited as if scrupulously to detach from its stem the flower of irony that had sprouted in this speech, and while she inhaled it she gave her visible attention only to the little hole in the lawn that she continued to prick with the point of her parasol. 'If that's a graceful way of asking me,' she returned at last, 'whether the end of my visit here isn't near at hand, perhaps the best satisfaction I can give you is to say that I shall probably stay on at least as long as Miss Martle. What I meant, however, just now,' she pursued, 'by saying that I'm more on the spot than heretofore, is simply that while I do stay I stay to be vigilant. That's what I hurried out to let you definitely know, in case you should be going home without our meeting again. I told you before I went into the house that I trusted you – I needn't recall to you for what. Mr Beever after a while came in and told me that Miss Martle had refused him. Then I felt that, after what had passed between us, it was only fair to say to you—'

'That you've ceased to trust me?' Tony interjected.

'By no means. I don't give and take back.' And though his companion's handsome head, with its fixed, pale face, rose high, it became appreciably handsomer and reached considerably higher, while she wore once more the air of looking at his mistake through the enlarging blur of tears. 'As I believe you did, in honour, what you could for Mr Beever, I trust you perfectly still.'

Tony smiled as if he apologised, but as if also he couldn't but wonder. 'Then it's only fair to say to me—?'

'That I don't trust Miss Martle.'

'Oh, my dear woman!' Tony precipitately laughed.

But Rose went on with all deliberation and distinctness. 'That's what has made the difference – that's what has brought me, as you say, round to a sense of my possible use, or rather of my clear obligation. Half an hour ago I knew how much you loved her. Now I know how much she loves you.'

Tony's laugh suddenly dropped; he showed the face of a man for whom a joke has sharply turned grave. 'And what is it that, in possession of this admirable knowledge, you see—?'

Rose faltered; but she had not come so far simply to make a botch of it. 'Why, that it's the obvious interest of the person we speak of not to have too stupid a patience with any obstacle to her marrying you.'

This speech had a quiet lucidity of which the odd action was for an instant to make him lose breath so violently that, in his quick gasp, he felt sick. In the indignity of the sensation he struck out. 'Pray, why is it the person's obvious interest any more than it's yours?'

'Seeing that I love you quite as much as she does? Because you don't love me quite so much as you love *her*. That's exactly "why", dear Tony Bream!' said Rose Armiger.

She turned away from him sadly and nobly, as if she had done with him and with the subject, and he stood where she had left him, gazing at the foolish greenness at his feet and slowly passing his hand over his head. In a few seconds, however, he

heard her utter a strange, short cry, and, looking round, saw her
face to face – across the interval of sloping lawn – with a
gentleman whom he had been sufficiently prepared to recognise
on the spot as Dennis Vidal.

CHAPTER 23

He had, in this preparation, the full advantage of Rose, who, quite thrown for the moment off her balance, was vividly unable to give any account of the apparition which should be profitable to herself. The violence of her surprise made her catch the back of the nearest chair, on which she covertly rested, directing at her old suitor from this position the widest eyes the master of Bounds had ever seen her unwittingly open. To perceive this, however, was to be almost simultaneously struck, and even to be not a little charmed, with the clever quickness of her recovery – that of a person constitutionally averse to making unmeasured displays. Rose was capable of astonishment, as she was capable of other kinds of emotion; but she was as little capable of giving way to it as she was of giving way to other kinds; so that both of her companions immediately saw her moved by the sense that a perturbing incident could at the worst do her no such evil turn as she might suffer by taking it in the wrong way. Tony became aware, in addition, that the fact communicated to him by Mrs Beever gave him an advantage even over the poor fellow whose face, as he stood there, showed the traces of an insufficient forecast of two things: one of them the influence on all his pulses of the sight again, after such an interval, and in the high insolence of life and strength, of the woman he had lost and still loved; the other the instant effect on his imagination of his finding her intimately engaged with the man who had been, however without fault, the occasion of her perversity. Vidal's marked alertness had momentarily failed him; he paused in his advance long enough to give Tony, after noting and regretting his agitation, time to feel that Rose was already as colourlessly bland as a sensitive woman could wish to be.

All this made the silence, however brief – and it was much briefer than my account of it – vibrate to such a tune as to prompt Tony to speak as soon as possible in the interest of harmony. What directly concerned him was that he had last seen Vidal as his own duly appreciative guest, and he offered him a hand freely charged with reminders of that quality. He was refreshed and even a little surprised to observe that the young man took it, after all, without stiffness; but the strangest thing in the world was that as he cordially brought him up the bank he had a mystic glimpse of the fact that Rose Armiger, with her heart in her throat, was waiting for some sign as to whether she might, for the benefit of her intercourse with himself, safely take the ground of having expected what had happened – having perhaps even brought it about. She naturally took counsel of her fears, and Tony, suddenly more elated than he could have given a reason for being, was ready to concur in any attempt she might make to save her appearance of knowing no reproach. Yet, foreseeing the awkwardness that might arise from her committing herself too rashly, he made haste to say to Dennis that he would have been startled if he had not been forewarned: Mrs Beever had mentioned to him the visit she had just received.

'Ah, she told you?' Dennis asked.

'Me only – as a great sign of confidence,' Tony laughed.

Rose, at this, could be amazed with superiority. 'What? – you've already been here?'

'An hour ago,' said Dennis. 'I asked Mrs Beever not to tell you.'

That was a chance for positive criticism. 'She obeyed your request to the letter. But why in the world such portentous secrecy?' Rose spoke as if there was no shade of a reason for his feeling shy, and now gave him an excellent example of the right tone. She had emulated Tony's own gesture of welcome, and he said to himself that no young woman could have stretched a more elastic arm across a desert of four cold years.

'I can explain to you better,' Dennis replied, 'why I emerged than why I vanished.'

'You emerged, I suppose, because you wanted to see me.' Rose spoke to one of her admirers, but she looked, she even laughed, at the other, showing him by this time an aspect completely and inscrutably renewed. 'You knew I was here?'

'At Wilverley?' Dennis hesitated. 'I took it for granted.'

'I'm afraid it was really for Miss Armiger you came,' Tony

remarked in the spirit of pleasantry. It seemed to him that the spirit of pleasantry would help them on.

It had its result – it proved contagious. 'I would still say so – before her – even if it weren't!' Dennis returned.

Rose took up the joke. 'Fortunately it's true – so it saves you a fib.'

'It saves me a fib!' Dennis said.

In this way the trick was successfully played – they found their feet; with the added amusement for Tony of hearing the necessary falsehood uttered neither by himself nor by Rose, but by a man whose veracity, from the first, on that earlier day, of looking at him, he had felt to be almost incompatible with the flow of conversation. It was more and more distinct while the minutes elapsed that the secondary effect of her old friend's reappearance was to make Rose shine with a more convenient light; and she met her embarrassment, every way, with so happy an art that Tony was moved to deplore afresh the complication that estranged him from a woman of such gifts. It made up indeed a little for this that he was also never so possessed of his own as when there was something to carry off or to put, as the phrase was, through. His light hand, his slightly florid facility were the things that in managing, in presiding, had rendered him so widely popular; and wasn't he, precisely, a little presiding, wasn't he a good deal managing just now? Vidal would be a blessed diversion – especially if he should be pressed into the service as one: Tony was content for the moment to see this with eagerness rather than to see it whole. His eagerness was quite justified by the circumstance that the young man from China did somehow or other – the reasons would appear after the fact – represent relief, relief not made vain by the reflection that it was perhaps only temporary. Rose herself, thank heaven, was, with all her exaltation, only temporary. He could already condone the officiousness of a gentleman too interested in Effie's equilibrium: the grounds of that indiscretion gleamed agreeably through it as soon as he had seen the visitor's fingers draw together over the hand held out by Rose. It was matter to whistle over, to bustle over, that, as had been certified by Mrs Beever, the passion betrayed by that clasp had survived its shipwreck, and there wasn't a rope's end Tony could throw, or a stray stick he could hold out, for which he didn't immediately cast about him. He saw indeed from this moment his whole comfort in the idea of an organised rescue and of making the struggling swimmer know, as a preliminary, how little any one at the other house was interested in preventing him to land.

Dennis had, for that matter, not been two minutes in touch with him before he really began to see this happy perception descend. It was, in a manner, to haul him ashore to invite him to dine and sleep; which Tony lost as little time as possible in doing; expressing the hope that he had not gone to the inn and that even if he had he would consent to the quick transfer of his effects to Bounds. Dennis showed that he had still some wonder for such an overture, but before he could respond to it the words were taken out of his mouth by Rose, whose recovery from her upset was complete from the moment she could seize a pretext for the extravagance of tranquillity.

'Why should you take him away from us and why should he consent to be taken? Won't Mrs Beever,' Rose asked of Dennis – 'since you're not snatching the fearful joy of a clandestine visit to her – expect you, if you stay anywhere, to give her the preference?'

'Allow me to remind you, and to remind Mr Vidal,' Tony returned, 'that when he was here before he gave her the preference. Mrs Beever made no scruple of removing him bodily from under my roof. I forfeited – I was obliged to – the pleasure of a visit to him. But that leaves me with my loss to make up and my revenge to take – I repay Mrs Beever in kind.' To find Rose disputing with him the possession of their friend filled him with immediate cheer. 'Don't you recognise,' he went on to him, 'the propriety of what I propose? I take you and deal with Mrs Beever, as she took you and dealt with me. Besides, your things have not even been brought here as they had of old been brought to Bounds. I promise to share you with these ladies and not to grudge you the time you may wish to spend with Miss Armiger. I understand but too well the number of hours I shall find you putting in. You shall pay me a long visit and come over here as often as you like, and your presence at Bounds may even possibly have the consequence of making them honour me there a little oftener with their own.'

Dennis looked from one of his companions to the other; he struck Tony as slightly mystified, but not beyond the point at

which curiosity was agreeable. 'I think I had better go to Mr
Bream,' he after a moment sturdily said to Rose. 'There's a
matter on which I wish to talk with you, but I don't see that
that need prevent.'

'It's for you to determine. There's a matter on which I find
myself, to you also, particularly glad of the opportunity of
saying a word.'

Tony glanced promptly at his watch and at Rose, 'Your
opportunity's before you – say your word now. I've a little job
in the town,' he explained to Dennis; 'I must attend to it quickly
and I can easily stop at the hotel and give directions for the
removal of your traps. All you will have to do then will be to
take the short way, which you know – over the bridge there and
through my garden – to my door. We shall dine at an easy
eight.'

Dennis Vidal assented to this arrangement without qualifica-
tion and indeed almost without expression: there evidently
lingered in him an operative sense that there were compensations
Mr Bream might be allowed the luxurious consciousness of
owing him. Rose, however, showed she still had a communication to make to Tony, who had begun to move in the quarter
leading straight from Eastmead to the town, so that he would
have to pass near the house on going out. She introduced it with
a question about his movements. 'You'll stop, then, on your
way and tell Mrs Beever—?'

'Of my having appropriated our friend? Not this moment,'
said Tony – 'I've to meet a man on business, and I shall only
just have time. I shall if possible come back here, but meanwhile
perhaps you'll kindly explain. Come straight over and take
possession,' he added, to Vidal; 'make yourself at home – don't
wait for me to return to you.' He offered him a hand-shake
again, and then, with his native impulse to accommodate and to
harmonise making a friendly light in his face, he offered one to
Rose herself. She accepted it so frankly that she even for a
minute kept his hand – a response that he approved with a smile
so encouraging that it scarcely needed even the confirmation of
speech. They stood there while Dennis Vidal turned away as if
they might have matters between them, and Tony yielded to the
impulse to prove to Rose that though there were things he kept
from her he kept nothing that was not absolutely necessary.

'There's something else I've got to do – I've got to stop at the Doctor's.'

Rose raised her eyebrows. 'To consult him?'

'To ask him to come over.'

'I hope you're not ill.'

'Never better in my life. I want him to see Effie.'

'She's not ill surely?'

'She's not right – with the fright Gorham had this morning. So I'm not satisfied.'

'Let him then by all means see her,' Rose said.

Their talk had, through the action of Vidal's presence, dropped from its chilly height to the warmest domestic level, and what now stuck out of Tony was the desire she should understand that on such ground as that he was always glad to meet her. Dennis Vidal faced about again in time to be called, as it were, if only by the tone of his host's voice, to witness this. 'A bientôt. Let me hear from you – and from him – that in my absence you've been extremely kind to our friend here.'

Rose, with a small but vivid fever-spot in her cheek, looked from one of the men to the other, while her kindled eyes showed a gathered purpose that had the prompt and perceptible effect of exciting suspense. 'I don't mind letting you know, Mr Bream, in advance exactly how kind I shall be. It would be affectation on my part to pretend to be unaware of your already knowing something of what has passed between this gentleman and me. He suffered, at my hands, in this place, four years ago, a disappointment – a disappointment into the rights and wrongs, into the good reasons of which I won't attempt to go further than just to say that an inevitable publicity then attached to it.' She spoke with slow and deliberate clearness, still looking from Tony to Dennis and back again; after which her strange intensity fixed itself on her old suitor. 'People saw, Mr Vidal,' she went on, 'the blight that descended on our long relations, and people believed – and I was at the time indifferent to their believing – that it had occurred by my act. I'm not indifferent now – that is to any appearance of having been wanting in consideration for such a man as you. I've often wished I might make you some reparation – some open atonement. I'm sorry for the distress that I'm afraid I caused you, and here, before the principal witness of the indignity you so magnanimously met, I very

sincerely express my regret and very humbly beg your forgive-
ness.' Dennis Vidal, staring at her, had turned dead white as she
kept it up, and the elevation, as it were, of her abasement had
brought tears into Tony's eyes. She saw them there as she looked
at him once more, and she measured the effect she produced
upon him. She visibly and excusably enjoyed it and after a
moment's pause she handsomely and pathetically completed it.
'*That*, Mr Bream – for your injunction of kindness – is the
kindness I'm capable of showing.'

Tony turned instantly to their companion, who now stood
staring hard at the ground. 'I change, then, my appeal – I make
it, with confidence, to *you*. Let me hear, Mr Vidal, when we
meet again, that you've not been capable of less!' Dennis, deeply
moved, it was plain, but self-conscious and stiff, gave no sign of
having heard him; and Rose, on her side, walked a little away
like an actress who has launched her great stroke. Tony, between
them, hesitated; then he laughed in a manner that showed he
felt safe. 'Oh, you're both all right!' he declared; and with
another glance at his watch he bounded off to his business. He
drew, as he went, a long breath – filled his lungs with the sense
that he should after all have a margin. She would take Dennis
back.

CHAPTER 24

'Why did you do that?' Dennis asked as soon as he was alone with Rose.

She had sunk into a seat at a distance from him, all spent with her great response to her sudden opportunity for justice. His challenge brought her flight to earth; and after waiting a moment she answered him with a question that betrayed her sense of coming down. 'Do you really care, after all this time, what I do or don't do?'

His rejoinder to this was in turn only another demand. 'What business is it of his that you may have done this or that to me? What has passed between us is still between us: nobody else has anything to do with it.'

Rose smiled at him as if to thank him for being again a trifle sharp with her. 'He wants me, as he said, to be kind to you.'

'You mean he wants you to do *that* sort of thing?' His sharpness brought him step by step across the lawn and nearer to her. 'Do you care so very much what he wants?'

Again she hesitated; then, with her pleased, patient smile, she tapped the empty place on the bench. 'Come and sit down beside me, and I'll tell you how much I care.' He obeyed her, but not precipitately, approaching her with a deliberation which still held her off a little, made her objective to his inspection or his mistrust. He had said to Mrs Beever that he had not come to watch her, but we are at liberty to wonder what Mrs Beever might have called the attitude in which, before seating himself, he stopped before her with a silent stare. She met him at any rate with a face that told him there was no scrutiny she was now enough in the wrong to fear, a face that was all the promise of confession and submission and sacrifice. She tapped again upon her bench, and at this he sat down. Then she went on: 'When did you come back?'

'To England? The other day – I don't remember which of

them. I think you ought to answer my question,' Dennis said, 'before asking any more of your own.'

'No, no,' she replied, promptly but gently; 'there's an inquiry it seems to me I've a right to make of you before I admit yours to make any at all.' She looked at him as if to give him time either to assent or to object; but he only sat rather stiffly back and let her see how fine and firm the added years had hammered him. 'What are you really here for? Has it anything to do with *me*?'

Dennis remained profoundly grave. 'I didn't know you were here – I had no reason to,' he at last replied.

'Then you simply desired the pleasure of renewing your acquaintance with Mrs Beever?'

'I came to ask her about you.'

'How beautiful of you!' – and Rose's tone, untinged with irony, rang out as clear as the impulse it praised. 'Fancy your caring!' she added; after which she continued: 'As I understand you, then, you've had your chance, you've talked with her?'

'A very short time. I put her a question or two.'

'I won't ask you what they were,' said Rose, 'I'll only say that, since I happen to be here, it may be a comfort to you not to have to content yourself with information at second-hand. Ask *me* what you like. I'll tell you everything.'

Her companion considered. 'You might then begin by telling me what I've already asked.'

She took him up before he could go on. 'Oh, why I attached an importance to his hearing what I just now said? Yes, yes; you shall have it.' She turned it over as if with the sole thought of giving it to him with the utmost lucidity; then she was visibly struck with the help she should derive from knowing just one thing more. 'But first – are you at all jealous of him?'

Dennis Vidal broke into a laugh which might have been a tribute to her rare audacity, yet which somehow, at the same time, made him seem only more serious. 'That's a thing for you to find out for yourself!'

'I see – I see.' She looked at him with musing, indulgent eyes. 'It would be too wonderful. Yet otherwise, after all, why should you care?'

'I don't mind telling you frankly,' said Dennis, while, with two fingers softly playing upon her lower lip, she sat estimating the possibility she had named – 'I don't mind telling you frankly that I asked Mrs Beever if you were still in love with him.'

She clasped her hands so eagerly that she almost clapped them. 'Then you do care?'

He was looking beyond her now – at something at the other end of the garden; and he made no other reply than to say: 'She didn't give you away.'

'It was very good of her; but I would tell you myself, you know, perfectly, if I were.'

'You didn't tell me perfectly four years ago,' Dennis returned.

Rose hesitated a minute; but this didn't prevent her speaking with an effect of great promptitude. 'Oh, four years ago I was the biggest fool in England!'

Dennis, at this, met her eyes again. 'Then what I asked Mrs Beever—'

'Isn't true?' Rose caught him up. 'It's an exquisite position,' she said, 'for a woman to be questioned as you question me, and to have to answer as I answer you. But it's your revenge, and you've already seen that to your revenge I minister with a certain amount of resolution.' She let him look at her a minute; at last she said without flinching: 'I'm not in love with Anthony Bream.'

Dennis shook his head sadly. 'What does that do for my revenge?'

Rose had another quick flush. 'It shows you what I consent to discuss with you,' she rather proudly replied.

He turned his eyes back to the quarter to which he had directed them before. 'You do consent?'

'Can you ask – after what I've done?'

'Well, then, *he* no longer cares—?'

'For me?' said Rose. 'He never cared.'

'Never?'

'Never.'

'Upon your honour?'

'Upon my honour.'

'But you had an idea – ?' Dennis bravely pursued.

Rose as dauntlessly met him. 'I had an idea.'

'And you've had to give it up?'

'I've had to give it up.'

Dennis was silent; he slowly got upon his feet. 'Well, *that* does something.'

'For your revenge?' She sounded a bitter laugh. 'I should think it might! What it does is magnificent!'

He stood looking over her head till at last he exclaimed: 'So, apparently, is the child!'

'She has come?' Rose sprang up to find that Effie had been borne toward them, across the grass, in the arms of the muscular Manning, who, having stooped to set her down and given her a vigorous impulsion from behind, recovered the military stature and posture.

'You're to take her, miss, please – from Mrs Beever. And you're to keep her.'

Rose had already greeted the little visitor. 'Please assure Mrs Beever that I will. She's with Miss Martle?'

'She is indeed, miss.'

Manning always spoke without emotion, and the effect of it on this occasion was to give her the air of speaking without pity.

Rose, however, didn't mind that. 'She may trust me,' she said, while Manning saluted and retired. Then she stood before her old suitor with Effie blooming on her shoulder.

He frankly wondered and admired. 'She's magnificent – she's magnificent!' he repeated.

'She's magnificent!' Rose ardently echoed. 'Aren't you, my very own?' she demanded of the child, with a sudden passion of tenderness.

'What did he mean about her wanting the Doctor? She'll see us *all* through – every blessed one of us!' Dennis gave himself up to his serious interest, an odd, voracious manner of taking her in from top to toe.

'You look at her like an ogre!' Rose laughed, moving away from him with her burden and pressing to her lips as she went a little plump pink arm. She pretended to munch it; she covered it with kisses; she gave way to the joy of her renounced abstention. 'See us all through? I hope so! Why shouldn't you, darling, why shouldn't you? You've got a *real* friend, you have, you duck; and she sees you know what you've got by the wonderful way you look at her!' This was to attribute to the little girl's solemn stare a vividness of meaning which moved Dennis to hilarity; Rose's profession of confidence made her immediately turn her round face over her friend's shoulder to the gentleman who was strolling behind and whose public criticism, as well as his public mirth, appeared to arouse in her only a soft sense of superiority. Rose sat down again where she had sat before, keeping Effie in her lap and smoothing out her fine feathers. Then their companion, after a little more detached contemplation, also took his former place.

'She makes me remember!' he presently observed.

'That extraordinary scene – poor Julia's message? You can fancy whether *I* forget it!'

Dennis was silent a little; after which he said quietly: 'You've more to keep it in mind.'

'I can assure you I've plenty!' Rose replied.

'And the young lady who was also present – isn't she the Miss Martle—?'

'Whom I spoke of to that woman? She's the Miss Martle. What about her?' Rose asked with her cheek against the child's.

'Does she also remember?'

'Like you and me? I haven't the least idea.'

Once more Dennis paused; his pauses were filled with his friendly gaze at their small companion. 'She's here again – like you?'

'And like you?' Rose smiled. 'No, not like either of us. She's always here.'

'And it's from her you're to keep a certain little person?'

'It's from her.' Rose spoke with rich brevity.

Dennis hesitated. 'Would you trust the little person to another little person?'

'To you – to hold?' Rose looked amused. 'Without a pang!' The child, at this, profoundly meditative and imperturbably "good", submitted serenely to the transfer and to the prompt, long kiss which, as he gathered her to him, Dennis, in his turn, imprinted on her arm. 'I'll stay with *you!*' she declared with expression; on which he renewed, with finer relish, the freedom she permitted, assuring her that this settled the question and that he was her appointed champion. Rose watched the scene between them, which was charming; then she brought out abruptly: 'What I said to Mr Bream just now I didn't say for Mr Bream.'

Dennis had the little girl close to him; his arms were softly round her and, like Rose's just before, his cheek, as he tenderly bent his head, was pressed against her cheek. His eyes were on their companion. 'You said it for Mr Vidal? He liked it, all the same, better than I,' he replied in a moment.

'Of course he liked it! But it doesn't matter what he likes,' Rose added. 'As for you – I don't know that your "liking" it was what I wanted.'

'What then did you want?'

'That you should see me utterly abased – and all the more utterly that it was in the cruel presence of another.'

Dennis had raised his head and sunk back into the angle of the bench, separated from her by such space as it yielded. His face, presented to her over Effie's curls, was a combat of mystifications. 'Why in the world should that give me pleasure?'

'Why in the world shouldn't it?' Rose asked. 'What's your revenge but pleasure?'

She had got up again in her dire restlessness; she glowed there in the perversity of her sacrifice. If he hadn't come to Wilverley to watch her, his wonder-stricken air much wronged him. He shook his head again with his tired patience. 'Oh, damn pleasure!' he exclaimed.

'It's nothing to you?' Rose cried. 'Then if it isn't, perhaps you pity me?' She shone at him as if with the glimpse of a new hope.

He took it in, but he only, after a moment, echoed, ambiguously, her word. 'Pity you?'

'I think you would, Dennis, if you understood.'

He looked at her hard; he hesitated. At last he returned quietly, but relentingly: 'Well, Rose, I *don't* understand.'

'Then I must go through it all – I must empty the cup. Yes, I must tell you.'

She paused so long, however, beautiful, candid and tragic, looking in the face her necessity, but gathering herself for her effort, that, after waiting a while, he spoke. 'Tell me what?'

'That I'm simply at your feet. That I'm yours to do what you will with – to take or to cast away. Perhaps you'll care a little for your triumph,' she said, 'when you see in it the grand opportunity I give you. It's *your* turn to refuse now – you can treat me exactly as you were treated!'

A deep, motionless silence followed, between them, this speech, which left them confronted as if it had rather widened than bridged their separation. Before Dennis found his answer to it the sharp tension snapped in a clear, glad exclamation. The child threw out her arms and her voice: 'Auntie Jean, Auntie Jean!'

The others had been so absorbed that they had not seen Jean Martle approach, and she, on her side, was close to them before appearing to perceive a stranger in the gentleman who held Effie in his lap and whom she had the air of having assumed, at a greater distance, to be Anthony Bream. Effie's reach towards her friend was so effective that, with Vidal's obligation to rise, it enabled her to slip from his hands and rush to avail herself of the embrace offered her, in spite of a momentary arrest, by Jean. Rose, however, at the sight of this movement, was quicker than Jean to catch her; she seized her almost with violence, and, holding her as she had held her before, dropped again upon the bench and presented her as a yielding captive. This act of appropriation was confirmed by the flash of a fine glance – a single gleam, but direct – which, however, producing in Jean's fair face no retort, had only the effect of making her look, in gracious recognition, at Dennis. He had evidently, for the moment, nothing but an odd want of words to meet her with; but this, precisely, gave her such a sense of having disturbed a scene of intimacy that, to be doubly courteous, she said: 'Perhaps you remember me. We were here together—'

'Four years ago – perfectly,' Rose broke in, speaking for him with an amenity that might have been intended as a quick corrective of any impression conveyed by her grab of the child. 'Mr Vidal and I were just talking of you. He has come back, for the first time since then, to pay us a little visit.'

'Then he has things to say to you that I've rudely interrupted. Please excuse me – I'm off again,' Jean went on to Dennis. 'I only came for the little girl.' She turned back to Rose. 'I'm afraid it's time I should take her home.'

Rose sat there like a queen-regent with a baby sovereign on her knee. 'Must I give her up to you?'

'I'm responsible for her, you know, to Gorham,' Jean returned.

Rose gravely kissed her little ward, who, now that she was apparently to be offered the entertainment of a debate in which she was so closely concerned, was clearly prepared to contribute to it the calmness of impartial beauty at a joust. She was just old enough to be interested, but she was just young enough to be judicial; the lap of her present friend had the compass of a small child-world, and she perched there in her loveliness as if she had been Helen on the walls of Troy. 'It's not to Gorhan *I'm* responsible,' Rose presently answered.

Jean took it good-humouredly. 'Are you to Mr Bream?'

'I'll tell you presently to whom.' And Rose looked intelligently at Dennis Vidal.

Smiled at in alternation by two clever young women, he had yet not sufficiently to achieve a jocose manner shaken off his sense of the strange climax of his conversation with the elder of them. He turned away awkwardly, as he had done four years before, for the hat it was one of the privileges of such a colloquy to make him put down in an odd place. 'I'll go over to Bounds,' he said to Rose. And then to Jean, to take leave of her: 'I'm staying at the other house.'

'Really? Mr Bream didn't tell me. But I must never drive you away. You've more to say to Miss Armiger than I have. I've only come to get Effie,' Jean repeated.

Dennis, at this, brushing off his recovered hat, gave way to his thin laugh. 'That apparently may take you some time!'

Rose generously helped him off. 'I've more to say to Miss Martle than I've now to say to you. I think that what I've already said to you is quite enough.'

'Thanks, thanks – quite enough. I'll just go over.'

'You won't go first to Mrs Beever?'

'Not yet – I'll come in this evening. Thanks, thanks!' Dennis repeated with a sudden dramatic gaiety that was presumably intended to preserve appearances – to acknowledge Rose's aid and, in a spirit of reciprocity, cover any exposure she might herself have incurred. Raising his hat, he passed down the slope and disappeared, leaving our young ladies face to face.

Their situation might still have been embarrassing had Rose not taken immediate measures to give it a lift. 'You must let me have the pleasure of making you the first person to hear of a matter that closely concerns me.' She hung fire, watching her companion; then she brought out: 'I'm engaged to be married to Mr Vidal.'

'Engaged?' – Jean almost bounded forward, holding up her relief like a torch.

Rose greeted with laughter this natural note. 'He arrived half an hour ago, for a supreme appeal – and it has not, you see, taken long. I've just had the honour of accepting him.'

Jean's movement had brought her so close to the bench that, though slightly disconcerted by its action on her friend, she could only, in consistency, seat herself. 'That's very charming – I congratulate you.'

'It's charming of you to be so glad,' Rose returned. 'However, you've the news in all its freshness.'

'I appreciate that too,' said Jean. 'But fancy my dropping on a conversation of such importance!'

'Fortunately you didn't cut it short. We had settled the question. He had got his answer.'

'If I had known it I would have congratulated Mr Vidal,' Jean pursued.

'You would have frightened him out of his wits – he's so dreadfully shy,' Rose laughed.

'Yes – I could see he was dreadfully shy. But the great thing,' Jean candidly observed, 'is that he was not too dreadfully shy to come back to you.'

Rose continued to be moved to mirth. 'Oh, I don't mean with *me*! He's as bold with me as I am – for instance – with you.' Jean had not touched the child, but Rose smoothed our her ribbons as if to redress some previous freedom. 'You'll think that says everything. I can easily imagine how you judge my frankness,' she added. 'But of course I'm grossly immodest – I always was.'

Jean wistfully watched her light hands play here and there over Effie's adornments. 'I think you're a person of great courage – if you'll let me also be frank. There's nothing in the world I admire so much – for I don't consider that I've, myself, a great deal. I daresay, however, that I should let you know just as soon if I were engaged.'

'Which, unfortunately, is exactly what you're not!' Rose,

having finished her titivation of the child, sank comfortably back on the bench. 'Do you object to my speaking to you of that?' she asked.

Jean hesitated; she had only after letting them escape become conscious of the reach of her words, the inadvertence of which showed how few waves of emotion her scene with Paul Beever had left to subside. She coloured as she replied: 'I don't know how much you know.'

'I know everything,' said Rose. 'Mr Beever has already told me.'

Jean's flush, at this, deepened. 'Mr Beever already doesn't care!'

'That's fortunate for you, my dear! Will you let me tell you,' Rose continued, 'how much I do?'

Jean again hesitated, looking, however, through her embarrassment, very straight and sweet. 'I don't quite see that it's a thing you should tell me or that I'm really obliged to hear. It's very good of you to take an interest—'

'But however good it may be, it's none of my business: is that what you mean?' Rose broke in. 'Such an answer is doubtless natural enough. My having hoped you would accept Paul Beever, and above all my having rather publicly expressed that hope, is an apparent stretch of discretion that you're perfectly free to take up. But you must allow me to say that the stretch is more apparent than real. There's discretion and discretion – and it's all a matter of motive. Perhaps you can guess mine for having found a reassurance in the idea of your definitely bestowing your hand. It's a very small and a very pretty hand, but its possible action is out of proportion to its size and even to its beauty. It was not a question of meddling in your affairs – your affairs were only one side of the matter. My interest was wholly in the effect of your marriage on the affairs of others. Let me say, moreover,' Rose went smoothly and inexorably on, while Jean, listening intently, drew shorter breaths and looked away, as if in growing pain, from the wonderful white, mobile mask that supplied half the meaning of this speech – 'let me say, moreover, that it strikes me you hardly treat me with fairness in forbidding me an allusion that has after all so much in common with the fact, in my own situation, as to which you've no scruple in showing me your exuberant joy. You clap your hands over *my* being – if you'll forgive the vulgarity of my calling things by their names – got out of the way; yet I must suffer in silence to see you rather more in it than ever.'

Jean turned again upon her companion a face bewildered and alarmed: unguardedly stepping into water that she had believed shallow, she found herself caught up in a current of fast-moving depths – a cold, full tide that set straight out to sea. 'Where *am* I?' her scared silence seemed for the moment to ask. Her quick intelligence indeed, came to her aid, and she spoke in a voice out of which she showed that she tried to keep her heart-beats. 'You call things, certainly, by names that are extraordinary; but I, at any rate, follow you far enough to be able to remind you that what I just said about your engagement was provoked by your introducing the subject.'

Rose was silent a moment, but without prejudice, clearly, to her firm possession of the ground she stood on – a power to be effectively cool in exact proportion as her interlocutress was troubled. 'I introduced the subject for two reasons. One of them was that your eager descent upon us at that particular moment seemed to present you in the light of an inquirer whom it would be really rude not to gratify. The other was just to see if you would succeed in restraining your glee.'

'Then your story isn't true?' Jean asked with a promptitude that betrayed the limits of her circumspection.

'There you are again!' Rose laughed. 'Do you know your apprehensions are barely decent? I haven't, however, laid a trap with a bait that's all make-believe. It's perfectly true that Mr Vidal has again pressed me hard – it's not true that I've yet given him an answer completely final. But as I mean to at the earliest moment, you can say so to whomever you like.'

'I can surely leave the saying so to *you*!' Jean returned. 'But I shall be sorry to appear to have treated you with a want of confidence that may give you a complaint to make on the score of my manners – as to which you set me too high an example by the rare perfection of your own. Let me simply let you know, then, to cover every possibility of that sort, that I intend, under no circumstances – ever – ever – to marry. So far as that knowledge may satisfy you, you're welcome to the satisfaction. Perhaps in consideration of it,' Jean wound up, with an effect that must have struck her own ear as the greatest she had ever produced – 'perhaps in consideration of it you'll kindly do what I ask you.'

The poor girl was destined to see her effect reduced to her mere personal sense of it. Rose made no movement save to lay her hands on Effie's shoulders, while that young lady looked up at the friend of other occasions in round-eyed detachment, following the talk enough for curiosity, but not enough either for comprehension or for agitation. 'You take my surrender for granted, I suppose, because you've worked so long to produce the impression, which no one, for your good fortune, has gainsaid, that she's safe only in your hands. But *I* gainsay it at last, for her safety becomes a very different thing from the moment you give such a glimpse of your open field as you must excuse my still continuing to hold that you do give. My "knowledge" – to use your term – that you'll never marry has exactly as much and as little weight as your word for it. I leave it to your conscience to estimate that wonderful amount. You say too much – both more than I ask you and more than I can oblige you by prescribing to myself to take seriously. You do thereby injustice to what must be always on the cards for you – the possible failure of the great impediment. *I'm* disinterested in the matter – I shall marry, as I've had the honour to inform you, without having to think at all of impediments or failures. That's the difference between us, and it seems to me that it alters everything. I had a delicacy – but now I've nothing in the world but a fear.'

Jean had got up before these remarks had gone far, but even though she fell back a few steps her dismay was a force that condemned her to take them in. 'God forbid I should understand you,' she panted; 'I only make out that you say and mean horrible things and that you're doing your best to seek a quarrel with me from which you shall derive some advantage that, I'm happy to feel, is beyond my conception.' Both the women were now as pale as death, and Rose was brought to her feet by the pure passion of this retort. The manner of it was such as to leave Jean nothing but to walk away, which she instantly proceeded to do. At the end of ten paces, however, she turned to look at their companion, who stood beside Rose, held by the hand, and whom, as if from a certain consideration for infant innocence and a certain instinct of fair play, she had not attempted to put on her side by a single direct appeal from intimate eyes. This appeal she now risked, and the way the little girl's face mutely met it suddenly precipitated her to blind supplication. She became weak – she broke down. 'I beseech you to let me have her.'

Rose Armiger's countenance made no secret of her appreciation of this collapse. 'I'll let you have her on one condition,' she presently replied.

'What condition?'

'That you deny to me on the spot that you've but one feeling in your soul. Oh, don't look vacant and dazed,' Rose derisively pursued; 'don't look as if you didn't know what feeling I mean! Renounce it – repudiate it, and I'll never touch her again!'

Jean gazed in sombre stupefaction. 'I know what feeling you mean,' she said at last, 'and I'm incapable of meeting your condition. I "deny", I "renounce", I "repudiate" as little as I hope, as I dream, or as I feel that I'm likely ever again even to utter—!' Then she brought out in her baffled sadness, but with so little vulgarity of pride that she sounded, rather, a note of compassion for a perversity so deep: 'It's because of *that* that I want her!'

'Because you adore him – and she's his?'

Jean faltered, but she was launched. 'Because I adore him – and she's his.'

'*I* want her for another reason,' Rose declared. 'I adored her poor mother – and she's hers. That's *my* ground, that's *my* love, that's *my* faith.' She caught Effie up again; she held her in two strong arms and dealt her a kiss that was a long consecration. 'It's as your dear dead mother's, my own, my sweet, that – if it's time – I shall carry you to bed!' She passed swiftly down the slope with her burden and took the turn which led her out of sight. Jean stood watching her till she disappeared and then waited till she had emerged for the usual minute on the rise in the middle of the bridge. She saw her stop again there, she saw her again, as if in the triumph – a great open-air insolence – of possession, press her face to the little girl's. Then they dipped together to the further end and were lost, and Jean, after taking a few vague steps on the lawn, paused, as if sick with the aftertaste of her encounter, and turned to the nearest seat. It was close to Mrs Beever's blighted tea-table, and when she had sunk into the chair she threw her arms upon this support and wearily dropped her head.

CHAPTER 26

At the end of some minutes, with the sense of being approached, she looked up and saw Paul Beever. Returning to the garden, he had stopped short at sight of her, and his arrival made her spring to her feet with the fear of having, in the belief that she was unobserved, shown him something she had never shown. But as he bent upon her his kind, ugly face there came into her own the comfort of a general admission, the drop of all attempt at a superfine surface: they stood together without saying a word, and there passed between them something sad and clear, something that was in its essence a recognition of the great, pleasant oddity of their being drawn closer by their rupture. They knew everything about each other now and, young and clean and good as they were, could meet not only without attenuations, but with a positive friendliness that was for each, from the other, a moral help. Paul had no need of speech to show Jean how he thanked her for understanding why he had not besieged her with a pressure more heroic, and she, on her side, could enter with the tread of a nurse in a sick-room into the spirit of that accommodation. They both, moreover, had been closeted with his mother – an experience on which they could, with some dumb humour, compare notes. The girl, finally, had now, to this dear boy she didn't love, something more to give than she had ever given; and after a little she could see the dawn of suspicion of it in the eyes with which he searched her grave face.

'I knew Miss Armiger had come back here, and I thought I should find her,' he presently explained.

'She was here a few minutes ago – she has just left me,' Jean said.

'To go in again?' Paul appeared to wonder he had not met her on his way out.

'To go over to Bounds.'

He continued to wonder. 'With Mr Bream?'

'No – with his little girl.'

Paul's surprise increased. 'She has taken *her* up?'

Jean hesitated; she uneasily laughed. 'Up – up – up: away up in her arms!'

Her companion was more literal. 'A young woman of Effie's age must be a weight!'

'I know what weight – I've carried her. Miss Armiger did it precisely to prevent that.'

'To prevent your carrying her?'

'To prevent my touching or, if possible, looking at her. She snatched her up and fled with her – to get her away from me.'

'Why should she wish to do that?' Paul inquired.

'I think you had better ask her directly.' Then Jean added: 'As you say, she has taken her up. She's *her* occupation, from this time.'

'Why, suddenly, from this time?'

'Because of what has happened.'

'Between you and me?'

'Yes – that's one of her reasons.'

'One of them?' laughed Paul. 'She has so many?'

'She tells me she has two.'

'Two? She speaks of it?'

Jean saw, visibly, that she mystified him; but she as visibly tried to let him see that this was partly because she spared him. 'She speaks of it with perfect frankness.'

'Then what's her second reason?'

'That if I'm not engaged' – Jean hung fire, but she brought it out – 'at least she herself is.'

'She herself? – instead of you?'

Paul's blandness was so utter that his companion's sense of the comic was this time, and in spite of the cruelty involved in a correction, really touched. 'To you? No, not to you, my dear Paul. To a gentleman I found with her here. To that Mr Vidal,' said Jean.

Paul gasped. 'You found that Mr Vidal with her?' He looked bewilderedly about. 'Where then *is* he?'

'He went over to Bounds.'

'And she went with him?'

'No, she went after.'

Still Paul stood staring. 'Where the dickens did he drop from?'

'I haven't the least idea.'

The young man had a sudden light. 'Why, I saw him with mamma! He was here when I came off the river – he borrowed the boat.'

'But you didn't know it was he?'

'I never dreamed – and mamma never told me.'

Jean thought a moment. 'She was afraid. You see I'm not.'

Paul Beever more pitifully wondered; he repeated again the word she had left ringing in his ears. 'She's "engaged"?'

'So she informed me.'

His little eyes rested on her with a stupefaction so candid as almost to amount to a challenge; then they moved away, far away, and he stood lost in what he felt. She came, tenderly, nearer to him, and they turned back to her: on which she saw they were filled with the tears that another failure she knew of had no power to draw to them. 'It's awfully odd!' he said.

'I've had to hurt you,' she replied. 'I'm very sorry for you.'

'Oh, don't mind it!' Paul smiled.

'These are things for you to hear of – straight.'

'From *her*? Ah, I don't want to do that! You see, of course, I shan't say anything.' And he covered, for an instant, working it clumsily, one of his little eyes with the base of one of his big thumbs.

Jean held out her hand to him. 'Do you love her?'

He took it, embarrassed, without meeting her look; then, suddenly, something of importance seemed to occur to him and he replied with simple alertness: 'I never mentioned it!'

Dimly, but ever so kindly, Jean smiled. 'Because you hadn't had your talk with *me*?' She kept hold of his hand. 'Dear Paul, I must say it again – you're beautiful!'

He stared, not as yet taking this approval home; then with the same prompt veracity, 'But she knows it, you know, all the same!' he exclaimed.

Jean laughed as she released him; but it kept no gravity out of the tone in which she presently repeated: 'I'm sorry for you.'

'Oh, it's all right! May I light a cigarette?' he asked.

'As many as you like. But I must leave you.'

He had struck a match, and at this he paused. 'Because I'm smoking?'

'Dear, no. Because I must go over to see Effie.' Facing wistfully to her little friend's quarter, Jean thought aloud. 'I always bid her "Goodnight". I don't see why – on her birthday, of all evenings – I should omit it.'

'Well, then, bid her "Goodnight" for me too.' She was halfway down the slope; Paul went in the same direction, puffing his cigarette hard. Then, stopping short, 'Tony puts him up?' he abruptly asked.

'Mr Vidal? So it appears.'

He gazed a little, blowing his smoke, at this appearance. 'And she has gone over to see him?'

'That may be a part of her errand.'

He hesitated again. 'They can't have lost much time!'

'Very little indeed.'

Jean went on again; but again he checked her with a question. 'What has he, what has the matter you speak of, to do with her cutting in—?' He paused as if in the presence of things painfully obscure.

'To the interest others take in the child? Ah,' said Jean, 'if you feel as you do' – she hesitated – 'don't ask me. Ask her!'

She went her way, and, standing there in thought, he waited for her to come, after an interval, into sight on the curve of the bridge. Then as the minutes elapsed without her doing so, he lounged, heavy and blank, up again to where he had found her. Manning, while his back was turned, had arrived with one of her aids to carry off the tea-things; and from a distance, planted on the lawn, he bent on these evolutions an attention unnaturally fixed. The women marched and countermarched, dismantling the table; he broodingly and vacantly watched them; then, as he lighted a fresh cigarette, he saw his mother come out of the house to give an eye to their work. She reached the spot and dropped a command or two; after which, joining him, she took in that her little company had dispersed.

'What has become of every one?'

Paul's replies were slow; but he gave her one now that was distinct. 'After the talk on which I lately left you I should think you would know pretty well what had become of *me*.'

She gave him a keen look; her face softened. 'What on earth's the matter with you?'

He placidly smoked. 'I've had my head punched.'

'Nonsense – for all you mind me!' She scanned him again. 'Are you ill, Paul?'

'I'm all right,' he answered philosophically.

'Then kiss your old mammy.' Solemnly, silently he obeyed her; but after he had done so she still held him before her eyes. She gave him a sharp pat. 'You're worth them all!'

Paul made no acknowledgement of this tribute save to remark after an instant rather awkwardly: 'I don't know where Tony is.'

'I can do without Tony,' said his mother. 'But where's Tony's child?'

'Miss Armiger has taken her home.'

'The clever thing!' Mrs Beever fairly applauded the feat. 'She was here when you came out?'

'No, but Jean told me.'

'Jean was here?'

'Yes; but she went over.'

'Over to Bounds – after what has happened?' Mrs Beever looked at first incredulous; then she looked stern again. 'What in the name of goodness possesses her?'

'The wish to bid Effie goodnight.'

Mrs Beever was silent a moment. 'I wish to heaven she'd leave Effie alone!'

'Aren't there different ways of looking at that?' Paul indulgently asked.

'Plenty, no doubt – and only one decent one.' The grossness of the girl's error seemed to loom larger. 'I'm ashamed of her!' she declared.

'Well, I'm not!' Paul quietly returned.

'Oh, you – of course you excuse her!' In the agitation that he had produced Mrs Beever bounced across an interval that brought her into view of an object from which, as she stopped short at the sight of it, her emotion drew fresh sustenance. 'Why, there's the boat!'

'Mr Vidal has brought it back,' said Paul.

She faced round in surprise. 'You've seen him?'

'No, but Jean told me.'

The lady of Eastmead stared. '*She* has seen him? Then where on earth is he?'

'He's staying at Bounds,' said Paul.

His mother's wonderment deepened. 'He has got there already?'

Paul smoked a little: then he explained. 'It's not very soon for Mr Vidal – he puts things through. He's already engaged to her.'

Mystified, at sea, Mrs Beever dropped upon a bench. 'Engaged to Jean?'

'Engaged to Miss Armiger.'

She tossed her head with impatience. 'What news is that? He was engaged to her four years ago!'

'Well, then he is still. They've patched it up.'

Mrs Beever was on her feet. 'She has seen him?'

Tony Bream at this moment came rapidly down the lawn and had the effect of staying Paul's answer. The young man gave a jerk to the stump of his cigarette and turned away with marked nervousness.

CHAPTER 27

The lady of Eastmead fronted her neighbour with a certain grimness. 'She has seen him – they've patched it up.'

Breathless with curiosity, Tony yet made but a bite of her news. 'It's on again – it's all right?'

'It's whatever you like to call it. I only know what Paul tells me.'

Paul, at this, stopped in his slow retreat, wheeling about. 'I only know what I had just now from Jean.'

Tony's expression, in the presence of his young friend's, dropped almost comically into the considerate. 'Oh, but I daresay it's so, old man. I was there when they met,' he explained to Mrs Beever, 'and I saw for myself pretty well how it would go.'

'I confess I didn't,' she replied. Then she added: 'It must have gone with a jump!'

'With a jump, precisely – and the jump was hers!' laughed Tony. 'All's well that ends well!' He was heated – he wiped his excited brow, and Mrs Beever looked at him as if it struck her that she had helped him to more emotion than she wished him. 'She's a most extraordinary girl,' he went on, 'and the effort she made there, all unprepared for it' – he nodded at the very spot of the exploit – 'was magnificent in its way, one of the finest things I've ever seen.' His appreciation of the results of this effort seemed almost feverish, and his elation deepened so that he turned, rather blindly, to poor Paul. 'Upon my honour she's cleverer, she has more domestic resources, as one may say, than – I don't care whom!'

'Oh, we all know how clever she is!' Mrs Beever impatiently grunted.

Tony's enthusiasm, none the less, overflowed; he was nervous for joy. 'I thought I did myself, but she had a lot more to show me!' He addressed himself again to Paul. 'She told you – with her coolness?'

Paul was occupied with another cigarette; he emitted no sound, and his mother, with a glance at him, spoke for him. 'Didn't you hear him say it was Jean who told him?'

'Oh, Jean!' – Tony looked graver. 'She told Jean?' But his gaiety, at this image, quickly came back. 'That was charming of her!'

Mrs Beever remained cold. 'Why on earth was it charming?'

Tony, though he reddened, was pulled up but an instant – his spirits carried him on. 'Oh, because there hasn't been much between them, and it was a pretty mark of confidence.' He glanced at his watch. 'They're in the house?'

'Not in mine – in yours.'

Tony looked surprised. 'Rose and Vidal?'

Paul spoke at last. 'Jean also went over – went after them.'

Tony thought a moment. '"After them" – Jean? How long ago?'

'About a quarter of an hour,' said Paul.

Tony continued to wonder. 'Aren't you mistaken? They're not there now.'

'How do you know,' asked Mrs Beever, 'if you've not been home?'

'I *have* been home – I was there five minutes ago.'

'Then how did you get here?'

'By the long way. I took a fly. I went back to get a paper I had stupidly forgotten and that I needed for a fellow with whom I had to talk. Our talk was a bore for the want of it, so I drove over there and got it, and, as he had his train to catch, I then overtook him at the station. I ran it close, but I saw him off; and here I am.' Tony shook his head. 'There's no one at Bounds.'

Mrs Beever looked at Paul. 'Then where's Effie?'

'Effie's not here?' Tony asked.

'Miss Armiger took her home,' said Paul.

'You saw them go?'

'No, but Jean told me.'

'Then where's Miss Armiger?' Tony continued. 'And where's Jean herself?'

'Where's Effie herself – that's the question,' said Mrs Beever.

'No,' Tony laughed, 'the question's Where's Vidal? *He's* the fellow I want to catch. I asked him to stay with me, and he said he'd go over, and it was my finding just now he hadn't come over that made me drive on here from the station to pick him up.'

Mrs Beever gave ear to this statement, but she gave nothing else. 'Mr Vidal can take care of himself; but if Effie's not at home, where is she?' She pressed her son. 'Are you sure of what Jean said to you?'

Paul bethought himself. 'Perfectly, mamma. She said Miss Armiger carried off the little girl.'

Tony appeared struck with this. 'That's exactly what Rose told me she meant to do. Then they're simply in the garden – they simply hadn't come in.'

'They've been in gardens enough!' Mrs Beever declared. 'I should like to know the child's simply in bed.'

'So should I,' said Tony with an irritation that was just perceptible, 'but I none the less deprecate the time-honoured custom of a flurry – I may say indeed of a panic – whenever she's for a moment out of sight.' He spoke almost as if Mrs Beever were trying to spoil for him by the note of anxiety the pleasantness of the news about Rose. The next moment, however, he questioned Paul with an evident return of the sense that toward a young man to whom such a hope was lost it was a time for special tact. 'You, at any rate, dear boy, saw Jean go?'

'Oh, yes – I saw Jean go.'

'And you understood from her that Rose and Effie went with Vidal?'

Paul consulted his memory. 'I think Mr Vidal went first.'

Tony thought a moment. 'Thanks so much, old chap.' Then with an exaggerated gaiety that might have struck his companions had it not been the sign of so much of his conversation: 'They're all a jolly party in the garden together. I'll go over.'

Mrs Beever had been watching the bridge. 'Here comes Rose – she'll tell us.'

Tony looked, but their friend had already dropped on the hither side, and he turned to Paul. 'You wouldn't object – a – to dining—?'

'To meet Mr Vidal?' Mrs Beever interposed. 'Poor Paul,' she laughed, 'you're between two fires! You and your guest,' she said to her neighbour, 'had better dine here.'

'Both fires at once?' – Tony smiled at her son. 'Should you like that better?'

Paul, where he stood, was lost in the act of watching for Rose. He shook his head absently. 'I don't care a rap!' Then he turned away again, and his mother, addressing Tony, dropped her voice.

'He won't show.'

'Do you mean his feelings?'

'I mean for either of us.'

Tony observed him a moment. 'Poor lad, I'll bring him round!' After which, 'Do you mind if I speak to her of it?' he abruptly inquired.

'To Rose – of this news?' Mrs Beever looked at him hard, and it led her to reply with severity: 'Tony Bream, I don't know what to make of you!' She was apparently on the point of making something rather bad, but she now saw Rose at the bottom of the slope and straightway hailed her. 'You took Effie home?'

Rose came quickly up. 'Not I! She isn't here?'

'She's gone,' said Mrs Beever. 'Where is she?'

'I'm afraid I don't know. I gave her up.' Paul had wheeled round at her first negation; Tony had not moved. Bright and handsome, but a little out of breath, she looked from one of her friends to the other. 'You're sure she's not here?' Her surprise was fine.

Mrs Beever's, however, had greater freedom. 'How can she be, when Jean says you took her away?'

Rose Armiger stared; she threw back her head. '"Jean says"?' She looked round her. 'Where is "Jean"?'

'She's nowhere about – she's not in the house.' Mrs Beever challenged the two men, echoing the question as if it were indeed pertinent. 'Where is the girl?'

'She has gone to Bounds,' said Tony. 'She's not in my garden?'

'She wasn't five minutes ago – I've just come out of it.'

'Then what took you there?' asked Mrs Beever.

'Mr Vidal.' Rose smiled at Tony: 'You know what!' She turned again to Mrs Beever, looking her full in the face. 'I've seen him. I went over with him.'

'Leaving Effie with Jean – precisely,' said Tony, in his arranging way.

'She came out – she begged so hard,' Rose explained to Mrs Beever. 'So I gave in.'

'And yet Jean says the contrary?' this lady demanded in stupefaction of her son.

Rose turned, incredulous, to Paul. 'She said to *you* – anything so false?'

'My dear boy, you simply didn't understand!' Tony laughed. 'Give me a cigarette.'

Paul's eyes, contracted to the pin-points we have already seen them become in his moments of emotion, had been attached, while he smoked still harder, to Rose's face. He turned very red and, before answering her, held out his cigarette-case. 'That was what I remember she said – that you had gone with Effie to Bounds.'

Rose stood wonderstruck. 'When she had taken her from me herself—?'

Mrs Beever referred her to Paul. 'But she wasn't with Jean when he saw her!'

Rose appealed to him. 'You saw Miss Martle alone?'

'Oh yes, quite alone.' Paul now was crimson and without visible sight.

'My dear boy,' cried Tony, impatient, 'you simply *don't* remember.'

'Yes, Tony. I remember.'

Rose had turned grave – she gave Paul a sombre stare. 'Then what on earth had she done with her?'

'What she had done was evident: she had taken her home!' Tony declared with an air of incipient disgust. They made a silly mystery of nothing.

Rose gave him a quick, strained smile. 'But if the child's not there—?'

'You just told us yourself she isn't!' Mrs Beever reminded him.

He hunched his shoulders as if there might be many explanations. 'Then she's somewhere else. She's wherever Jean took her.'

'But if Jean was here without her?'

'Then Jean, my dear lady, had come back.'

'Come back to lie?' asked Mrs Beever.

Tony coloured at this, but he controlled himself. 'Dearest Mrs Beever, Jean doesn't lie.'

'Then somebody does!' Mrs Beever roundly brought out.

'It's not you, Mr Paul, I know!' Rose declared, discomposed but still smiling. 'Was it you who saw her go over?'

'Yes; she left me here.'

'How long ago?'

Paul looked as if fifty persons had been watching him. 'Oh, not long!'

Rose addressed herself to the trio. 'Then why on earth haven't I met her? She must explain her astounding statement!'

'You'll see that she'll explain it easily,' said Tony.

'Ah, but, meanwhile, where's your daughter, don't you know?' Rose demanded with resentment.

'I'm just going over to see.'

'Then please go!' she replied with a nervous laugh. She presented to the others, as a criticism of his inaction, a white, uneasy face.

'I want first,' said Tony, 'to express to you my real joy. Please believe in it.'

She thought – she seemed to come back from a distance. 'Oh, you know?' Then to Paul: 'She told you? It's a detail,' she added impatiently. '*The* question' – she thought again – 'is the poor child.' Once more she appealed to Paul. 'Will you go and see?'

'Yes, go, boy.' Tony patted his back.

'Go this moment,' his mother put in.

He none the less lingered long enough to offer Rose his blind face. 'I want also to express—'

She took him up with a wonderful laugh. '*Your* real joy, dear Mr Paul?'

'Please believe in that too.' And Paul, at an unwonted pace, took his way.

'I believe in everything – I believe in every one,' Rose went on. 'But I don't believe—' She hesitated, then checked herself. 'No matter. Can you forgive me?' she asked of Mrs Beever.

'For giving up the child?' The lady of Eastmead looked at her hard. 'No!' she said curtly, and, turning straight away, went and dropped into a seat from which she watched the retreating figures of her two parlourmaids, who carried off between them a basket containing the paraphernalia of tea. Rose, with a queer expression, but with her straight back to the painful past, quietly transferred her plea to Tony. 'It was his coming – it made the difference. It upset me.'

'Upset you? You were splendid!'

The light of what had happened was in her face as she considered him. '*You* are!' she replied. Then she added: 'But he's finer than either of us!'

'I told you four years ago what he is. He's all right.'

'Yes,' said Rose – 'he's all right. And *I* am – now,' she went on. 'You've been good to me.' She put out her hand. 'Goodbye.'

'Goodbye? You're going?'

'He takes me away.'

'But not tonight!' – Tony's native kindness, expressed in his inflection, felt that it could now risk almost all the forms he essentially liked.

From the depth of Rose's eyes peeped a distracted, ironic sense of this. But she said with all quietude: 'Tomorrow early. I may not see you.'

'Don't be absurd!' laughed Tony.

'Ah, well – if you will!' She stood a moment looking down; then raising her eyes, 'Don't hold my hand so long,' she abruptly said. 'Mrs Beever, who has dismissed the servants, is watching us.'

Tony had the appearance of having felt as if he had let it go; but at this, after a glance at the person indicated, staring and smiling with a clear face, he retained his grasp of it. 'How in the world, with your back turned, can you see that?'

'It's with my back turned that I see most. She's looking at us hard.'

'I don't care a hang!' said Tony gaily.

'Oh, I don't say it for myself!' But Rose withdrew her hand.

Tony put both his own into his pockets. 'I hope you'll let me say to you – very simply – that I believe you'll be very happy.'

'I shall be as happy as a woman can be who has abandoned her post.'

'Oh, your post!' – Tony made a joke of that now. But he instantly added: 'Your post will be to honour us with your company at Bounds again; which, as a married woman, you see, you'll be perfectly able to do.'

She smiled at him. 'How you arrange things!' Then with a musing headshake: 'We leave England.'

'How *you* arrange them!' Tony exclaimed. 'He goes back to China?'

'Very soon – he's doing so well.'

Tony hesitated. 'I hope he has made money.'

'A great deal. I should look better – shouldn't I? – if he hadn't. But I show you enough how little I care how I look. I blow hot and cold; I'm all there – then I'm off. No matter,' she repeated. In a moment she added: 'I accept your hopes for my happiness. It will do, no doubt, soon as I learn—!' Her voice dropped for impatience; she turned to the quarter of the approach from the other house.

'That Effie's all right?' Tony saw their messenger already in the shrubbery. 'Here comes Paul to tell us.'

Mrs Beever rejoined them as he spoke. 'It wasn't Paul on the bridge. It was the Doctor – without his hat.'

'Without his hat?' Rose murmured.

'He has it in his hand,' Tony cheerfully asserted as their good friend emerged from cover.

But he hadn't it in his hand, and at sight of them on the top of the slope he stopped short, stopped long enough to give Rose time to call eagerly: 'Is Effie there?'

It was long enough also to give them all time to see, across the space, that his hair was disordered and his look at them strange; but they had no sooner done so than he made a violent gesture – a motion to check the downward rush that he evidently felt his aspect would provoke. It was so imperative that, coming up, he was with them before they had moved, showing them splashed, wet clothes and a little hard white face that Wilverley had never seen. 'There has been an accident.' Neither had Wilverley, gathered into three pair of ears, heard that voice.

The first effect of these things was to hold it an instant while Tony cried: 'She's hurt?'

'She's killed?' cried Mrs Beever.

'Stay where you are!' was the Doctor's stern response. Tony had given a bound, but, caught by the arm, found himself jerked, flaming red, face to face with Rose, who had been caught as tightly by the wrist. The Doctor closed his eyes for a second with this effort of restraint, but in the force he had put into it, which was not all of the hands, his captives submissively quivered. 'You're not to go!' he declared – quite as if it were for their own good.

'She's dead?' Tony panted.

'Who's *with* her – who *was*?' cried Rose.

'Paul's with her – by the water.'

'By the water?' Rose shrieked.

'My child's *drowned*?' Tony's cry was strange.

The Doctor had been looking from one of them to the other; then he looked at Mrs Beever, who, instantly, admirably, with a strength quickly acknowledged by the mute motion of his expressive little chin toward her, had stilled herself into the appeal of a blanched, breathless wait. 'May *I* go?' sovereignly came from her.

'Go. There's no one else,' he said as she bounced down the bank.

'No one else? Then where's that girl?' Rose's question was fierce. She gave, as fiercely, to free herself, a great wrench of her arm, but the Doctor held her as if still to spare her what he himself had too dreadfully seen. He looked at Tony, who said with quick quietness—

'Ramage, have I lost my child?'

'You'll see – be brave. Not *yet* – I've told Paul. Be quiet!' the Doctor repeated; then his hand dropped on feeling that the movement he had meant to check in his friend was the vibration of a man stricken to weakness and sickened on the spot. Tony's face had turned black; he was rooted to the ground; he stared at Rose, to whom the Doctor said: 'Who, Miss Armiger, was with her?'

All her lividness wondered. 'When *was* it—?'

'God knows! She was there – against the bridge.'

'Against the bridge – where I passed just now? *I* saw nothing!' Rose jerked, while Tony dumbly closed his eyes.

'I came over because she wasn't at the house, and – from the bank – *there* she was. I reached her – with the boat, with a push. She might have been half an hour—'

'It was half an hour ago she took her!' Rose broke in. 'She's not there?'

The Doctor looked at her hard. 'Of whom do you speak?'

'Why, of Miss Martle – whose hands are never off her.' Rose's mask was the mask of Medusa. 'What has become of Miss Martle?'

Doctor Ramage turned with the question to Tony, whose eyes, open now, were half out of his head. 'What has become of her?'

'She's not there?' Tony articulated.

'There's no one there.'

'Not Dennis?' sprang bewilderedly from Rose.

The Doctor stared. 'Mr Vidal? No, thank God – only Paul.' Then pressing Tony: 'Miss Martle was with her?'

Tony's eyes rolled over all space. 'No – not Miss Martle.'

'But *somebody* was!' Rose clamoured. 'She wasn't alone!'

Tony fixed her an instant. 'Not Miss Martle,' he repeated.

'But who then? And where is she now?'

'It's positive she's not here?' the Doctor asked of Rose.

'Positive – Mrs Beever knew. Where *is* she?' Rose rang out.

'Where in the name—?' passed, as with the dawn of a deeper horror, from their companion to Tony.

Tony's eyes sounded Rose's, and hers blazed back. His silence was an anguish, his face a convulsion; 'It isn't half an hour,' he at last brought out.

'Since it happened?' The Doctor blinked at his sudden knowledge. 'Then when—?'

Tony looked at him straight. 'When I was there.'

'And when was that?'

'After I called for you.'

'To leave word for me to go?' The Doctor set his face. 'But you were not going home then.'

'I did go – I had a reason. You know it,' Tony said to Rose.

'When you went for your paper?' She thought. 'But Effie wasn't there then.'

'Why not? She was there, but Miss Martle wasn't with her.'

'Then, in God's name, who was?' cried the Doctor.

'*I* was,' said Tony.

Rose gave the inarticulate cry of a person who has been holding her breath, and the Doctor an equally loud, but more stupefied 'You?'

Tony fixed upon Rose a gaze that seemed to count her respirations. 'I was with her,' he repeated; 'and I was with her alone. And what was done – *I* did.' He paused while they both gasped: then he looked at the Doctor. 'Now you know.' They continued to gasp; his confession was a blinding glare, in the shock of which the Doctor staggered back from Rose and she fell away with a liberated spring. 'God forgive me!' howled Tony – he broke now into a storm of sobs. He dropped upon a bench with his wretched face in his hands, while Rose, with a passionate wail, threw herself, appalled, on the grass, and their companion, in a colder dismay, looked from one prostrate figure to the other.

BOOK THREE

CHAPTER 28

The greatest of the parlourmaids came from the hall into
the drawing-room at Eastmead – the high, square temple of
mahogany and tapestry in which, the last few years, Mrs Beever
had spent much time in rejoicing that she had never set up
new gods. She had left it, from the first, as it was – full of
the old things that, on succeeding to her husband's mother,
she had been obliged, as a young woman of that period, to
accept as dolefully different from the things thought beautiful
by other young women whose views of drawing-rooms, all
about her, had also been intensified by marriage. She had not
unassistedly discovered the beauty of her heritage, and she had
not from any such subtle suspicion kept her hands off it. She
had never in her life taken any course with regard to any object
for reasons that had so little to do with her duty. Everything in
her house stood, at an angle of its own, on the solid rock of the
discipline it had cost her. She had therefore lived with mere dry
wistfulness through the age of rosewood, and had been
rewarded by finding that, like those who sit still in runaway
vehicles, she was the only person not thrown out. Her mahogany
had never moved, but the way people talked about it had, and
the people who talked were now eager to sit down with her
on everything that both she and they had anciently thought
plainest and poorest. It was Jean, above all, who had opened
her eyes – opened them in particular to the great wine-dark
doors, polished and silver-hinged, with which the lady of
Eastmead, arriving at the depressed formula that they were
'gloomy', had for thirty years, prudently on the whole, as she
considered, shut out the question of taste. One of these doors
Manning now softly closed, standing, however, with her hand
on the knob and looking across, as if, in the stillness, to listen at
another which exactly balanced with it on the opposite side of
the room. The light of the long day had not wholly faded, but

what remained of it was the glow of the western sky, which showed through the wide, high window that was still open to the garden. The sensible hush in which Manning waited was broken after a moment by a movement, ever so gentle, of the other door. Mrs Beever put her head out of the next room; then, seeing her servant, closed the door with precaution and came forward. Her face, hard but overcharged, had pressingly asked a question.

'Yes, ma'am – Mr Vidal. I showed him, as you told me, into the library.'

Mrs Beever thought. 'It may be wanted. I'll see him here.' But she checked the woman's retreat. 'Mr Beever's in his room?'

'No, ma'am – he went out.'

'But a minute ago?'

'Longer, ma'am. After he carried in –'

Mrs Beever stayed the phrase on Manning's lips and quickly supplied her own. 'The dear little girl – yes. He went to Mr Bream?'

'No, ma'am – the other way.'

Mrs Beever thought afresh. 'But Miss Armiger's in?'

'Oh, yes – in her room.'

'She went straight?'

Manning, on her side, reflected. 'Yes, ma'am. She always goes straight.'

'Not always,' said Mrs Beever. 'But she's quiet there?'

'Very quiet.'

'Then call Mr Vidal.' While Manning obeyed she turned to the window and stared at the gathering dusk. Then the door that had been left open closed again, and she faced about to Dennis Vidal.

'Something dreadful has happened?' he instantly asked.

'Something dreadful has happened. You've come from Bounds?'

'As fast as I could run. I saw Doctor Ramage there.'

'And what did he tell you?'

'That I must come straight here.'

'Nothing else?'

'That you would tell me,' Dennis said. 'I saw the shock in his face.'

'But you didn't ask?'

'Nothing. Here I am.'

'Here you are, thank God!' Mrs Beever gave a muffled moan.

She was going on, but, eagerly, he went before her. 'Can I help you?'

'Yes – if there *is* help. You can do so first by not asking me a question till I have put those I wish to yourself.'

'Put them – put them!' he said impatiently.

At his peremptory note she quivered, showing him she was in the state in which every sound startles. She locked her lips and closed her eyes an instant; she held herself together with an effort. 'I'm in great trouble, and I venture to believe that if you came back to me today it was because—'

He took her up shorter than before. 'Because I thought of you as a friend? For God's sake, think of *me* as one!'

She pressed to her lips while she looked at him the small tight knot into which her nerves had crumpled her pocket-handker-chief. She had no tears – only a visible terror. 'I've never appealed to anyone,' she replied, 'as I shall appeal to you now. Effie Bream is dead.' Then as instant horror was in his eyes: 'She was found in the water.'

'The water?' Dennis gasped.

'Under the bridge – at the other side. She had been caught, she was held, in the slow current by some obstruction, and by the pier. Don't ask me *how* – when I arrived, by the mercy of heaven, she had been brought to the bank. But she was gone.' With a movement of the head toward the room she had quitted, 'We carried her back here,' she went on. Vidal's face, which was terrible in the intensity of its sudden vision, struck her appar-ently as for the instant an echo, wild but interrogative, of what she had last said; so she explained quickly: 'To think – to get more time.' He turned straight away from her; he went, as she had done, to the window and, with his back presented, stood looking out in the mere rigour of dismay.

She was silent long enough to show a respect for the particular consternation that her manner of watching him betrayed her impression of having stirred; then she went on: 'How long were you at Bounds with Rose?'

Dennis turned round without meeting her eyes or, at first, understanding her question. 'At Bounds?'

'When, on your joining her, she went over with you.'

He thought a moment. 'She didn't go over with me. I went alone – after the child came out.'

'You were there when Manning brought her?' – Mrs Beever wondered. 'Manning didn't tell me that.'

'I found Rose on the lawn – with Mr Bream – when I brought back your boat. He left us together – after inviting me to Bounds – and then the little girl arrived. Rose let me hold her, and I was with them till Miss Martle appeared. Then I – rather uncivilly – went off.'

'You went without Rose?' Mrs Beever asked.

'Yes – I left her with the little girl and Miss Martle.' The marked effect of this statement made him add: 'Was it your impression I didn't?'

His companion, before answering him, dropped into a seat and stared up at him; after which she articulated: 'I'll tell you later. You left them,' she demanded, 'in the garden with the child?'

'In the garden with the child.'

'Then you hadn't taken her?'

Dennis had for some seconds a failure either of memory or of courage; but whichever it was he completely overcame it. 'By no means. She was in Rose's arms.'

Mrs Beever, at this image, lowered her eyes to the floor; after which, raising them again, she continued: 'You went to Bounds?'

'No – I turned off short. I *was* going, but if I had a great deal to think of,' Dennis pursued, 'after I had learned from you she was here, the quantity wasn't of course diminished by our personal encounter.' He hesitated. 'I had seen her with *him*.'

'Well?' said Mrs Beever as he paused again.

'I asked you if she was in love with him.'

'And I bade you find out for yourself.'

'I've found out,' Dennis said.

'Well?' Mrs Beever repeated.

It was evidently, even in this tighter tension, something of an ease to all his soreness to tell her. 'I've never seen anything like it – and there's not much I've not seen.'

'That's exactly what the Doctor says!'

Dennis stared, but after a moment, 'And does the Doctor say Mr Bream cares?' he somewhat artlessly inquired.

'Not a farthing.'

'Not a farthing. I'm bound to say – I could see it for myself,' he declared, 'that he has behaved very well.' Mrs Beever, at this, turning in torment on her seat, gave a smothered wail which pulled him up so that he went on in surprise: 'Don't you think that?'

'I'll tell you later,' she answered. 'In the presence of this misery I don't judge him.'

'No more do I. But what I was going to say was that, all the same, the way he has with a woman, the way he had with *her* there, and his damned good looks and his great happiness—'

'His great happiness? God help him!' Mrs Beever broke out, springing up again in her emotion. She stood before him with pleading hands. 'Where *were* you then?'

'After I left the garden? I was upset, I was dissatisfied – I didn't go over. I lighted a cigar; I passed out of the gate by your little closed pavilion and kept on by the river.'

'By the river?' – Mrs Beever was blank. 'Then why didn't you see—?'

'What happened to the child? Because if it happened near the bridge I had left the bridge behind.'

'But you were in sight—'

'For five minutes,' Dennis said. 'I was in sight perhaps even for ten. I strolled there, I turned things over, I watched the stream and, finally – just at the sharp bend – I sat a little on the stile beyond that smart new boat-house.'

'It's a horrid thing.' Mrs Beever considered. 'But you see the bridge from the boat-house.'

Dennis hesitated. 'Yes – it's a good way, but you've a glimpse.'

'Which showed you nothing at all?'

'Nothing at all?' – his echo of the question was interrogative, and it carried him uneasily to the window, where he again, for a little, stared out. The pink of the sky had faded and dusk had begun in the room. At last he faced about. 'No – I saw something. But I'll not tell you what it was, please, till I've myself asked you a thing or two.'

Mrs Beever was silent at this: they stood face to face in the twilight. Then she slowly exhaled a throb of her anguish. 'I think you'll be a help.'

'How much of one,' he bitterly demanded, 'shall I be to myself?' But he continued before she could meet the question: 'I went back to the bridge, and as I approached it Miss Martle came down to it from your garden.'

Mrs Beever grabbed his arm. 'Without the child?' He was silent so long that she repeated it: 'Without the child?'

He finally spoke. 'Without the child.'

She looked at him as she showed that she felt she had never looked at any man. 'On your sacred honour?'

'On my sacred honour.'

She closed her eyes as she had closed them at the beginning of their talk, and the same defeated spasm passed over her face. 'You *are* a help,' she said.

'Well,' Dennis replied straightforwardly, 'if it's being one to let you know that she was with me from that moment—'

Breathless she caught him up. 'With *you?* – till when?'

'Till just now, when we again separated at the gate-house: I to go over to Bounds, as I had promised Mr Bream, and Miss Martle—'

Again she snatched the words from him. 'To come straight in? Oh, glory be to God!'

Dennis showed some bewilderment. 'She *did* come—?'

'Mercy, yes – to meet this horror. She's with Effie.' She returned to it, to have it again. 'She was *with* you?'

'A quarter of an hour – perhaps more.' At this Mrs Beever dropped upon her sofa again and gave herself to the tears that had not sooner come. She sobbed softly, controlling them, and Dennis watched her with hard, haggard pity; after which he said: 'As soon as I saw her I spoke to her – I felt that I wanted her.'

'You wanted her?' – in the clearer medium through which Mrs Beever now could look up there were still obscurities.

He hesitated. 'For what she might say to me. I told you, when we spoke of Rose after my arrival, that I had not come to watch her. But while I was with them' – he jerked his head at the garden – 'something remarkable took place.'

Mrs Beever rose again. 'I know what took place.'

He seemed struck. 'You know it?'

'She told Jean.'

Dennis stared. 'I think not.'

'Jean didn't speak of it to you?'

'Not a word.'

'She spoke of it to Paul,' said Mrs Beever. Then, to be more specific: 'Something highly remarkable. I mean your engagement.'

Dennis was mute; but at last, in the gathered gloom, his voice was stranger than his silence. 'My engagement?'

'Didn't you, on the spot, induce her to renew it?'

Again, for some time, he was dumb. 'Has she said so?' he then asked.

'To every one.'

Once more he waited. 'I should like to see her.'

'Here she is.'

The door from the hall had opened as he spoke: Rose Armiger stood there. She addressed him straight and as if she had not seen Mrs Beever. 'I knew you'd be here – I must see you.'

Mrs Beever passed quickly to the side of the room at which she had entered, where her fifty years of order abruptly came out to Dennis. 'Will you have lights?'

It was Rose who replied. 'No lights, thanks.' But she stayed her hostess. 'May I see her?'

Mrs Beever fixed a look through the dusk. 'No!' And she slipped soundlessly away.

CHAPTER 29

Rose had come for a purpose, Vidal saw, to which she would make but a bound, and she seemed in fact to take the spring as she instantly broke out: 'For what did you come back to me? – for what did you come back?' She approached him quickly, but he made, more quickly, a move that gained him space and that might well have been the result of two sharp impressions: one of these the sense that in a single hour she had so altered as to be ugly, without a trace of the charm that had haunted him; and the other the sense that, thus ravaged and disfigured, wrecked in the gust that had come and gone, she required of him something that she had never required. A monstrous reality flared up in their relation, the perception of which was a shock that he was conscious for the moment of betraying that he feared, finding no words to answer her and showing her, across the room, while she repeated her question, a face blanched by the change in her own. 'For what did you come back to me? -- for what did you come back?'

He gaped at her; then as if there were help for him in the simple fact that on his own side he could immediately recall, he stammered out: 'To you – to you? I hadn't the slightest notion you were here!'

'Didn't you come to see where I was? Didn't you come absolutely and publicly *for* me?' He jerked round again to the window with the vague, wild gesture of a man in horrible pain, and she went on without vehemence, but with clear, deep intensity: 'It was exactly when you found I was here that you did come back. You had a perfect chance, on learning it, not to show; but you didn't take the chance, you quickly put it aside. You reflected, you decided, you insisted we should meet.' Her voice, as if in harmony with the power of her plea, dropped to a vibration more muffled, a soft but inexorable pressure. 'I hadn't called you, I hadn't troubled you, I left you as perfectly alone as

I've *been* alone. It was your own passion and your own act – you've dropped upon me, you've overwhelmed me. You've overwhelmed me, I say, because I speak from the depths of *my* surrender. But you didn't do it, I imagine, to be cruel, and if you didn't do it to be cruel you did it to take what it would give you.' Gradually, as she talked, he faced round again; she stood there supported by the high back of a chair, either side of which she held tight. 'You know what I am, if any man has known, and it's to the thing I am – whatever that is – you've come back at last from so far. It's the thing I am – whatever that is – I now count on you to stand by.'

'Whatever that is?' – Dennis mournfully marvelled. 'I feel, on the contrary, that I've never, never known!'

'Well, it's before anything a woman who has such a need as no woman has ever had.' Then she eagerly added: 'Why on earth did you descend on me if you hadn't need of *me*?'

Dennis took for an instant, quite as if she were not there, several turns in the wide place; moving in the dumb distress of a man confronted with the greatest danger of his life and obliged, while precious minutes lapse, to snatch at a way of safety. His whole air was an instinctive retreat from being carried by assault, and he had the effect both of keeping far from her and of revolving blindly round her. At last, in his hesitation, he pulled up before her. 'What makes, all of a sudden, the tremendous need you speak of? Didn't you remind me but an hour ago of how remarkably low, at our last meeting, it had dropped?'

Rose's eyes, in the dimness, widened with their wonder. 'You can speak to me in harshness of what I did an hour ago? You can taunt me with an act of penance that might have moved you – that did move you? Does it mean,' she continued, 'that you've none the less embraced the alternative that seems to you most worthy of your courage? Did I only stoop, in my deep contrition, to make it easier for you to knock me down? I gave you your chance to refuse me, and what you've come back for then will have been only, most handsomely, to take it. In that case you did injustice there to the question of your revenge. What fault have you to find with anything so splendid?'

Dennis had listened with his eyes averted, and he met her own again as if he had not heard, only bringing out his previous words with a harder iteration: 'What makes your tremendous need? what makes your tremendous need?' – he spoke as if that tone were the way of safety. 'I don't in the least see why it should have taken such a jump. You must do justice, even after your act of this afternoon – a demonstration far greater than any I dreamed of asking of you – you must do justice to my absolute necessity for seeing everything clear. I didn't there in the garden see anything clear at all – I was only startled and wonder-struck and puzzled. Certainly I was touched, as you say – I was so touched that I particularly suffered. But I couldn't pretend I was satisfied or gratified, or even that I was particularly convinced. You often failed of old, I know, to give me what I really wanted from you, and yet it never prevented the success of your effect on – what shall I call it?' He stopped short. 'On God knows what baser, obscurer part of me! I'm not such a brute as to say,' he quickly went on, 'that that effect was not produced this afternoon—'

'You confine yourself to saying,' Rose interrupted, 'that it's not produced in our actual situation.'

He stared through the thicker dusk; after which, 'I don't understand you!' he dropped. 'I do say,' he declared, 'that, whatever your success today may be admitted to consist of, I didn't at least then make the admission. I didn't at that moment understand you any more than I do now; and I don't think I said anything to lead you to suppose I did. I showed you simply that I was bewildered, and I couldn't have shown it more than by the abrupt way I left you. I don't recognise that I'm committed to anything that deprives me of the right of asking you for a little more light.'

'Do you recognise by chance,' Rose returned, 'the horrible blow—?'

'That has fallen on all this wretched place? I'm unutterably shocked by it. But where does it come into our relations?'

Rose smiled in exquisite pity, which had the air, however, of being more especially for herself. 'You say you were painfully affected; but you really invite me to go further still. Haven't I put the dots on all the horrid i's and dragged myself through the dust of enough confessions?'

Dennis slowly and grimly shook his head; he doggedly clung to his only refuge. 'I don't understand you – I don't understand you.'

Rose, at this, surmounted her scruples. 'It would be inexpressibly horrible to me to appear to be free to profit by Mr Bream's misfortune.'

Dennis thought a moment. 'To appear, you mean, to have an interest in the fact that the death of his daughter leaves him at liberty to invite you to become his wife?'

'You express it to admiration.'

He discernibly wondered. 'But why should you be in danger of that torment to your delicacy if Mr Bream has the best of reasons for doing nothing to contribute to it?'

'The best of Mr Bream's reasons,' Rose rejoined, 'won't be nearly so good as the worst of mine.'

'That of your making a match with some one else? I see,' her companion said. 'That's the precaution I'm to have the privilege of putting in your power.'

She gave the strangest of smiles; the whites of her excited eyes shimmered in the gloom. 'Your loyalty makes my position perfect.'

Dennis hesitated. 'And what does it make my own?

'Exactly the one you came to take. You *have* taken it by your startling presence; you're up to your eyes in it, and there's nothing that will become you so as to wear it bravely and gallantly. If you don't like it,' Rose added, 'you should have thought of that before!'

'You like it so much on your side,' Dennis retorted, 'that you appear to have engaged in measures to create it even before the argument for it had acquired the force that you give such a fine account of.'

'Do you mean by giving it out as an accomplished fact? It was never too soon to give it out; the right moment was the moment you were there. Your arrival changed everything; it gave me on the spot my advantage; it precipitated my grasp of it.'

Vidal's expression was like a thing battered dead, and his voice was a sound that matched it. 'You call your grasp your announcement—?'

She threw back her head. 'My announcement *has* reached you? Then you know I've cut off your retreat.' Again he turned away from her; he flung himself on the sofa on which, shortly before, Mrs Beever had sunk down to sob, and, as if with the need to hold on to something, buried his face in one of the hard, square cushions. She came a little nearer to him; she went on with her low-lucidity: 'So you can't abandon me – you can't. You came to me through doubts – you spoke to me through fears. You're mine!'

She left him to turn this over; she moved off and approached the door at which Mrs Beever had gone out, standing there in strained attention till, in the silence, Dennis at last raised his head. 'What is it you look to me to do?' he asked.

She came away from the door. 'Simply to see me through.'

He was on his feet again. 'Through what, in the name of horror?'

'Through everything. If I count on you, it's to support me. If I say things, it's for you to say them.'

'Even when they're black lies?' Dennis brought out.

Her answer was immediate. 'What need should I have of you if they were white ones?' He was unable to tell her, only meeting her mettle with his stupor, and she continued, with the lightest hint of reproach in her quiet pain: 'I thank you for giving that graceful name to my weak boast that you admire me.'

He had a sense of comparative idiocy. 'Do you expect me – on that admiration – to marry you?'

'Bless your innocent heart, no! – for what do you take me? I expect you simply to make people believe that you mean to.'

'And how long will they believe it if I don't?'

'Oh, if it should come to that,' said Rose, 'you can easily make them believe that you *have*!' She took a step so rapid that it was almost a spring; she had him now and, with her hands on his shoulders, she held him fast. 'So you see, after all, dearest, how little I ask!'

He submitted, with no movement but to close his eyes before the new-born dread of her caress. Yet he took the caress when it came – the dire confession of her hard embrace, the long entreaty of her stony kiss. He might still have been a creature trapped in steel; after she had let him go he still stood at a loss how to turn. There was something, however, that he presently opened his eyes to try. 'That you went over with *me* – that's what you wish me to say?'

'Over to Bounds? Is that what *I* said? I can't think.' But she thought all the same. 'Thank you for fixing it. If it's that, stick to it!'

'And to our having left the child with Miss Martle?'

This brought her up a moment. 'Don't ask me – simply meet the case as it comes. I give you,' she added in a marvellous manner, 'a perfectly free hand!'

'You're very liberal,' said Dennis, 'but I think you simplify too much.'

'I can hardly do that if to simplify is to leave it to your honour. It's the beauty of my position that *you're* believed.'

'That, then, gives me a certain confidence in telling you that Miss Martle was the whole time with me.'

Rose stared. 'Of what time do you speak?'

'The time after you had gone over to Bounds with Effie.'

Rose thought again. 'Where was she with you?'

'By the river, on this side.'

'On this side? You didn't go to Bounds?'

'Not when I left you for the purpose. I obeyed an impulse that made me do just the opposite. You see,' said Dennis, 'that there's a flaw in my honour! You had filled my cup too full – I couldn't carry it straight. I kept by the stream – I took a walk.'

Rose gave a low, vague sound. 'But Miss Martle and I were there together.'

'You were together till you separated. On my return to the bridge I met her.'

Rose hesitated. 'Where was she going?'

'Over to Bounds – but I prevented her.'

'You mean she joined you?'

'In the kindest manner – for another turn. I took her the same way again.'

Once more Rose thought. 'But if she was going over, why in the world should she have let you?'

Dennis considered. 'I think she pitied me.'

'Because she spoke to you of me?'

'No; because she didn't. But I spoke to her of you,' said Dennis.

'And what did you say?'

He hung fire a moment. 'That – a short time before – I saw you cross to Bounds.'

Rose slowly sat down. 'You saw me?'

'On the bridge, distinctly. With the child in your arms.'

'Where were you then?'

'Far up the stream – beyond your observation.'

She looked at him fixedly, her hands locked together between her knees. 'You were watching me?' Portentous and ghostly, in the darker room, had become their confronted estrangement.

Dennis waited as if he had a choice of answers; but at last he simply said: 'I saw no more.'

His companion as slowly rose again and moved to the window, beyond which the garden had now grown vague. She stood before it a while; then, without coming away, turned her back to it, so that he saw her handsome head, with the face obscure, against the evening sky. 'Shall I tell you who did it?' she asked.

Dennis Vidal faltered. 'If you feel that you're prepared.'

'I've been preparing. I see it's best.' Again, however, she was silent.

This lasted so long that Dennis finally spoke. 'Who did it?'

'Tony Bream – to marry Jean.'

A loud sound leaped from him, which was thrown back by the sudden opening of the door and a consequent gush of light. Manning marched in with a high lamp, and Doctor Ramage stood on the threshold.

CHAPTER 30

The Doctor remained at the door while the maid put down her lamp, and he checked her as she proceeded to the blinds and the other duties of the moment.

'Leave the windows, please; it's warm. That will do – thanks.' He closed the door on her extinguished presence and he held it a little, mutely, with observing eyes, in that of Dennis and Rose.

'Do you want *me*?' the latter promptly asked, in the tone, as he liked, of readiness either to meet him or to withdraw. She seemed to imply that at such an hour there was no knowing what any one might want. Dennis's eyes were on her as well as the Doctor's, and if the lamp now lighted her consciousness of looking horrible she could at least support herself with the sight of the crude embarrassment of others.

The Doctor, resorting to his inveterate practice when confronted with a question, consulted his watch. 'I came in for Mr Vidal, but I shall be glad of a word with you after I've seen him. I must ask you, therefore' – and he nodded at the third door of the room – 'kindly to pass into the library.'

Rose, without haste or delay, reached the point he indicated. 'You wish me to wait there?'

'If you'll be so good.'

'While you talk with *him*?'

'While I talk with "him".'

Her eyes held Vidal's a minute. 'I'll wait.' And she passed out.

The Doctor immediately attacked him. 'I must appeal to you for a fraction of your time. I've seen Mrs. Beever.'

Dennis hesitated. 'I've done the same.'

'It's because she has told me of your talk that I mention it. She sends you a message.'

'A message?' Dennis looked as if it were open to him to question indirectness. 'Where then is she?'

'With that distracted girl.'

'Miss Martle?' Dennis hesitated. 'Miss Martle so greatly feels the shock?'

'"Feels" it, my dear sir?' the Doctor cried. 'She has been made so pitifully ill by it that there's no saying just what turn her condition may take, and she now calls for so much of my attention as to force me to plead, with you, that excuse for my brevity. Mrs Beever,' he rapidly pursued, 'requests you to regard this hurried inquiry as the sequel to what you were so good as to say to her.'

Dennis thought a moment; his face had changed as if by the action of Rose's disappearance and the instinctive revival, in a different relation, of the long, stiff habit of business, the art of treating affairs and meeting men. This was the art of not being surprised, and, with his emotion now controlled, he was discernibly on his guard. 'I'm afraid,' he replied, 'that what I said to Mrs Beever was a very small matter.'

'She doesn't think it at all a small matter to have said you'd help her. You can do so – in the cruel demands our catastrophe makes of her – by considering that I represent her. It's in her name, therefore, that I ask you if you're engaged to be married to Miss Armiger.'

Dennis had an irrepressible start; but it might have been quite as much at the freedom of the question as at the difficulty of the answer. 'Please say to her that – I *am*.' He spoke with a clearness that proved the steel surface he had in a few minutes forged for his despair.

The Doctor took the thing as he gave it, only drawing from his pocket a key, which he held straight up. 'Then I feel it to be only right to say to you that this locks' – and he indicated the quarter to which Rose had retired – 'the other door.'

Dennis, with a diffident hand out, looked at him hard; but the good man showed with effect that he was professionally used to that. 'You mean she's a prisoner?'

'On Mr Vidal's honour.'

'But whose prisoner?'

'Mrs Beever's.'

Dennis took the key, which passed into his pocket. 'Don't you forget,' he then asked with inscrutable gravity, 'that we're here, all round, on a level—'

'With the garden?' the Doctor broke in. 'I forget nothing. We've a friend on the terrace.'

'A friend?'

'Mr Beever. A friend of Miss Armiger's,' he promptly added.

Still showing nothing in his face, Dennis perhaps showed something in the way that, with his eyes bent on the carpet and his hands interclenched behind him, he slowly walked across the room. At the end of it he turned round. 'If I have this key, who has the other?'

'The other?'

'The key that confines Mr Bream.'

The Doctor winced, but he stood his ground. 'I have it.' Then he said as if with a due recognition of the weight of the circumstance: 'She has told you?'

Dennis turned it over. 'Mrs Beever?'

'Miss Armiger.' There was a faint sharpness in the Doctor's tone.

It had something evidently to do with the tone in which Dennis replied. 'She has told me. But if you've left him—'

'I've not left him. I've brought him over.'

Dennis showed himself at a loss. 'To see *me*?'

The Doctor raised a solemn, reassuring hand; then, after an instant, 'To see his child,' he colourlessly said.

'He desires that?' Dennis asked with an accent that emulated this detachment.

'He desires that.' Dennis turned away, and in the pause that followed the air seemed charged with a consciousness of all that between them was represented by the unspoken. It lasted indeed long enough to give to an auditor, had there been one, a sense of the dominant unspeakable. It was as if each were waiting to have something from the other first, and it was eventually clear that Dennis, who had not looked at his watch, was prepared to wait longest. The Doctor had moreover to recognise that he himself had sought the interview. He impatiently summed up his sense of their common attitude. 'I do full justice to the difficulty created for you by your engagement. That's why it was important to have it from your own lips.' His companion said nothing, and he went on: 'Mrs Beever, all the same, feels that it mustn't prevent us from putting you another question, or rather from reminding you that there's one that you led her just now to expect that you'll answer.' The Doctor paused again, but he perceived he must go all the way. 'From the bank of the river you saw something that bears upon this' – he hesitated; then daintily selected his words – 'remarkable performance. We appeal to your sense of propriety to tell us what you saw.'

Dennis considered. 'My sense of propriety is strong; but so – just now – is my sense of some other things. My word to Mrs Beever was contingent. There are points *I* want made clear.'

'I'm here,' said the Doctor, 'to do what I can to satisfy you. Only be so good as to remember that time is everything.' He added, to drive this home, in his neat, brisk way: 'Some action has to be taken.'

'You mean a declaration made?'

'Under penalty,' the Doctor assented, 'of consequences sufficiently tremendous. There has been an accident of a gravity—'

Dennis, with averted eyes, took him up. 'That can't be explained away?'

The Doctor looked at his watch; then, still holding it, he quickly looked up at Dennis. 'You wish her presented as dying of a natural cause?'

Vidal's haggard face turned red, but he instantly recovered himself. 'Why do you ask, if you've a supreme duty?'

'I haven't *one* – worse luck. I've fifty.'

Dennis fixed his eyes on the watch. 'Does that mean you can keep the thing quiet?'

The Doctor put his talisman away. 'Before I say I must know what you'll do for me.'

Dennis stared at the lamp. 'Hasn't it gone too far?'

'I know *how* far: not so far, by a peculiar mercy, as it might have gone. There has been an extraordinary coincidence of chances – a miracle of conditions. Everything appears to serve.' He hesitated; then with great gravity: 'We'll call it a providence and have done with it.'

Dennis turned this over. 'Do you allude to the absence of witnesses—?'

'At the moment the child was found. Only the blessed three of us. And she had been there—' Stupefaction left him counting.

Dennis jerked out a sick protest. 'Don't tell me how long! What do *I* want—?' What he wanted proved, the next moment, to be more knowledge. 'How do you meet the servants?'

'Here? By giving a big name to her complaint. None of them have seen her. She was carried in with a success—!' The Doctor threw up triumphant little hands.

'But the people at the other house?'

'They know nothing but that over here she has had an attack which it will be one of the fifty duties of mine I mentioned to you to make sufficiently remarkable. She was out of sorts this morning – this afternoon I was summoned. That call of Tony's at my house is the providence!'

But still Dennis questioned. 'Hadn't she some fond nurse – some devoted dragon?'

'The great Gorham? Yes: she didn't want her to come; she was cruelly overborne. Well,' the Doctor lucidly pursued, 'I must face the great Gorham. I'm already keeping her at bay – doctors, you see, are so luckily despots! They're blessedly bullies. She'll be tough – but it's all tough!'

Dennis, pressing his hand to his head, began wearily to pace again: it was far too tough for *him*. But he suddenly dropped upon the sofa, all but audibly moaning, falling back in the despair that broke through his false pluck. His interlocutor watched his pain as if he had something to hope from it; then abruptly the young man began: 'I don't in the least conceive how—' He stopped short: even this he couldn't bring out.

'How was it done? Small blame to you! It was done in one minute – with the aid of a boat and the temptation (we'll call it!) of solitude. The boat's an old one of Tony's own – pad-locked, but with a long chain. To see the place,' said the Doctor after an instant, 'is to see the deed.'

Dennis threw back his head; he covered his distorted face with his two hands. 'Why in thunder should I see it?'

The Doctor had moved towards him; at this he seated himself beside him and, going on with quiet clearness, applied a controlling, soothing grasp to his knee. 'The child was taken into the boat and it was tilted: that was enough – the trick was played.' Dennis remained motionless and dumb, and his companion completed the picture. 'She was immersed – she was held under water – she was made sure of. Oh, I grant you it took a hand – and it took a spirit! But they were there. Then she was left. A pull of the chain brought back the boat; and the author of the crime walked away.'

Dennis slowly shifted his position, dropped his head, dropped his hands, sat staring lividly at the floor. 'But how could she be *caught*?'

The Doctor hesitated, as if in the presence of an ambiguity. 'The poor little girl? You'd see if you saw the place.'

'I passed it to come back here,' Dennis said. 'But I didn't look, for I didn't know.'

The Doctor patted his knee. 'If you had known you would have looked still less. She rose; she drifted some yards; then she was washed against the base of the bridge, and one of the openings of her little dress hooked itself to an old loose clamp. There she was kept.'

'And no one came by?'

'No one came till, by the mercy of God, *I* came!'

Dennis took it in as if with a long, dry gulp, and the two men sat for a minute looking at each other. At last the younger one got up. 'And yet the risk of anything but a straight course is hideous.'

The Doctor kept his place. 'Everything's hideous. I appreciate greatly,' he added, 'the gallantry of your reminding me of my danger. Don't think I don't know exactly what it is. But I have to think of the danger of others. I can measure mine; I can't measure theirs.'

'I can return your compliment,' Dennis replied. ' "Theirs", as you call it, seems to me such a fine thing for you to care for.'

The Doctor, with his plump hands folded on his stomach, gave a small stony smile. 'My dear man, I care for my friends!'

Dennis stood before him; he was visibly mystified. 'There's a person whom it's very good of you to take this occasion of calling by that name!'

Doctor Ramage stared; with his vision of his interlocutor's mistake all his tight curves grew tense. Then, as he sprang to his feet, he seemed to crack in a grim little laugh. 'The person you allude to is, I confess, not, my dear sir—'

'One of the persons,' said Dennis, 'whom you wish to protect? It certainly would have surprised me to hear it! But you spoke of your "friends". Who then is your second one?'

The Doctor looked astonished at the question. 'Why, sweet Jean Martle.'

Dennis equally wondered. 'I should have supposed her the first! Who then is the other?'

The Doctor lifted his shoulders. 'Who but poor Tony Bream?'

Dennis thought a moment. 'What's *his* danger?'

The Doctor grew more amazed. 'The danger we've been talking of!'

'Have we been talking of *that*?'

'You ask me, when you told me you knew—?'

Dennis, hesitating, recalled. 'Knew that he's accused—?'

His companion fairly sprang at him. 'Accused by *her* too?'

Dennis fell back at his onset. 'Is he by anybody else?'

The Doctor, turning crimson, had grabbed his arm; he blazed up at him. 'You don't know it all?'

Dennis faltered. 'Is there any more?'

'Tony cries on the housetops that *he* did it!'

Dennis, blank and bewildered, sank once more on his sofa. '*He* cries—?'

'To cover Jean.'

Dennis took it in. 'But if she *is* covered?'

'Then to shield Miss Armiger.'

Poor Dennis gazed aghast. 'Who meanwhile denounces him?' He was on his feet again; again he moved to the open window and stood there while the Doctor in silence waited. Presently he turned round. 'May I see him?'

The Doctor, as if he had expected this, was already at the door. 'God bless you!' And he flashed out.

Dennis, left alone, remained rigid in the middle of the room, immersed apparently in a stupor of emotion; then, as if shaken out of it by a return of conscious suffering, he passed in a couple of strides to the door of the library. Here, however, with his hand on the knob, he yielded to another impulse, which kept him irresolute, listening, drawing his breath in pain. Suddenly he turned away – Tony Bream had come in.

CHAPTER 31

'If in this miserable hour I've asked you for a moment of your time,' Dennis immediately said, 'I beg you to believe it's only to let you know that anything in this world I can do for you—' Tony raised a hand that mutely discouraged as well as thanked him, but he completely delivered himself: 'I'm ready, whatever it is, to do on the spot.'

With his handsome face smitten, his red eyes contracted, his thick hair disordered and his black garments awry, Tony had the handled, hustled look of a man just dragged through some riot or some rescue and only released to take breath. Like Rose, for Dennis, he was deeply disfigured, but with a change more passive and tragic. His bloodshot eyes fixed his interlocutor's. 'I'm afraid there's nothing any one can do for me. My disaster's overwhelming; but I must meet it myself.'

There was courtesy in his voice; but there was something hard and dry in the way he stood there, something so opposed to his usual fine overflow that for a minute Dennis could only show by pitying silence the full sense of his wretchedness. He was in the presence of a passionate perversity – an attitude in which the whole man had already petrified. 'Will it perhaps help you to think of something,' he presently said, 'if I tell you that your disaster is almost as much mine as yours, and that what's of aid to one of us may perhaps therefore be of aid to the other?'

'It's very good of you,' Tony replied, 'to be willing to take upon you the smallest corner of so big a burden. Don't do that – don't do that, Mr Vidal,' he repeated, with a heavy head-shake. 'Don't come near such a thing; don't touch it; don't know it!' He straightened himself as if with a long, suppressed shudder; and then with a sharper and more sombre vehemence, 'Stand from under it!' he exclaimed. Dennis, in deeper compassion, looked at him with an intensity that might have suggested submission, and Tony followed up what he apparently took for an advantage. 'You came here for an hour, for your own reasons, for your relief: you came in all kindness and trust. You've encountered an unutterable horror, and you've only one thing to do.'

'Be so good as to name it,' said Dennis.

'Turn your back on it for ever – go your way this minute. I've come to you simply to say that.'

'Leave you, in other words—?'

'By the very first train that will take you.'

Dennis appeared to turn this over; then he spoke with a face that showed what he thought of it. 'It has been my unfortunate fate in coming to this place – so wrapped, as one might suppose, in comfort and peace – to intrude a second time on obscure, unhappy things, on suffering and danger and death. I should have been glad, God knows, not to renew the adventure, but one's destiny kicks one before it, and I seem myself not the least part of the misery I speak of. You must accept that as my excuse for not taking your advice. I must stay at least till you understand me.' On this he waited a moment; after which, abruptly, impatiently, 'For God's sake, Mr Bream, believe in me and meet me!' he broke out.

'Meet you?'

'Make use of the hand I hold out to you!'

Tony had remained just within the closed door, as if to guard against its moving from the other side. At this, with a faint flush in his dead vacancy, he came a few steps further. But there was something still locked in his conscious, altered eyes, and coldly absent from the tone in which he said: 'You've come, I think, from China?'

'I've come, Mr Bream, from China.'

'And it's open to you to go back?'

Dennis frowned. 'I can do as I wish.'

'And yet you're not off like a shot?'

'My movements and my inclinations are my own affair. You won't accept my aid?'

Tony gave his sombre stare. 'You ask me, as you call it, to meet you. I beg you to excuse me if on my side I first inquire on what definite ground—?'

Dennis took him straight up. 'On the definite ground on

which Doctor Ramage is good enough to do so. I'm afraid there's no better ground than my honour.'

Tony's stare was long and deep; then he put out his hand, and while Dennis held it, 'I understand you,' he said. 'Goodbye.'

Dennis kept hold of him. 'Goodbye?'

Tony had a supreme hesitation. 'She's safe.'

Dennis had a shorter one. 'Do you speak of Miss Martle?'

'Not of Miss Martle.'

'Then I can. *She's* safe.'

'Thank you,' said Tony. He drew away his hand.

'As for the person you do speak of, if *you* say it—' and Dennis paused.

'She's safe,' Tony repeated.

'That's all I ask of you. The Doctor will do the rest.'

'I know what the Doctor will do.' Tony was silent a moment. 'What will you do?'

Dennis waited, but at last he spoke. 'Everything but marry her.'

A flare of admiration rose and fell in Tony's eyes. 'You're beyond me!'

'I don't in the least know where I am, save that I'm in a black, bloody nightmare and that it's not I, it's not she, it's not you, it's not any one. I shall wake up at last, I suppose, but meanwhile—'

'There's plenty more to come? Oh, as much as you like!' Tony excitedly declared.

'For me, but not for you. For you the worst's over,' his companion boldly observed.

'Over? with all my life made hideous?'

There was a certain sturdiness in Vidal's momentary silence. 'You think so now—!' Then he added more gently: 'I grant you it's hideous enough.'

Tony stood there in the agony of the actual; the tears welled into his hot eyes. 'She murdered – she tortured my child. And she did it to incriminate Jean.'

He brought it all back to Dennis, who exclaimed with simple solemnity: 'The dear little girl – the sweet, kind little girl!' With a sudden impulse that, in the midst of this tenderness, seemed almost savage, he laid on Tony's shoulder a hard, conscientious hand. 'She forced her in. She held her down. She left her.'

The men turned paler as they looked at each other. 'I'm infamous – I'm infamous,' said Tony.

There was a long pause that was like a strange assent from Dennis, who at last, however, brought out in a different tone: 'It was her passion.'

'It was her passion.'

'She loves you—!' Dennis went on with a drop, before the red real, of all vain terms.

'She loves me!' – Tony's face reflected the mere monstrous fact. 'It has made what it has made – her awful act and my silence. My silence is a part of the crime and the cruelty – I shall live to be a horror to myself. But I see it, none the less, as I see it, and I shall keep the word I gave her in the first madness of my fear. It came to me – there it is.'

'I know what came to you,' Dennis said.

Tony wondered. 'Then you've seen her?'

Dennis hesitated. 'I know it from the Doctor.'

'I see—' Tony thought a moment. 'She, I imagine—'

'Will keep it to herself? Leave that to me!' Dennis put out his hand again. 'Goodbye.'

'You take her away?'

'Tonight.'

Tony kept his hand. 'Will her flight help Ramage?'

'Everything falls in. Three hours ago I came for her.'

'So it will seem pre-arranged?'

'For the event she announced to you. Our happy union!' said Dennis Vidal.

He reached the door to the hall, where Tony checked him. 'There's nothing, then, I shall do for *you*?'

'It's done. We've helped each other.'

What was deepest in Tony stirred again. 'I mean when your trouble has passed.'

'It will never pass. Think of that when you're happy yourself.'

Tony's grey face stared. 'How shall I ever be—?'

The door, as he spoke, opened from the room to which Mrs Beever had returned, and Jean Martle appeared to them. Dennis retreated. '*Ask her*!' he said from the threshold.

CHAPTER 32

Rushing to Tony, she wailed under her breath: 'I must speak to you – I must speak to you! But how can you ever look at me? – how can you ever forgive me?' In an instant he had met her; in a flash the gulf was bridged: his arms had opened wide to her and she had thrown herself into them. They had only to be face to face to let themselves go; he making no answer but to press her close against him, she pouring out her tears upon him as if the contact quickened the source. He held her and she yielded with a passion no bliss could have given; they stood locked together in their misery with no sound and no motion but her sobs. Breast to breast and cheek to cheek, they felt simply that they had ceased to be apart. This long embrace was the extinction of all limits and questions – swept away in a flood which tossed them over the years and in which nothing remained erect but the sense and the need of each other. These things had now the beauty of all the tenderness that they had never spoken and that, for some time, even as they clung there, was too strange and too deep for speech. But what was extraordinary was that as Jean disengaged herself there was neither wonder nor fear between them; nothing but a recognition in which everything swam and, on the girl's part, the still higher tide of the remorse that harried her and that, to see him, had made her break away from the others. 'They tell me I'm ill, I'm insane,' she went on – 'they want to shut me up, to give me things – they tell me to lie down, to try to sleep. But it's all to me, so dreadfully, as if it were *I* who had done it, that when they admitted to me that you were here I felt that if I didn't see you it would make me as crazy as they say. It's to have seen her go – to have seen her go: that's what I can't bear – it's too horrible!' She continued to sob; she stood there before him swayed to and fro in her grief. She stirred up his own, and that added to her pain; for a minute, in their separate sorrow, they moved asunder like creatures too stricken to communicate. But they were quickly face to face again, more intimate, with more understood, though with the air, on either side and in the very freedom of their action, of a clear vision of the effect of their precipitated union – the instinct of not again touching it with unconsecrated hands. Tony had no idle words, no easy consolation; she only made him see more vividly what had happened, and they hung over it together while she accused and reviled herself. 'I let her go – I let her go; that's what's so terrible, so hideous. I might have got her – have kept her; I might have screamed, I might have rushed for help. But how could I know or dream? How could the worst of my fears—?' She broke off, she shuddered and dropped; she sat and sobbed while he came and went. 'I see her little face as she left me – she looked at me as if she knew. She wondered and dreaded: she knew – she knew! It was the last little look I was to have from her, and I didn't even answer it with a kiss. She sat there where I could seize her, but I never raised a hand. I was close, I was *there* – she must have called for me in her terror! I didn't listen – I didn't come – I only gave her up to be murdered! And now I shall be punished for ever: I shall see her in those arms – in those arms!' Jean flung herself down and hid her face; her smothered wild lament filled the room.

Tony stopped before her, seeing everything she brought up, but only the more helpless in his pity. 'It was the only little minute in all the years that you had been forced to fail her. She was always more yours than mine.'

Jean could only look out through her storm-beaten window. 'It was just because she was yours that she was mine. It was because she was yours from the first hour that I—!' She broke down again; she tried to hold herself; she got up. 'What could I do, you see? To you I couldn't be kind.' She was as exposed in her young, pure woe as a bride might have been in her joy.

Tony looked as if he were retracing the saddest story on earth. 'I don't see how you could have been kinder.'

She wondered with her blinded eyes. 'That wasn't what thought I was – it *couldn't* be, ever, ever. Didn't I try not to think of you? But the child was a beautiful part of you – the child I could take and keep. I could take her altogether, without thinking or remembering. It was the only thing I could do for you, and you let me, always, and *she* did. So I thought it would go on, for wasn't it happiness enough? But all the horrible things – I didn't know them till today! There they were – so near to us; and there they closed over her, and – oh!' She turned away in a fresh wild spasm, inarticulate and distracted.

They wandered in silence, as if it made them more companions; but at last Tony said: 'She was a little radiant, perfect thing. Even if she had not been mine you would have loved her.' Then he went on, as if feeling his way through his thickest darkness: 'If she had not been mine she wouldn't be lying there as I've seen her. Yet I'm glad she was mine!' he said.

'She lies there because I loved her and because I so insanely showed it. That's why it's I who killed her!' broke passionately from Jean.

He answered nothing till he quietly and gently answered: 'It was *I* who killed her.'

She roamed to and fro, slowly controlling herself, taking this at first as a mere torment like her own. 'We seem beautifully eager for the guilt!'

'It doesn't matter what any one else seems. I must tell you all – now. I've taken the act on myself.'

She had stopped short, bewildered. 'How have you taken it—?'

'To meet whatever may come.'

She turned as white as ashes. 'You mean you've accused yourself?'

'Any one may accuse me. Whom is it more natural to accuse? What had she to gain? My own motive is flagrant. There it is,' said Tony.

Jean withered beneath this new stroke. 'You'll say you did it?'

'I'll say I did it.'

Her face grew old with terror. 'You'll lie? You'll perjure yourself?'

'I'll say I did it for you.'

She suddenly turned crimson. 'Then what do you think *I'll* say?'

Tony coldly considered. 'Whatever you say will tell against me.'

'Against you?'

'If the crime was committed for you.'

'"For" me?' she echoed again.

'To enable us to marry.'

'Marry? – *we*?' Jean looked at it in blighted horror.

'It won't be of any consequence that we shan't, that we can't: it will only stand out clear that we *can*.' His sombre ingenuity halted, but he achieved his demonstration. 'So I shall save – whom I wish to save.'

Jean gave a fiercer wail. 'You wish to save *her*?'

'I don't wish to hand her over. You can't conceive it?'

'I?' The girl looked about her for a negation not too vile. 'I wish to hunt her to death! I wish to burn her alive!' All her emotion had changed to stupefaction; the flame in her eyes had dried them. 'You mean she's not to suffer?'

'You want her to suffer – all?'

She was ablaze with the light of justice. 'How can anything be enough? I could tear her limb from limb. That's what she tried to do to me!'

Tony lucidly concurred. 'Yes – what she tried to do to you.'

But she had already flashed round. 'And yet you condone the atrocity—?'

Tony thought a moment. 'Her doom will be to live.'

'But how will such a fiend be suffered to live – when she went to it before my eyes?' Jean stared at the mountain of evidence; then eagerly: 'And Mr Vidal – her very lover, who'll swear what he knows – what he saw!'

Tony stubbornly shook his head. 'Oh, Mr Vidal!'

'To make me,' Jean cried, 'seem the monster—!'

Tony looked at her so strangely that she stopped. 'She made it for the moment possible—'

She caught him up. 'To suspect me—?'

'I was mad – and you're weren't there.' With a muffled moan she sank down again; she covered her face with her hands. 'I must tell you all – I must tell you all,' he said. 'He knows nothing – he saw nothing – he'll swear nothing. He's taking her away.'

Jean started as if he had struck her. 'She's here?'

Tony wondered. 'You didn't know it?'

'She came back?' the girl panted.

'You thought she had fled?'

Jean hung there like a poised hawk. 'Where *is* she?'

Tony gave her, with a grave gesture, a long, absolute look before which, gradually, her passion fell. 'She has gone. Let her go.'

She was silent a little. 'But others: how will they—?'

'There are no others.' After a moment he added: 'She would have died for me.'

The girl's pale wrath gave a flare. 'So you want to die for *her*?'

'I shan't die. But I shall remember.' Then, as she watched him, 'I must tell you all,' he said once more. 'I knew it – I always knew it. And I made her come.'

'You were kind to her – as you're always kind.'

'No; I was more than that. And I should have been less.' His face showed a rift in the blackness. 'I remember.'

She followed him in pain and at a distance. 'You mean you liked it?'

'I liked it – while I was safe. Then I grew afraid.'

'Afraid of what?'

'Afraid of everything. You don't know – but we're abysses. At least *I'm* one!' he groaned. He seemed to sound this depth. 'There are other things. They go back far.'

'Don't tell me all,' said Jean. She had evidently enough to turn over. 'What will become of her?' she asked.

'God knows. She goes forth.'

'And Mr Vidal with her?'

'Mr Vidal with her.'

Jean gazed at the tragic picture. 'Because he still loves her?'

'Yes,' said Tony Bream.

'Then what will he do?'

'Put the globe between them. Think of her torture,' Tony added.

Jean looked as if she tried. 'Do you mean *that*?'

He meant another matter. 'To have only made us free.'

Jean protested with all her woe. 'It's her triumph – that our freedom is horrible!'

Tony hesitated; then his eyes distinguished in the outer dusk Paul Beever, who had appeared at the long window which in the mild air stood open to the terrace. 'It's horrible,' he gravely replied.

Jean had not seen Paul; she only heard Tony's answer. It touched again the source of tears; she broke again into stifled sobs. So, blindly, slowly, while the two men watched her, she passed from the room by the door at which she had entered.

CHAPTER 33

'You're looking for me?' Tony quickly asked.

Paul, blinking in the lamplight, showed the dismal desert of his face. 'I saw you through the open window, and I thought I would let you know—'

'That someone wants me?' Tony was all ready.

'She hasn't asked for you; but I think that if you could do it—'

'I can do anything,' said Tony. 'But of whom do you speak?'

'Of one of your servants – poor Mrs Gorham.'

'Effie's nurse? – she has come over?'

'She's in the garden,' Paul explained. 'I've been floundering about – I came upon her.'

Tony wondered. 'But what's she doing?'

'Crying very hard – without a sound.'

'And without coming in?'

'Out of discretion.'

Tony thought a moment. 'You mean because Jean and the Doctor—?'

'Have taken complete charge. She bows to that, but she sits there on a bench—'

'Weeping and wailing?' Tony asked. 'Dear thing, I'll speak to her.'

He was about to leave the room in the summary manner permitted by the long window when Paul checked him with a quiet reminder. 'Hadn't you better have your hat?'

Tony looked about him – he had not brought it in. 'Why? – if it's a warm night?'

Paul approached him, laying on him as if to stay him a heavy but friendly hand. 'You never go out without it – don't be too unusual.'

'I see what you mean – I'll get it.' And he made for the door to the hall.

But Paul had not done with him. 'It's much better you should see her – it's unnatural you shouldn't. But do you mind my just thinking for you the least bit – asking you for instance what it's your idea to say to her?'

Tony had the air of accepting this solicitude; but he met the inquiry with characteristic candour. 'I think I've no idea but to talk with her of Effie.'

Paul visibly wondered. 'As dangerously ill? That's all she knows.'

Tony considered an instant. 'Yes, then – as dangerously ill. Whatever she's prepared for.'

'But what are *you* prepared for? You're not afraid—?' Paul hesitated.

'Afraid of what?'

'Of suspicions – importunities; her making some noise.'

Tony slowly shook his head. 'I don't think,' he said very gravely, 'that I'm afraid of poor Gorham.'

Paul looked as if he felt that his warning half failed. 'Every one else is. She's tremendously devoted.'

'Yes – that's what I mean.'

Paul sounded him a moment. 'You mean to *you*?'

The irony was so indulgent – and all irony on this young man's part was so rare – that Tony was to be excused for not perceiving it. 'She'll do anything. We're the best of friends.'

'Then get your hat,' said Paul.

'It's much the best thing. Thank you for telling me.' Even in a tragic hour there was so much in Tony of the ingenuous that, with his habit of good-nature and his hand on the door, he lingered for the comfort of his friend. 'She'll be a resource – a fund of memory. She'll know what I mean – I shall want some one. So we can always talk.'

'Oh, *you're* safe!' Paul went on.

It had now all come to Tony. 'I see my way with her.'

'So do I!' said Paul.

Tony fairly brightened through his gloom. 'I'll keep her on!' And he took his course by the front.

Left alone Paul closed the door on him, holding it a minute and lost evidently in reflections of which he was the subject. He exhaled a long sigh that was burdened with many things; then as he moved away his eyes attached themselves as if in sympathy with a vague impulse to the door of the library. He stood a moment irresolute; after which, deeply restless, he went to take up the hat that, on coming in, he had laid on one of the tables. He was in the act of doing this when the door of the library opened and Rose Armiger stood before him. She had since their last meeting changed her dress and, arrayed for a journey, wore a bonnet and a long, dark mantle. For some time after she appeared no word came from either; but at last she said: 'Can you endure for a minute the sight of me?'

'I was hesitating – I thought of going to you,' Paul replied. 'I knew you were there.'

At this she came into the room. 'I knew you were here. You passed the window.'

'I've passed and repassed – this hour.'

'I've known that too, but this time I heard you stop. I've no light there,' she went on, 'but the window, on this side, is open. I could tell that you had come in.'

Paul hesitated. 'You ran a danger of not finding me alone.'

'I took my chance – of course I knew. I've been in dread, but in spite of it I've seen nobody. I've been up to my room and come down. The coast was clear.'

'You've not then seen Mr Vidal?'

'Oh yes – *him*. But he's nobody.' Then as if conscious of the strange sound of this: 'Nobody, I mean, to fear.'

Paul was silent a moment. 'What in the world is it *you* fear?'

'In the sense of the awful things – you know? Here on the spot nothing. About those things I'm quite quiet. There may be plenty to come; but what I'm afraid of now is my safety. There's something in that—!' She broke down; there was more in it than she could say.

'Are you so sure of your safety?'

'You see how sure. It's in your face,' said Rose. 'And your face – for what it says – is terrible.'

Whatever it said remained there as Paul looked at her. 'Is it as terrible as yours?' he asked.

'Oh, mine – mine must be hideous; unutterably hideous for-ever! Yours is beautiful. Everything, every one here is beautiful.'

'I don't understand you,' said Paul.

'How should you? It isn't to ask you to do that that I've come to you.'

He waited in his woeful wonder. 'For what have you come?'

'You *can* endure it, then, the sight of me?'

'Haven't I told you that I thought of going to you?'

'Yes – but you didn't go,' said Rose. 'You came and went like a sentinel, and if it was to watch me—'

Paul interrupted her. 'It wasn't to watch you.'

'Then what was it for?'

'It was to keep myself quiet,' said Paul.

'But you're anything but quiet.'

'Yes!' he dismally allowed; 'I'm anything but quiet.'

'There's something then that may help you: it's one of two things for which I've come to you. And there's no one but you to care. You may care a very little; it may give you a grain of comfort. Let your comfort be that I've failed.'

Paul, after a long look at her, turned away with a vague, dumb gesture, and it was a part of his sore trouble that, in his wasted strength, he had no outlet for emotion, no channel even for pain. She took in for a moment his clumsy, massive misery. 'No – you loathe my presence,' she said.

He stood awhile in silence with his back to her, as if within him some violence were struggling up; then with an effort, almost with a gasp, he turned round, his open watch in his hand. 'I saw Mr Vidal,' was all he produced.

'And he told you too he would come back for me?'

'He said there was something he had to do, but that he would meanwhile get ready. He would return immediately with a carriage.'

'That's why I've waited,' Rose replied. 'I'm ready enough. But he won't come.'

'He'll come,' said Paul. 'But it's more than time.'

She drearily shook her head. 'Not after getting off – not back to the horror and the shame. He thought so; no doubt he has tried. But it's beyond him.'

'Then what are you waiting for?'

She hesitated. 'Nothing – now. Thank you.'

She looked about her. 'How shall I go?'

Paul went to the window; for a moment he listened. 'I thought I heard wheels.'

She gave ear; but once more she shook her head. 'There are no wheels, but I can go that way.'

He turned back again, heavy and uncertain; he stood wavering and wondering in her path. 'What will become of you?' he asked.

'How do I know and what do I care?'

'What will become of you? what will become of you?' he went on as if he had not heard her.

'You pity me too much,' she answered after an instant. 'I've failed, but I did what I could. It was all that I saw – it was all that was left me. It took hold of me, it possessed me: it was the last gleam of a chance.'

Paul flushed like a sick man under a new wave of weakness. 'Of a chance for what?'

'To make him take her. You'll say my calculation was grotesque – my stupidity as ignoble as my crime. All I can answer is that I might none the less have succeeded. People *have* – in worse conditions. But I don't defend myself – I'm face to face with my mistake. I'm face to face with it forever – and that's how I wish you to see me. Look at me well!'

'I would have done anything for you!' Paul as if all talk with her were vain, wailed under his breath.

She considered this; her dreadful face was lighted by the response it kindled. 'Would you do anything now?' He answered nothing; he seemed lost in the vision of what was carrying her through. 'I saw it as I saw it,' she continued: 'there it was and there it is. There it is – there it is,' she repeated in a tone sharp, for a flash, with all the excitement she contrived to keep under. 'It has nothing to do now with any part or any other possibility even of what may be worst in me. It's a storm that's past, it's a debt that's paid. I may literally be better.' At the expression this brought out in him she interrupted herself. 'You don't understand a word I utter!'

He was following her – as she showed she could see – only in the light of his own emotion; not in that of any feeling that she herself could present. 'Why didn't you speak to me – why didn't you tell me what you were thinking? There was nothing you couldn't have told me, nothing that wouldn't have brought me nearer. If I had known your abasement—'

'What would you have done?' Rose demanded.

'I would have saved you.'

'What would you have done?' she pressed.

'Everything.'

She was silent while he went to the window. 'Yes, I've lost you – I've lost you,' she said at last. 'And you were the thing I might have had. *He* told me that, and I knew it.'

'"He" told you?' Paul had faced round.

'He tried to put me off on you. That was what finished me. Of course they'll marry,' she abruptly continued.

'Oh yes, they'll marry.'

'But not soon, do you suppose?'

'Not soon. But sooner than they think.'

Rose looked surprised. 'Do you already know what they think?'

'Yes – that it will never be.'

'Never?'

'Coming about so horribly. But some day – it will be.'

'It will be,' said Rose. 'And I shall have done it for him. That's more,' she said, 'than even you would have done for *me*.'

Strange tears had found their way between Paul's closed lids. 'You're too horrible,' he breathed; 'you're too horrible.'

'Oh, I talk only to you: it's *all* for you. Remember, please, that I shall never speak again. You see,' she went on, 'that he daren't come.'

Paul looked afresh at his watch. 'I'll go with you.'

Rose hesitated. 'How far?'

'I'll go with you,' he simply repeated.

She looked at him hard; in her eyes too there were tears. 'My safety – my safety!' she murmured as if awestruck.

Paul went round for his hat, which on his entrance he had put down. 'I'll go with you,' he said once more.

Still, however, she hesitated. 'Won't *he* need you?'

'Tony? – for what?'

'For help.'

It took Paul a moment to understand. 'He wants none.'

'You mean he has nothing to fear?'

'From any suspicion? Nothing.'

'That's his advantage,' said Rose. 'People like him too much.'

'People like him too much,' Paul replied. Then he exclaimed: 'Mr Vidal!' – to which, as she looked, Rose responded with a low, deep moan.

Dennis had appeared at the window; he gave signal in a short, sharp gesture and remained standing in the dusk of the terrace. Paul put down his hat; he turned away to leave his companion free. She approached him while Dennis waited; she lingered desperately, she wavered, as if with a last word to speak. As he only stood rigid, however, she faltered, choking her impulse and giving her word the form of a look. The look held her a moment, held her so long that Dennis spoke sternly from the darkness: 'Come!' At this, for a space as great, she fixed her eyes on him; then while the two men stood motionless she decided and reached the window. He put out a hand and seized her, and they passed quickly into the night. Paul, left alone, again sounded a long sigh; this time it was the deep breath of a man who has seen a great danger averted. It had scarcely died away before Tony Bream returned. He came in from the hall as eagerly as he had gone out, and, finding Paul, gave him his news: 'Well – I took her home.'

Paul required a minute to carry his thoughts back to Gorham. 'Oh, she went quietly?'

'Like a bleating lamb. She's too glad to stay on.'

Paul turned this over; but as if his confidence now had solid ground he asked no question. 'Ah, you're all right!' he simply said.

Tony reached the door through which Jean had left the room; he paused there in surprise at this incongruous expression. Yet there was something absent in the way he echoed 'All right?'

'I mean you have such a pull. You'll meet nothing but sympathy.'

Tony looked indifferent and uncertain; but his optimism finally assented. 'I daresay I shall get on. People perhaps won't challenge me.'

'They like you too much.'

Tony, with his hand on the door, appeared struck with this; but it embittered again the taste of his tragedy. He remembered with all his vividness to what tune he had been 'liked', and he wearily bowed his head. 'Oh, too much, Paul!' he sighed as he went out.

SUGGESTIONS FOR FURTHER READING

———

Edel, Leon, *The Middle Years: 1890–95* (Rupert Hart-Davis, 1962).
——, *The Treacherous Years: 1895–1900* (Rupert Hart-Davis, 1969).
Egan, Michael, *Henry James: The Ibsen Years* (Vision Press, 1972).
Poole, Adrian, *Henry James* (Harvester New Readings, 1991).

TEXT SUMMARY

Book One

Chapter 1

Introduction to Mrs Beever, lady of Eastmead, and to her concerns: her business and neighbourly association with the Breams; her son Paul and her plans for his life, including marriage to Jean Martle. Tony Bream is her business partner. Married with a young wife and baby he is an attractive man. Rose Armiger is his wife Julia's best friend, in attendance at Eastmead for the birth of Julia's child and recuperation of the mother. She is expecting her lover to return from China.

Chapter 2

Jean Martle and Rose Armiger meet at Bounds. Though Julia Bream is ill it is thought not be serious. Doctor Ramage attends to her.

Chapter 3

Relations between Rose and Mrs Beever are prickly. Mrs Beever is sensitive of Rose's intimacy with Tony Bream.

Chapter 4

Julia prepares for death and settles her personal affairs.

Chapter 5

The arrival of Dennis Vidal, Rose's lover.

Chapter 6

Dennis and Rose have not seen each other for a long time and their relations are strained. He is keen to marry her as soon as possible. Tony announces that Julia has asked him not to remarry after her death, in the lifetime of their child.

Chapter 7

Julia wishes happiness on Dennis and Rose, but no one is convinced that she is about to die.

Chapter 8
Dennis begins to perceive that his feelings for Rose are not entirely reciprocated. He notes the intimacy between Rose and Tony. But while Julia is ill Rose claims she is unable to concentrate on her own affairs.

Chapter 9
Dennis forces his credentials upon Rose. She asks for more time to consider his proposal. He accepts this as a rejection.

Chapter 10
Before he can quit Bounds, Dennis is roped into Julia's illness and makes an errand to Eastmead to fetch Mrs Beever for Julia. Tony speaks to Rose of Mrs Beever's wish for Rose's marriage to Dennis. Rose declares that Dennis has rejected her.

Chapter 11
Mrs Beever arrives under the impression from Dennis that Rose has rejected him. Julia's health continues to decline.

Chapter 12
Tony rests alone and drifts into sleep to awaken to Jean Martle gazing on him. He entertains her with the baby, Effie. Rose, Dennis and Mrs Beever enter upon the scene. Mrs Beever announces, formally, that Julia requests that Tony not remarry after her death in the lifetime of their child. Effie shall have no stepmother. Tony swears in front of the company. Doctor Ramage informs him that Julia is seriously ill.

Book Two

Chapter 13
Fours years have passed since Julia's death. It is Effie and Jean's joint birthdays and the celebration is to be held in Mrs Beever's garden. In those four years Jean has spent much time at Bounds but it is the first revisit from Rose, who is Mrs Beever's guest but at the request of Tony. Rose's presence also bears upon Mrs Beever's desire that Jean should marry Paul. Dennis Vidal has, coincidentally, picked this day for his first return visit.

Mrs Beever believes Tony to have a love interest in both Rose and Jean. It is apparent to all that Rose is in love with Tony, but believes that he will never break his vow not to remarry.

Chapter 14

Dennis speaks privately with Mrs Beever, who informs him of Rose's presence. He is unsure whether or not to confront her and adjourns to the river to contemplate.

Chapter 15

First meeting with Paul Beever. He is prompted by his mother to propose, again, to Jean. Six months earlier he had asked for her hand and she had postponed her decision. His closeness to Rose is more apparent.

Chapter 16

Rose encourages Paul in his plan to marry Jean.

Chapter 17

Tony Bream arrives, but without Effie who is mildly ill. Jean visits the sick child. Rose and Tony are left alone and he realises, for the first time, the full force of Rose's intentions towards him and the danger of their situation.

Chapter 18

In confused conversation, Tony misunderstands that Rose is interested in marrying Paul. What she in fact wants Tony to do is help bring about the union of Paul and Jean.

Chapter 19

Jean returns to the garden, with Effie. Left alone with her, Tony puts to her arguments in Paul's favour but she is adamant that she will never marry him.

Chapter 20

Jean is aware that Paul is not in love with her. When he proposes his case, she rejects him.

Chapter 21

Mrs Beever is displeased by the rejection and unamused to discover that Tony had pleaded for Paul's case. She accuses him of being in love with Jean and that his words to her were given in an attempt to rid himself of the danger of her availability.

Chapter 22

Tony becomes aware that Jean has rejected Paul for him, and he knows that he cannot marry her himself. Rose confronts Tony with her love for him. But she knows that, though he loves her too, he loves Jean more and that she loves him. Effie stands as an obstacle to any marriage. Rose turns away from Tony to stand face to face with Dennis.

Chapter 23
After a momentary lapse in composure, Rose takes the situation in hand and, before Tony, abjectly apologises to Dennis for her treatment of him four years earlier. It convinces Tony that she will have Dennis back. He leaves them alone to attend to business.

Chapter 24
Rose denies to Dennis her love for Tony and offers herself to him in marriage. They are joined by Effie, of whom a great fuss is made, and they are eventually joined by Jean.

Chapter 25
Dennis leaves Jean and Rose in the garden of Eastmead for Bounds. Rose informs Jean of her engagement. Jean claims that she will never marry. The two women are forced to confront the issue of Tony Bream which comes between them. Rose, refusing to give Effie back to Jean, leaves with her for Bounds.

Chapter 26
Paul discovers Jean alone in despair. She relates to him what has passed with Rose, then leaves for Bounds. Mrs Beever arrives to be told by Paul of the latest events.

Chapter 27
Tony returns to the garden of Eastmead to find Mrs Beever and Paul talking over Rose's engagement. He has just come from Bounds, but has not seen either Dennis, Rose, Effie or Jean there. Rose returns, claiming that Jean took Effie to Bounds. Paul contradicts her, knowing from Jean that Rose took Effie to Bounds herself. There is confusion and concern for the child's whereabouts. Paul is sent in search. Eventually, Doctor Ramage appears, obviously flustered, with the news that Effie's body has been found in the river. Rose maintains having no knowledge of the child's last moments, laying the blame with Jean. Tony claims responsibility for Effie's death.

Book Three

Chapter 28

Effie's death is confirmed and the investigation into it commences. Mrs Beever questions Dennis about events leading up to her disappearance. He reveals that when he left the Eastmead garden for Bounds he went and sat up river, where Jean Martle eventually joined him, without Effie, on her way over to Bounds.

Chapter 29

Rose appeals to Dennis to provide her with an alibi – that he was with her – and to stand by their engagement thus providing her with no motive for Effie's murder. Dennis tells her that he was in fact with Jean and that he saw Rose, from his vantage point up river, taking Effie across the bridge. Rose maintains that Jean killed Effie to facilitate her marriage to Tony.

Chapter 30

Ramage questions Dennis and the Doctor intimates that he understands Rose's guilt, but that he wishes to protect his friends by making the murder appear an accident.

Chapter 31

Tony and Dennis talk. Tony is sure of Rose's guilt, but feels partly responsible because she did it for the love of him. He is obliged to protect her: he invited her into his life and into an unpleasant situation. Dennis agrees to stand by his engagement and take Rose away from Eastmead that night, because he loves her.

Chapter 32

Jean enters and embraces Tony for the first time. She too carries guilt with her, having sensed Rose's intention. She cannot understand why Tony wants to protect Rose with his own name.

Chapter 33

An interview between Rose and Paul. She is remorseful. He declares that he would have done anything for her, and still will. He is on the verge of taking her away, when Dennis arrives to honour his word to Tony. They conclude that Tony and Jean will marry when the horror of the tragedy has died down. Rose has allowed this to happen by her action. Tony, Paul assures him, will be all right because he is so well liked. The death will be recorded as an accident and he will not be incriminated.

AMERICAN LITERATURE
IN EVERYMAN

The Marble Faun
NATHANIEL HAWTHORNE
*The product of Hawthorne's two
years in Italy, the thrilling story
of young Americans in Europe*
£5.99

The Portrait of a Lady
HENRY JAMES
*A masterpiece of psychological
and social examination, which
established James as a major
novelist*
£5.99

Billy Budd and Other Stories
HERMAN MELVILLE
*The compelling parable of
innocence destroyed by a fallen
world*
£4.99

The Red Badge of Courage
STEPHEN CRANE
*A vivid portrayal of a young
soldier's experience of the
American Civil War*
£3.99

**Leaves of Grass and
Selected Prose**
WALT WHITMAN
*The best of Whitman in
one volume*
£6.99

The Age of Innocence
EDITH WHARTON
*A tale of the conflict between love
and tradition by one of America's
finest women novelists*
£4.99

**Nineteenth-Century American
Short Stories**
edited by Christopher Bigsby
*A selection of the works of
Henry James, Edith Wharton,
Mark Twain and many other
great American writers*
£6.99

Selected Poems
HENRY LONGFELLOW
*A selection spanning the whole
of Longfellow's literary career*
£7.99

The Last of the Mohicans
JAMES FENIMORE COOPER
*The tale that shaped American
frontier myth*
£5.99

The Great Gatsby
F. SCOTT FITZGERALD
*Much loved story of passion
and betrayal, glamour and
the powerful allure of the
American dream*
£4.99

All books are available from your local bookshop or direct from:
Littlehampton Book Services Cash Sales, 14 Eldon Way, Lineside Estate,
Littlehampton, West Sussex BN17 7HE (*prices are subject to change*)

To order any of the books, please enclose a cheque (in sterling) made payable to
Littlehampton Book Services, or phone your order through with credit card details (Access,
Visa or Mastercard) on 01903 721596 (24 hour answering service) stating card number
and expiry date. (*Please add £1.25 for package and postage to the total of your order.*)

In the USA, for further information and a complete catalogue call 1-800-526-2778

CLASSIC FICTION
IN EVERYMAN

**The Impressions of
Theophrastus Such**
GEORGE ELIOT
*An amusing collection of character
sketches, and the only paperback
edition available*
£5.99

Frankenstein
MARY SHELLEY
*A masterpiece of Gothic terror in
its original 1818 version*
£3.99

East Lynne
MRS HENRY WOOD
*A classic tale of melodrama,
murder and mystery*
£7.99

**Holiday Romance and
Other Writings for Children**
CHARLES DICKENS
*Dickens's works for children,
including 'The Life of Our Lord'
and 'A Child's History of England',
with original illustrations*
£5.99

The Ebb-Tide
R. L. STEVENSON
*A compelling study of ordinary
people in extreme circumstances*
£4.99

The Three Impostors
ARTHUR MACHEN
*The only edition available
of this cult thriller*
£4.99

Mister Johnson
JOYCE CARY
*The only edition available of this
amusing but disturbing twentieth-
century tale*
£5.99

The Jungle Book
RUDYARD KIPLING
*The classic adventures of Mowgli
and his friends*
£3.99

Glenarvon
LADY CAROLINE LAMB
*The only edition available of the
novel which throws light on the
greatest scandal of the early nineteenth century – the infatuation of
Caroline Lamb with Lord Byron*
£6.99

**Twenty Thousand Leagues
Under the Sea**
JULES VERNE
*Scientific fact combines with
fantasy in this prophetic tale
of underwater adventure*
£4.99

All books are available from your local bookshop or direct from:
Littlehampton Book Services Cash Sales, 14 Eldon Way, Lineside Estate,
Littlehampton, West Sussex BN17 7HE (*prices are subject to change*)

To order any of the books, please enclose a cheque (in sterling) made payable to
Littlehampton Book Services, or phone your order through with credit card details (Access,
Visa or Mastercard) on 01903 721596 (24 hour answering service) stating card number
and expiry date. (*Please add £1.25 for package and postage to the total of your order.*)

In the USA, for further information and a complete catalogue call 1-800-526-2778

CLASSIC NOVELS
IN EVERYMAN

The Time Machine
H. G. WELLS
*One of the books which defined
'science fiction' – a compelling
and tragic story of a brilliant
and driven scientist*
£3.99

Oliver Twist
CHARLES DICKENS
*Arguably the best-loved of
Dickens's novels. With all the
original illustrations*
£4.99

Barchester Towers
ANTHONY TROLLOPE
*The second of Trollope's
Chronicles of Barsetshire,
and one of the funniest of all
Victorian novels*
£4.99

The Heart of Darkness
JOSEPH CONRAD
*Conrad's most intense, subtle,
compressed, profound and
proleptic work*
£3.99

Tess of the d'Urbervilles
THOMAS HARDY
*The powerful, poetic classic
of wronged innocence*
£3.99

Wuthering Heights and Poems
EMILY BRONTË
*A powerful work of genius – one of
the great masterpieces of literature*
£3.99

Pride and Prejudice
JANE AUSTEN
*Proposals, rejections, infidelities,
elopements, happy marriages –
Jane Austen's most popular novel*
£2.99

North and South
ELIZABETH GASKELL
*A novel of hardship, passion
and hard-won wisdom amidst the
conflicts of the industrial revolution*
£4.99

The Newcomes
W. M. THACKERAY
*An exposé of Victorian polite
society by one of the nineteenth-
century's finest novelists*
£6.99

Adam Bede
GEORGE ELIOT
*A passionate rural drama enacted
at the turn of the eighteenth
century*
£5.99

All books are available from your local bookshop or direct from:
Littlehampton Book Services Cash Sales, 14 Eldon Way, Lineside Estate,
Littlehampton, West Sussex BN17 7HE (*prices are subject to change*)

To order any of the books, please enclose a cheque (in sterling) made payable to
Littlehampton Book Services, or phone your order through with credit card details (Access,
Visa or Mastercard) on 01903 721596 (24 hour answering service) stating card number
and expiry date. (*Please add £1.25 for package and postage to the total of your order.*)

In the USA, for further information and a complete catalogue call 1-800-526-2778

DRAMA
IN EVERYMAN

The Oresteia
AESCHYLUS
New translation of one of the greatest Greek dramatic trilogies which analyses the plays in performance
£5.99

Everyman and Medieval Miracle Plays
edited by A. C. Cawley
A selection of the most popular medieval plays
£4.99

Complete Plays and Poems
CHRISTOPHER MARLOWE
The complete works of this great Elizabethan in one volume
£5.99

Restoration Plays
edited by Robert Lawrence
Five comedies and two tragedies representing the best of the Restoration stage
£7.99

Female Playwrights of the Restoration: Five Comedies
edited by Paddy Lyons
Rediscovered literary treasures in a unique selection
£5.99

Plays, Prose Writings and Poems
OSCAR WILDE
The full force of Wilde's wit in one volume
£4.99

A Dolls House/The Lady from the Sea/The Wild Duck
HENRIK IBSEN
introduced by Fay Weldon
A popular selection of Ibsen's major plays
£4.99

The Beggar's Opera and Other Eighteenth-Century Plays
JOHN GAY et. al.
Including Goldsmith's She Stoops To Conquer *and Sheridan's* The School for Scandal, *this is a volume which reflects the full scope of the period's theatre*
£6.99

Female Playwrights of the Nineteenth Century
edited by Adrienne Scullion
The full range of female nineteenth-century dramatic development
£6.99

SHORT STORY COLLECTIONS
IN EVERYMAN

The Strange Case of Dr Jekyll and Mr Hyde and Other Stories
R. L. STEVENSON
An exciting selection of gripping tales from a master of suspense
£1.99

Nineteenth-Century American Short Stories
edited by Christopher Bigsby
A selection of the works of Henry James, Edith Wharton, Mark Twain and many other great American writers
£6.99

The Best of Saki
edited by MARTIN STEPHEN
Includes Tobermory, Gabriel Ernest, Svedni Vashtar, The Interlopers, Birds on the Western Front
£4.99

Souls Belated and Other Stories
EDITH WHARTON
Brief, neatly crafted tales exploring a range of themes from big taboo subjects to the subtlest little ironies of social life
£6.99

The Night of the Iguana and Other Stories
TENNESSEE WILLIAMS
Twelve remarkable short stories, each a compelling drama in miniature
£4.99

Selected Short Stories and Poems
THOMAS HARDY
Hardy's most memorable stories and poetry in one volume
£4.99

Selected Tales
HENRY JAMES
Stories portraying the tensions between private life and the outside world
£5.99

The Best of Sherlock Homes
ARTHUR CONAN DOYLE
All the favourite adventures in one volume
£4.99

The Secret Self 1: *Short Stories by Women*
edited by Hermione Lee
'*A superb collection*' The Guardian
£4.99

All books are available from your local bookshop or direct from:
Littlehampton Book Services Cash Sales, 14 Eldon Way, Lineside Estate,
Littlehampton, West Sussex BN17 7HE (*prices are subject to change*)

To order any of the books, please enclose a cheque (in sterling) made payable to
Littlehampton Book Services, or phone your order through with credit card details (Access,
Visa or Mastercard) on 01903 721596 (24 hour answering service) stating card number
and expiry date. (*Please add £1.25 for package and postage to the total of your order.*)

In the USA, for further information and a complete catalogue call 1-800-526-2778